Figures of Space
Subject, Body, Place

THE SEA HORSE IMPRINT

Paola Mieli, *Publisher & Director*
Mark Stafford, *Editor*

This book is published under the aegis and with the financial assistance of Après-Coup Psychoanalytic Association, New York

Paola Mieli

Figures of Space
Subject, Body, Place

translated by Jacques Houis

Agincourt Press
New York, 2017

I'm grateful to Jacques Houis, who once more led me by the hand through an English version of my thoughts; to Gianpiero Doebler for the care with which he rendered Pontormo's writings; and to David Jacobson for his translations of earlier versions of my studies on "William Wilson" and Viennese architecture. The chapter "Of the Heavens on Stage" was translated by Gianpiero Doebler.

Copyright © 2017

ISBN: 978-1-946328-01-4

Copyedited
Zachary Slanger

Design and typesetting
Danilo Montanari

Agincourt Press
P.O. Box 1039
Cooper Station
New York, NY 10003
www.agincourtpress.org

Cover image: Cueva de la Manos, Río Pinturas, Santa Cruz, Argentina

The publisher welcomes enquiries from copyright-holders he has been unable to contact

*To Luigi,
The merry side of the fish*

Editorial Note

Freud's quotes have been translated directly from German every time we found the established English translation of the Standard Edition awkward, imprecise, or misleading.

For Lacan's quotes we have relied on the first complete English edition of the *Ecrits* translated by Bruce Fink (in collaboration with Héloïse Fink and Russell Grigg). The translation of all other texts by Lacan quoted here are ours.

Hier – das meint hier, wo die Kirschblüte schwärzer sein will als dort.
Hier – das meint diese Hand, die ihr hilft, es zu sein.
Hier – das meint jenes Schiff, auf dem ich den Sandstrom heraufkam:
vertäut
liegt es im Schlaf, den du streutest.

Hier – das meint einen Mann, den ich kenne:
seine Schläfe ist weiß,
wie die Glut, die er löschte.
Er warf mir sein Glas an die Stirn
und kam,
als ein Jahr herum war,
die Narbe zu küssen.
Er sprach den Fluch und den Segen
und sprach nicht wieder seither.

Hier – das meint diese Stadt,
die von dir und der Wolke regiert wird,
von ihren Abenden her.

                        Paul Celan, "Hier," *Von Schwelle zu Schwelle*, 1955

Here—that means here, where the cherry-blood blossom wants
to be blacker than there.
Here—that means this hand that helps it to be so.
Here—that means this ship on which I sailed up the sand-stream:
moored
it lies in sleep which you sprinkled around.

Here—that means the man I know:
his temple is white
as the glowing fire he quenched.
He threw his glass at my forehead
and came,
when a year had gone by,
to kiss the scar.
He spoke the curse and the blessing
And hasn't spoken since.

Here—that means this city,
that is ruled by you, and by the cloud
from its evenings.

Paul Celan, "Here," *From Threshold to Threshold*, 1955
Translation by David Young, 2010

TABLE OF CONTENTS

Foreword	13
Introduction	15
On the World Scene: Freudian Elements	21
Psychic Reality, External Reality	21
On the Advent of the Subject	22
Drive, Instinct	24
Need and Desire	26
Thought	28
Bejahung	29
Secondary Elaboration	30
Nachträglichkeit	32
Trauma: A Type of Necessity	33
Sexuality, Trauma, Seduction	34
Beyond	36
Inscription, Repetition	37
Phantasieren, Fantasm	39
Fading	42
Object: Between Less and More	45
Of the Subject in Question: The Space of an Edge	46
Space of the Drive	49
Psyche ist Ausgedehnt	51
Time Punctuated	52
The Space-Time of Identification	55
A Place with Several Dimensions	57
The Place in the Scene	61
The Place	61
Lalangue, the Call	62
The Space of Transmission	64

Table of Contents

In the Place: The Object Voice and the Object Gaze	68
Sound Architecture	71
Locus Amoenus et Gaudens	73
Playing with Words: Economy and Extension	74
Making Space	76
Moving, Walking	78
Walking, Horizon	80
Territory, Hands, Feet	82
Hands and Place	85
Positive, Negative	88
The Site, the Threshold	89
Between Two: A Threshold in the Frame	91
A Space for Representation	94
Dance and the Dit-mensions	99
The Abyss and Enthusiasm	101
Perspective and Gaze	105
The Screen	109
The Edge: Angst and the House of Man	110
Labyrinth-Space	113
See-Saw: Of Transitivism	116
Blindness in the Frame	120
Of the Uncanny and the Malevolent Gaze	123
Repetition and Enchantment	125
Phobic Strategy and the Limit of Place	128
Inside-Outside, Love-Hate	131
The Space of Hatred	133
Between the Two	135
Trespassing	138
To Die of Shoes	142
Producing a Place	146
Language and Place	148
Imponderabilia	153
Places on the Scene: Three Cases	159
Inhabiting the Place: History, Truth	159
1. Of the Scene within the Scene	165
Delano's Place	165
Benito Cereno	168
Of the Imaginary and the Real	171

2. Of the Heavens on Stage	177
The Open Book	177
Pontormo's Journal	178
The Body and the Sky	185
Rule, Hygiene, Work	187
The Body between Nature and Painting	191
Entrance, Exit	193
How is the Moon?	195
Liquefaction, Inundation, Deluge	199
Drawing and Designing	202
A Militant Work	206
3. The Nearby and the Open on Stage	211
The Ringstrasse and the Declaration of Styles	211
The Apple that Opens	216
The Particular and the Horizon	218
The Nearby Distant: Myth and Modernism	221
The Void and the Knot	225
The One and the Other	228
Punctuation at the Threshold	233
Bibliography	243

FOREWORD

In these pages I have gathered aspects of a reflection covering a thirty-year span. The practice of psychoanalysis and my involvement with art continue to raise questions for me regarding the human relation to the world and, within it, the way the subject inhabits space. When we say "space" we think we understand what we are talking about, even though the idea of space has given rise over the centuries to subtle philosophical, religious, and scientific debates that have yielded contrasting theories. Although my early background was philosophical, the reiterated experience of floating or suspended attention proper to psychoanalysis, as well as my interest in art, progressively distanced me from seductive but preconceived theories and prompted me to examine the evidence of the subject's relation to the world, made up of mostly common and familiar experiences. Seen from this angle, the relation to space appears above all libidinized, mediated by the signifying relation by means of which we approach the world. But this simple and obvious observation is not necessarily transparent. The very notions of subject, libido, psychic reality—introduced by Freud—often remain vague and misunderstood, and in particular the nature of the transferential relationship a human being has with the milieu to which s/he belongs. This is why I have decided to return to basic Freudian concepts in the first part of the book, to reaffirm their transformative trajectory and to trace the coordinates necessary to address the notions of subject and world—a platform allowing me to articulate the idea of *subjective place*. This seems all the more useful today, given a historical context in which the idealism intrinsic to the empirical and pragmatic vision of scientific discourse expresses a return to a mechanistic view of the human being. As Lacan has taught us, the return to Freud continues to convey innovative ethical and political values.

INTRODUCTION

Analytical reason treats the world as data, addressing it as an "immediate object"; what is assumed to be data is objectified.

But what does objectifying data mean? Werner Heisenberg gives the following definition: we "objectivate" a statement—for example, a statement relating to a material phenomenon—if we claim that its content doesn't depend on the conditions under which it can be verified.[1] A precise definition, derived from the history of modern Western science, but one which belies many of its premises and does not coincide with the prejudices that influence popular scientific discourse.

Descartes is considered the spokesman of modern scientific thought; his foundation of existence based on the *cogito* has proven useful for the development of science. By removing God from the world, by turning God into a necessary but separate point of reference, Descartes blazes the trail leading to the study of "natural" laws. The natural sciences blossom with Descartes' distinction between *res cogitans* and *res extensa*; Newtonian mechanics and classical physics develop thanks to the possibility of describing the world without dealing with either God or oneself.

While, on the one hand, the function of God as founding pillar of the laws of nature and the exactitude of knowledge or intuition begins to progressively fade,[2] on the other hand, the philosophical subdivision between *res cogitans* and *res extensa* persists as a platform for the conceptualization of the observer's relation to the world. Despite the contradictions and paradoxes to which it gives rise, this

---

[1] W. Heisenberg, "The Development of Philosophical Ideas since Descartes in Comparison with the New Situation in Quantum Theory," *Physics and Philosophy* (London: Allen and Unwin, 1959), 55–56.

[2] Asked by Napoleon what role God played in his understanding of the world, Laplace replied: "This hypothesis is no longer necessary." A. Koyré, *From the Closed World to the Infinite Universe* (Baltimore: Johns Hopkins UP, 1957), 276.

subdivision continues to influence the evolution of thought and constantly resurfaces in scientific discourse. Toward the end of the 1950s, Heisenberg pointed out that this subdivision contributed to the difficulty many scientists had accepting quantum theory and its implications, as was the case with Einstein.

The effects of the Cartesian conceptualization of the *res extensa* imply what Heisenberg defines as a metaphysical realism: for example, the idea that the world (i.e., things that extend) "*exist*." Heisenberg relates metaphysical realism to a dogmatic realism, according to which there are no statements concerning the material world *that cannot be objectivated*. And he contrasts it with practical realism, based on the supposition, however, that one objectify a statement only when claiming that its content *does not depend* on the conditions in which it can be verified. Statements of this type are possible and guide aspects of our daily life. Whereas practical realism is part and parcel of natural science, dogmatic realism, the spinal cord of classical physics, is not a necessary condition. This, according to Heisenberg, is one of the great lessons of quantum theory. Indeed, it demonstrates that there are statements concerning the material world that cannot be objectivated.

Quantum physics overturns the epistemological foundations of classical physics. Thanks to unexpected and remarkably advanced discoveries, it puts into a new perspective the relationship between the observer and the data, between the researcher and the object of research. It shakes the foundations of the subject/object separation particular to modern scientific thought. This reformulation is the result of an upheaval; it belongs to the *zeitgeist,* to the fecundity of Western thought during a period bridging the nineteenth and twentieth centuries, and it echoes the changes in perspective that occurred in other disciplines, from medicine to art, literature, and music. It is not by chance that its advent coincides with the advent of other discoveries just as transformative of the system of thought. Among these is that of psychoanalysis, Freud's Copernican revolution.

According to Freud, psychoanalysis inflicts a new narcissistic wound to the idea of the world: to the decentering of the earth in relation to the universe, constitutive of modern science, are added the decentering of man in relation to divine creation brought about by the Darwinian theory of evolution, and now the decentering of man in relation to himself, brought about by psychoanalysis. The discovery of the unconscious and the functioning of psychic causality entails a new conceptualization of subjectivity that upends the idea of the rational subject held by Cartesian modernity. The *I think, therefore I am* turns out to be the guarantee neither of the transparency of rational thought nor of existence. A subject harbors a knowledge that evades him or her, but which keeps producing effects in everyday life, be they slips of the tongue, unintended actions, dreams, symptoms, affects, and so on. When it is manifested, this presence surprises. One is stunned, sometimes taken aback, faced with what is intimate but which appears as "other." No self-reflection can exhaust the dimension of subjective reality. In the place where the subject thinks of itself as "me," the subject is never self-transparent; where s/he is to be found is where the subject does not think.

Although discoveries such as those of quantum theory or psychoanalysis, as distant from each other as they are, have had all kinds of practical consequences over the course of the twentieth century, oddly the reach of their conceptual revolution remains partly veiled. This is probably due to the persistence, to this day, of scientistic conceptions that predate the discoveries in question or to the strength of the mental habits that sustain specific prejudices of reason. The polarity *res cogitans/res extensa* has traversed diverse philosophical systems, from scientific modernity to idealism and to empiricism, for the most part leaving intact its characteristic distinction between body and soul or between matter and spirit, turning metaphysical realism and dogmatic realism into the norms of the study of the object and of the laws that regulate it. The force of this conception continues to imbue the conventional thinking and punditry of scientific discourse. Its foundations, moreover, fulfill the consumer's desire for simplification and serve as an excellent basis for the production of a multitude of consumer goods, in particular objects related to new scientific technologies. Dogmatic realism touches the individual closely, often regulating his or her relation to the body, as the many products of the current medical-pharmacological industry demonstrate.

Although stated, repeated, communicated, and commented upon, the implications of discoveries made in the early twentieth century continue to arouse incredulity and resistance in many people. Among these discoveries is the new conception of the subject introduced by Freud, and with it the question of the relationship between subject and world.

Introduction

In the *Traumdeutung*, Freud introduces the unconscious as *ein anderer Schauplatz*, another scene. From that point on, from the point the unconscious comes into play in the deciphering of the laws that regulate psychic causality, this definition, "the other scene," becomes essential. Lacan emphasizes that the other scene is a constituent modality of *"our reason"*: "This reason, we are seeking the path to determining its structures."[3] While the idea of studying the world "as it is" is based on the belief that the world can be observed without mediation, psychoanalysis examines the way the human being inhabits his or her world. Lacan answers dogmatic realism by stressing the distinction between world and scene:

> Now, the dimension of the scene, in its division from the place, worldly or not, cosmic or not, is where the spectator is indeed there to present to our eyes the radical distinction between the world and that place where things, be they the things of the world, can be said. All the things of the world come to be staged according to the laws of the signifier, laws which we can in no way claim to be from the outset homogenous to those of the world.[4]

Lacan calls *scene* the reality where the *parlêtre*,[5] a speaking being, lives and experiences the world, where the things of the world are said, are designated, and allow themselves to be studied, observed, classified. What we attribute to a first moment, the world "such as it is," which we believe we reach through our thinking about the world, boils down to the despoiled remains of the signifier that made access

---

[3] J. Lacan, *Le Séminaire livre X: L'angoisse* (Paris: Éditions du Seuil, 2004), 43.

[4] "Or, la dimension de la scène, dans sa division d'avec le lieu, mondain ou non, cosmique ou non, où est le spectateur, est bien là pour imager à nos yeux la distinction radicale du monde et de ce lieu où les choses, fût-ce les choses du monde, viennent à se dire. Toutes les choses du monde viennent à se mettre en scène selon les lois du signifiant, lois que nous ne saurions d'aucune façon tenir d'emblée pour homogènes à celle du monde." *Ibid*, 43-44.

[5] The term '*parlêtre*' is a neologism created by Lacan with the words '*parler*' and '*être*,' 'to speak' and 'to be.' It is also a pun that can be heard as *par-lettre*, 'through the letter.' There is no comparable neologism that can be created in English. *Parlêtre* is a concept that indicates the particularity of the human being as a being made of language. The way the neologism is constructed accentuates speaking over being, their intertwined nature. The concept challenges traditional ontology and indicates Lacan's effort to de-ontologize the notion of subject.

to it possible. Such a first moment turns out to be the effect of what is thought to have preceded it.

As Benveniste remarks, "It is what can be *said* that delimits and organizes what can be thought. Language furnishes the fundamental configuration of the properties of things recognized by the mind."[6] The world we speak of, the one that interests us insofar as it is where the subject first appears, is a scene, necessarily mediated by the signifier. It is on the scene of the world that we come and go.

---

[6] E. Benveniste "Catégorie de pensée et catégorie de langue," in *Problèmes de linguistique générale I* (Paris: Gallimard, 1966), 70.

ON THE WORLD SCENE: FREUDIAN ELEMENTS

Psychic Reality, External Reality

Liking scientific objectivity and the distinction between facts and the representation of facts, Freud quickly found himself confronted with the complexity of the idea of reality reflected in the subjective experience. It is well-known that when he abandoned his first theory of seduction (which made the "reality" of infantile seduction on the part of adults the cause of psychoneurosis), following the discovery of infantile sexuality and of the role played by fantasy in the relation of subject to world, Freud progressively came to recognize the nature of the psychic scene and the causality specific to it. Fantasy and reality turn out to have the same functional value in the psyche. In the psychic scene what is imagined can weigh as much as what is encountered in the outside world.

The discovery of the nature of psychic reality disrupts the comprehension of the relationship between subjective and objective as much as the comprehension of the way the subject articulates her or his own history and appropriates facts in general. It introduces a new perspective in the understanding of the relationship between thought and its objects, including the objects that thought considers as "givens"; this perspective overturns the separation between *res cogitans* and *res extensa* that animates metaphysical realism. The individual encounters the world through his or her own psychic reality and the world only presents itself through the filter of this reality:

> We do not even hope to be able to reach reality because we see that we have to translate any new acquisition into the language of our perceptions, which we are never really able to free ourselves of. But this is precisely what characterizes the nature and the narrowness of our science... The real will always remain unknowable.[7]

---

[7] S. Freud, "Das reale wird immer 'unerkennbar' bleiben," *Abriss der Psychoanalyse, 1938, Gesammelte Werke XVII* (Frankfurt am Main: S. Fischer Verlag, 1983), 126–127.

Thus Freud summarizes, in 1938, the fruits of the research that had guided him since the beginning of his theoretical reflections. Already on September 21, 1897, he had written to Fliess: "There exists in the unconscious no 'sign of reality,' so that it is impossible to distinguish between the truth and a fiction invested with affect."[8]

Psychic reality reflects the nature specific to the primary and secondary processes that articulate it; it is defined in opposition and in relation to 'external reality' or the 'outside world,' to employ Freud's terms, who generally uses one or the other expression interchangeably. We can define a thing as "external" if its presence is transmitted by a perception that an action can make disappear: "A perception made to disappear through muscular action is recognized as an external perception, as a reality; whereas, if an action of this type changes nothing, it means that the perception comes from within our own body, that it isn't real."[9] The status of reality is thereby associated with the structure of the apparatus that explores it. The idea of a material reality distinct from psychic reality is stressed by Freud not only to signal the difference between a factual event and a thought event, but also to indicate that a fact thought, and therefore desired, can have as much weight in a person's life as an action carried out.

On the Advent of the Subject

How shall we conceive of the territory where the subjective event is expressed? Physiological birth, the arrival into the world of a new body, does not guarantee a subjective birth. With the introduction of the difference between instinct and drive, between need and desire, Freud shows that the body cannot be reduced to its organic materiality. The body's physiological real accompanies and follows the forming of the erogenous body as an effect of the circuit of the drive. The body takes shape according to the rhythm of what the drive inscribes in it; it takes a subjective form as territory of the drive memory. But the drive, which takes off from the body, follows a path seeking the object

---

[8] S. Freud, *La naissance de la psychanalyse: Lettres à Fliess, Notes et plans (1887-1902)* (Paris: PUF, 1956), 191.

[9] S. Freud, "Metapsychologische Ergänzung zur Traumlehre" (1915), *Gesammelte Werke X* (Frankfurt am Main: S. Fischer Verlag, 1991), 423.

of satisfaction by unfolding in the domain of the Other. There is no subject without Other.

As soon as it enters the world, the infant is immersed in a reality defined by the presence of those who tend to its survival. From the outset, individual psychology is also social psychology.[10] The baby discovers the voice in the world of sounds: from the first days of life, it reacts to the mother's voice—to its tone, its pitch, the way the other addresses him or her—in an exchange that humanizes the physiological body. By perceiving the baby's cry as a call, as demand, the mother or the caretaker treats it as a signifying event and gives it a subjective meaning.[11] The subject is thus called to come into being from the place of the Other. In response, the infant progressively articulates a voice to be heard.

The fact that the infant's existence depends on the expectations and the fantasies that the adult manifests regarding her or him—the idea, for example, that the infant suffers, enjoys, fears, hates, understands or does not understand, and so on—influences its response to life as well as its physiological development. The study of the subject's relation to the other allows psychoanalytical care to intervene effectively on an entire range of infantile pathologies, from autism to developmental delays. Curiously, however, this undeniable fact continues to encounter all kinds of resistance. Ignorance and prejudice are for the most part rooted in a materialist and organicist view of the body, in a kind of dogmatic empiricism, which, holding to the primacy of matter, reproduces the old idolatry of the *res extensa*. Not enough attention is given to the innovative and subversive impact of the Freudian distinction between instinct and drive.[12]

---

[10] S. Freud, *Massenpsychologie und Ich-Analyse* (1921), *Gesammelte Werke XIII* (Frankfurt am Main: S. Fischer Verlag, 1987), 73.

[11] The term 'demand' translates in these pages the French "*demande*," which means 'asking for,' 'requesting,' 'demanding,' and so on, but whose primary meaning is 'asking for,' an address to the other. The concept of '*la demande*' is central to Lacan's articulation of the relation between "*demande*" and "*désir*," demand and desire. In these pages we will predominantly use 'demand' to refer to Lacan's concept.

[12] It is significant that to this day the official English translation of the title of Freud's text that establishes the notion of drive, "Triebe und Triebschicksale" (1915), remains "Instincts and Their Vicissitudes." While Freud introduced the new concept of *Trieb*, distinct from the concept of instinct, *laying the foundations of a new conception of the psyche*, his English translators took the initiative to eliminate the distinction, and with it the mean-

Drive, Instinct

Whereas the category of instinct covers a whole series of received animal behaviors, mainly concerned with the preservation of the species (reproduction) and of the individual for the purposes of the species (survival), behaviors that vary little from one individual to another, the concept of drive introduced by Freud is radically different from that of instinct. The drive, borderline concept between the somatic and the psychic—"the psychic representative of the stimuli originating from within the organism and reaching the psyche," "the measure of the operations asked of the psychic sphere by virtue of its connection to the bodily sphere"—is a constant propulsive force, untranslatable into pre-determined behaviors, devoted to its own satisfaction by means of eminently variable objects, independently of the organic cyclicity that rules certain animal behaviors.[13] The libido is its example, since the sexual drive precedes, accompanies, and follows organic fertility in the human being.

Nothing is more human than the concept (or "myth," as Freud calls it) of drive: the drive represents the fracture introduced by the human being in the evolution of the species.[14] To the extent that the human infant is born physiologically premature, that its survival requires a period of external care much longer than other primates require; to the extent that its upright posture involves the separation of perceptions directly linked to animal instincts (first of all the deviation from the cyclical function of reproduction guided by smell); to the extent that the development of the psychic organ ties the use of language to the handedness of action (left parietal lobe); to all these extents, the drive comes to represent as much the consequences of the intrinsically social nature of the speaking being as it does the passage from nature to *Kultur* characteristic of the arrival of human language. In the symbolic universe that characterizes the human being,

---

ing of such an innovation. The consequences of this are still present in the English-speaking world.

[13] S. Freud, "Triebe und Triebschicksale" (1915), *Gesammelte Werke X* (Frankfurt am Main: S. Fischer Verlag, 1991), 214.

[14] S. Freud, *Neue Folge der Vorlesungen zur Einführung in die Psychoanalyse* (1932), *Gesammelte Werke XV* (Frankfurt am Main: S. Fischer Verlag, 1991), 101.

the satisfaction of need passes through a demand that introduces the dimension of desire.

Françoise Dolto recounts a case (from World War II) of a baby only a few days old, suddenly separated from its mother.[15] After nursing her since birth, her mother was suddenly hospitalized because of a serious infection. Apart from her mother, the child rejected the bottle, her only sustenance. The family pediatrician placed an emergency call to Dolto, who advised wrapping the bottle in clothing worn by the mother at the hospital. The child accepted the bottle presented in this manner and began to nurse.

From the first days of life we can observe the difference between instinct and drive. What guides the psychic apparatus is not, as in the animal, the survival instinct, ruled by the need to eat, but the libido, the life drive, seconded here by the coalescence of partial drives. Only the libido is in a position to guarantee a pre-narcicisstic consistency to the body in the process of subjectivation. In the aforementioned case, the sense of smell, a complement to the oral and tactile drives, is able to activate the re-investment of the memory traces guided by desire.[16] In Freudian terms, the traces left by the odor, by the proximity of the mother's body, reactivate by contiguity the partial drives (oral, tactile) and orient desire, namely the attempt to rediscover in reality an object of satisfaction similar to the one of which the experience left a trace in the psychic apparatus. The repetition of the experience, even if it inscribes a difference, ensures a continuity necessary to the weaving of libidinal corporality, before a unitary experience of the body has been able to take place.

At the time of birth, the coalescence of the partial drives, derived from the exchange with the parental other, weaves a narcissistic base that allows for life. The persistence of the drives and the repetition of their inscription give to the becoming body its first consistency. Before any sense of subjectivity, we find the objects of the drive.

---

[15] F. Dolto, *L'image inconsciente du corps* (Paris: Éditions du Seuil, 1984).

[16] Freud's notion of 'investment' (*Besetzung*) was originally translated into English by J. Strachey as 'cathexis.' We take this opportunity to return to Freud's original use of *Besetzung* as 'investment.' Freud intentionally chose words from everyday language to define new psychoanalytic concepts.

Need and Desire

In the model of the psychic apparatus proposed by Freud in the *Traumdeutung*—directly inspired by Fechner's theory on the relationship between the tendency for stability and the pleasure-displeasure relation—the psychic apparatus is conceived of as a reflex apparatus, the function of which is to maintain the organism's internal energy at the lowest possible level, which is called the pleasure principle. The basic stimulation-response process of the reflex arc is disturbed by what Freud calls *die Not des Lebens*, vital urgency, the impossibility of having an automatic discharge of excitation.[17] Thus the process is complicated by the differentiation of diverse psychic agencies, through which the excitation undergoes a series of modifications before finding, or in order to find, the adequate discharge. Hence the distinction between primary and secondary processes and the necessary introduction of a reality principle that establishes a contrast between subjective and objective and allows rediscovering in reality an object corresponding to the object represented.

Freud proposes a construct, the *Befriedigungserlebnis*, the original experience of satisfaction, from which the apparatus is launched by a movement called *Wunsch*, desire, which leads to the hallucinatory re-investement of the memory traces left by the original satisfaction of the need. Mentioned in the *Project for a Scientific Psychology* and in Chapter VII of *The Interpretation of Dreams*, the *Befriedigungserlebnis* remains a permanent foundation of the Freudian conception of the primary process. It is conceived on the basis of the phenomenological given of the infant's original helplessness, requiring help to ensure its own survival because it is incapable of executing the specific action necessary to eliminate the excitation provoked by need (for example, by hunger). Once a first satisfaction is obtained, it will remain tied to the memory traces of the object that procured it and to the motor image of the movement that allowed its discharge. When the need reappears, satisfaction will be sought through the hallucinatory reactivation of the memory traces associated with the preceding experience of satisfaction.

---

[17] S. Freud, *Die Traumdeutung* (1901), *Gesammelte Werke II–III* (Frankfurt am Main: S. Fischer Verlag, 1976), 570.

The *Fiktion* of the first experience of satisfaction stages the mythical moment when desire emerges, breaking away from the drive impulses provoked by need: "Nothing but desire is capable of putting our psychic apparatus to work."[18] Need, which finds its satisfaction in the specific action procuring the real object, is therefore distinct from desire, which finds its fulfillment in the hallucinatory reproduction of the traces of perception.

Desire remains structurally tied to fantasy, a system of traces that convey fulfillment. The real object is distinguished by its inscription as a trace, the mark of the object and, at the same time, of its absence. The birth of desire is a response to a lack; as a psychic impulse, it remains by definition associated with the reactivation of a system of memory traces, henceforth regulating the tendency of the apparatus for fulfillment as well as the search for this fulfillment through an object in reality.

The *Befriedigungserlebnis* assembles, in a single and original moment, the arrival of desire, the structure of fantasy as a combination of signs conveying fulfillment, and the structure of sexuality, of the drives tending toward a fulfillment that is irreducible to the satisfaction of fundamental physiological needs. The psychic apparatus itself appears as the second act of a mythically inaugural experience, instituted by a lack.

According to Freud, the persistence of need forces the psychic apparatus to distinguish between fantasy and reality, to distinguish between the hallucinatory activation of perception and the perception of an object in reality. If the path of desire, the shortest path taken by the apparatus following its tendency to economize, turns out to be insufficient in suppressing the excitation provoked by need, the apparatus will complicate itself in the form of differentiated systems, allowing a motor discharge adequate to the stimulus (hence the development of a reality principle capable of verifying whether a representation is present in the outside world). But this complication implies the repetition of the experience—the repetition of attempts at satisfaction and of the frustration associated with it—as well as the inscription of new signifying traces. The articulation of the apparatus is an extension of the signifying network.

---

[18] *Ibid.*, 572.

Thought

In the Freudian conception, the complication of the psychic instrument is paired with the evolution of the thought process, with the development of a psychic activity capable of conceiving not only of the conditions proper to the apparatus, following the pleasure principle, but also of those belonging to the outside world. The function of thought is to inhibit the too intense hallucinatory investment, to defer automatic discharge in favor of a more advantageous use of psychic forces, for example an appropriate transformation of reality in view of satisfaction. It is a trial action (*Probehandeln*), a feeling one's way (*ein motorisches Tasten*) with a limited waste of energy. The economy achieved by thought as opposed to action is associated with an articulation of the apparatus: the premier function of the apparatus—to discharge excitation—results in its opposite, through the tendency to hold back. This antinomy between the discharge function and the tendency towards the economic principle of least waste, which characterizes the very model of the apparatus, becomes the basis for the successive Freudian formulations of the relationship between libido and death drive.

Thought is none other than the ersatz of hallucinatory desire: "All the complex activity of thought, which takes place from the memory image to the production of the identity of perception through the outside world, is none other than an *indirect* path, made necessary by experience, *to arrive at the fulfillment of desire*."[19] While desire is the apparatus' motor, it is up to the gap between drive fulfillment and need satisfaction to guide its articulation; the inextinguishability of the attempts to search for "the identity of perception" is its impetus. Sexuality and thought support each other thanks to the condition of failure introduced by the difference between the *jouissance* sought and the *jouissance* achieved, both made up of desire, "libidinal facts," two sides of the same coin of a movement as conservative as it is innovative.[20]

---

[19] S. Freud, *Die Traumdeutung*, op. cit., 572.

[20] The word *jouissance*, now a common psychoanalytic term, doesn't need extended explanation. Let's simply recall here that, in referring to the notion of enjoyment in terms of both rights and property, it indicates the satisfaction of the drive according to the pleasure principle and its beyond.

The idea of thought as a trial action establishes an intrinsic affinity between thought and action. Freud specifically brings up this bond again in 1925 in his text "Negation," where he stresses that it is indeed the intellectual action of judgment that puts an end to the postponement of thought as trial action and that guarantees the passage from thought to action. But the function of judgment derives from primary drive impulses: judgment might represent the ulterior and functional development of the original activity of inclusion in or exclusion from the ego, managed by the pleasure principle, which initiates the relationship between the subject and the world.

Bejahung

The original *Bejahung* introduced by Freud—the affirmation by which the pleasure-ego passes judgment on the thing's quality by introducing it in itself or excluding it outside of itself—represents the mythic moment of a primordial symbolization, as Lacan calls it, of an original inscription constitutive at the same time of the psychic scene and of the real as what is primordially excluded from it. Freud sums it up as follows: "'It shall be inside me' or 'it shall be outside me.' As I have shown elsewhere, the original pleasure-ego wants to introject into itself everything that is good and to eject from itself everything that is bad. What is bad, what is alien to the ego, and what is external are, to begin with, identical."[21]

The judgment of existence follows the judgment of quality, first institution of the psychic territory: it already concerns the "real definitive ego that developed from the initial pleasure-ego," able, by means of the examination of reality, to determine through a motor innervation if the perception can be made to disappear or whether it is resistant, able to distinguish between perception and representation. "The first immediate aim, therefore, of reality-testing is not to *find* an object in real perception that corresponds to the one presented, but to *refind* such an object, to convince oneself that it is still there."[22]

---

[21] S. Freud, "Negation," *The Standard Edition of the Complete Psychological Works of Sigmund Freud XIX* (London: Hogarth, 1961), 237.
[22] *Ibid.*, 237–38.

The domain of the reality that the subject must take into account in this second moment turns out to be regulated by what is already inscribed in the apparatus, by what already constitutes it as psychic reality, as a system of memory traces. The first act, the inaugural *Bejahung*, mythically institutes the psychic scene and the domain of the reality that touches the subject, its relationship with the world, with the external reality that concerns him or her; simultaneously, it institutes that which is completely excluded from this domain and which delineates it, the non-symbolized and non-symbolizable real.[23]

The *Bejahung*, the inaugural 'yes,' goes hand in hand with the 'no' of the *Ausstossung*; they are two sides of the same coin. The relationship between this 'no' and this 'yes,' their alliance, is resource, production, and necessary negativity. The judgment of quality establishes a border—a question of outside and inside, *eine Frage des Aussen und Innen*—which has a structurally constructive function in the definition of the relationship between subject and world, in the constitution of the scene where the subject is called to be. It is the introduction of a symbolic hole in the real. This border, ever present though always veiled on the world scene, is the imperceptible condition for the very existence of this scene.

Secondary Elaboration

According to Freud, secondary elaboration, the fruit of censorship, reflects the passage between the unconscious and the preconscious; it is the psychic activity at work in vigilant thought. Conscious thought thus shows itself to be the fruit of a psychic labor that necessarily leaves behind the unconscious knowledge of which it is the filtered and altered product. Its characteristic is to order representations, to create coherent relations among them. Its tendency to systematize is such that thought does not hesitate to produce a

---

[23] "For this is how we must understand '*Einbeziehung ins Ich*,' taking into the subject, and '*Ausstossung aus dem Ich*,' expelling from the subject. The latter constitutes the real insofar as it is the domain of that which subsists outside of symbolization." J. Lacan, "Response to Jean Hyppolite's Commentary on Freud's 'Verneinung,'" *Ecrits: The First Complete Edition in English*, trans. B. Fink in collaboration with H. Fink and R. Grigg (New York: Norton & Company, 2007), 324.

false coherence so long as coherence is achieved. This is the case for the secondary elaboration of dreams, delirium, obsessions, and phobias, and equally that of theories, philosophies, and religions, a need for coherence at all costs, for rational explanations, that comes from repression.

In *Totem and Taboo*, by showing the succession of the three great systems of thought—animist, religious, scientific—Freud stresses that the passage from one system to the next marks the passage from a more exhaustive worldview to one that is less so: the passage from the original omnipotence of thought to an incomplete construction, to loss, to the renunciation of a satisfaction, a passage that is at the same time the progressive acceptance of the unknowable and the acceptance of the provisional, limited, and relative nature of any thought construct. By including the provisional and error as necessary conditions, the Freudian notion of science reflects the preoccupations of twentieth-century epistemology; it is close to Popper's concept of science, according to which the validity of a scientific thesis is based on its own refutability.[24]

Freud progressively recognizes the fracture existing between knowledge and truth that is particular to the subject of language: "For each psychic event that is consciously judged, there can be two kinds of explanation, the one that has it as stemming from the system itself, and the one that is real but unconscious."[25] Thought inherits its messianic quality from desire, and its unquenchable questioning, its search for solutions, extends to a completeness mythically lost. To the specific suffering that emerges from the encounter with the unknowable, with what appears as a limit to the symbolizable, corresponds the clinging of rational thought to causal logic. Thus does theory produce its own fruits, its own constructs, faithful as it is to the explicative and lenitive tendency of secondary elaboration.

---

[24] This is a kind of paradox, however, since it is well known that Karl Popper is critical of psychoanalysis and concludes that it cannot be considered a science because of the non-refutability of the notion of the unconscious.

[25] S. Freud, *Totem und Tabu* (1912-1913), *Gesammelte Werke XI* (Frankfurt am Main: S. Fischer Verlag, 1986), 82.

Nachträglichkeit

At the time of his first seduction theory Freud discovered that trauma involves events separate in time, something that, from then on, would remain an essential element in his conceptualization of the functioning of psychic causality. An event originally experienced in an anodyne fashion acquires a traumatic meaning if a second event attributes to it a particular sexual connotation. By way of association, the second event retroactively evokes the first, and this scene thus acquires, *a posteriori,* the quality of the first. It is in this second moment that the subject is taken by surprise, unable to mobilize the necessary defenses against the sum of libido engendered in the present, which puts into motion the repression of the memory and the appearance of the symptom. The trauma is constituted in a temporal scansion that occurs *Nachträglichkeit,* in the aftermath.

This scansion does not signal a gap between stimulus and response, or a pause between action and reaction; it is *not* a deferred action. Rather, it indicates the efficacy of a present event that, by the very fact that it happens, invests a past inscription with a resounding meaning-effect, endowing it with the status of revelation. What happened 'after,' changes what preceded it into *'an occasion,'* an opportunity (and we should understand the word *'occasion'* here in its etymological sense of *chance* and *fall*). Psychic causality shows that what happens before does not necessarily determine what follows and that what follows can have a determining efficacy on what precedes it, which gives to the function of the fantasy—the motor of repression and symptom formation—all of its value.

Starting with his *Three Essays on the Theory of Sexuality,* Freud continually stresses the role played by the beginning in two stages of human sexuality and the function of the period of sexual latency, which, through forgetting and repression, allows infantile impressions to solidify. Latency consolidates the anteriority of the traumatic event and its first deciphering in the symptomatic manifestations of infantile neurosis. Adolescent sexuality and adult sexuality in general will therefore always have the character of an aftermath; physiological development will be accompanied by the logical pace of a psychic temporality that upends the idea of a linear progression of evolving events.

Trauma: A Type of Necessity

Once the theory of seduction was abandoned, the notion of trauma and its temporal scansion remained as central factors of psychic causality. According to Freud, the notion of trauma is structurally related to the prematuration of the human child, to the nature of libido, to the development in two stages of human sexuality, to sexual difference, to the assumption of the oedipal taboo, to primary repression as the mechanism constitutive of psychic structure. "No human being escapes traumatic experiences; no one avoids the repressions they entail," Freud writes in 1938.[26]

The role played by fantasy increases with the discovery of infantile sexuality and of the particular nature of the psychic scene, which, of course, does not constitute a denial of the pathogenic nature inherent to episodes experienced during childhood or later. It is not the notion of the reality of particular events that is called into question. What is new is the recognition of the role played by fantasies in subjective life and their function in determining the psychic scene. Paradoxically, traumatic experiences turn out to be a kind of necessity:

> The impression we derive from them is that these infantile events are in some way required by necessity, that they belong to the essential elements of a neurosis. If they are produced in reality, so much the better; but if reality refuses to furnish them, they are assembled through allusive traces and completed by fantasy. The result is the same and, until now, we have been unable to identify any degree of difference, as far as consequences, as to whether fantasy or reality played the more important role in these infantile events.[27]

Freud studies the function of fantasy in the psychic scene. He postulates the structural function of the *Urphantasien*, the primal fantasies, in the constitution of trauma. These fantasies—primal scene, seduction fantasy, castration fantasy—support and confirm in-

---

[26] S. Freud, *Abriss der Psychoanalyse* (1938), *Gesammelte Werke XVII* (Frankfurt am Main: S. Fischer Verlag, 1983), 111.

[27] S. Freud, *Vorlesungen zur Einführung in die Psychoanalyse* (1915–17), *Gesammelte Werke XI* (Frankfurt am Main: S. Fischer Verlag, 1986), 385.

fantile sexual theories.[28] Where the theories stop in the face of the unthinkable—the origin of the individual, of sexuality, and of sexual difference—fantasies offer a solution and answer fundamental enigmas related to origins; they give an explanation to an enigmatic cause that eludes symbolization.

The encounter with an unthinkable, a non-symbolizable—the advent of life, of sexuality, of sexual difference—proves to be necessarily traumatic. The primal fantasies translate their impact in the shape of violence. The solidarity that links the fantasy and the theory is thus highlighted. Fantasy and theory appear as the poles, the backstops of a tendency toward a mythic wholeness: fantasy as starting point and point of insistence of the primal hallucinatory solution, of the primitive sources of pleasure, and theory as a point of arrival and return, each time provisional, of messianic thought.

Sexuality, Trauma, Seduction

According to the model of the first topic, sexuality is structurally associated with the functioning of the apparatus; it possesses an immanent character and a spontaneity. However, its emergence is also necessarily linked to what reaches the subject from the outside world. The advent of sexuality is traumatic. The traumatic event cannot be assimilated in the psychic apparatus' network of representations, as its presence provokes an increase in tension that cannot find an adequate discharge. Through repression, the psychic apparatus isolates and excludes the inadmissible memory; however, being repressed, it acquires a permanent life in the unconscious. The repressed is condemned to return. Compulsion is an integral part of trauma.

Trauma inscribes *jouissance* in the body. Its repressed imprint constitutes a crystallization subject to the laws of the primary process, able to attract other intolerable representations. Already in his *Studies on Hysteria*, Freud points out that repression acts by isolating in the psyche a specific ideational group that acts like a detached psychic corpus. The "splitting of consciousness," such as he defines it

---

[28] For example, the castration fantasy confirms the infantile sexual theory of the penis' universality as an attribute of all living beings.

in this context, "the strange state at the same time of knowledge and non-knowledge" characteristic of subjective division, is a direct result of repression.[29] Repression acts neither on the drive nor on the affect, but rather on the ideational representatives of the drive (*Vorstellungsrepräsentanz*), commemorative traits of the traumatic experience. By striking the ideational representatives of the drive, repression "sets" an unconscious inscription, which the primary process will try to decipher.

Until the end of his theoretical elaboration, Freud maintained the relationship between sexuality and seduction: by taking care of the child's body, the mother, this original Other, becomes "the first seducer."[30] The care provokes a libidinal excitation: infantile sexuality organizes itself around the borders, the surfaces, and the organs of the body where a privileged exchange with the parental other occurs. Seduction is inevitable; it is the means through which the body becomes an erogenous zone. The care and the attentions of the adult affect the subject; they transmit a desire that guides the child's desire.

Trauma implies the fantasy's fulfillment. This is what Freud highlights by attributing to the *Urphantasien*, to the primal fantasies, the role of the driving force of trauma. The importance of the point stressed by Freud in his 1919 text, "A Child Is Being Beaten," can scarcely be overstated. Namely that, in all the substitutions of the subjective grammar articulated by the fantasy (the father beats a child; my father beats me; a child is beaten), the repressed time, the one that is untraceable because unconscious, ties *jouissance* to the trauma's invocation. This is precisely because the trauma stages a transmission between the subject and the Other, a transfusion of *jouissance* that is also an inscription. The repressed time—my father beats me; he loves me—designates the place occupied by the subject in the Other's fantasy; it is the proof of his desire, upon which the subject's recognition depends.

---

[29] S. Freud, *Studien über Hysterie* (1892–95), *Gesammelte Werke I* (Frankfurt am Main: S. Fischer Verlag, 1987), 232.

[30] S. Freud, *Abriss der Psychoanalyse*, op. cit., 115.

Beyond

The trauma is an event that exceeds the limits of the pleasure principle: it entails a *jouissance* that overcomes it. Based on clinical data about the repetition of painful experiences associated with an increase in stimulations, Freud introduces the notion of the "beyond," of the "other side," of the pleasure principle, which functions independently of the pleasure principle and, to a certain extent, without taking it into account, something that expresses the drive's most intimate character.

It is well known that Freud oscillated between, on the one hand, a tendency that sought to assimilate the pleasure principle to the principle of constancy—to the apparatus' internal tendency to maintain excitation at a constant level, to homeostasis—and, on the other hand, a conception that—making the pleasure principle correspond to the free flow of energy of the primary process and making constancy correspond to its link to the secondary process—tended to assimilate the pleasure principle to the Nirvana principle, to the tendency to reduce excitation to zero. The relationship between discharge and economy finds a new formulation with the introduction of the dualism between death drive (tending to the absolute resolution of tensions inherent to the organism) and life drive (tending to maintain and create vital units that presuppose a certain level of sometimes elevated tension).

In *Beyond the Pleasure Principle*, it is the drive itself that acquires a new and ulterior definition. *"The drive,"* concludes Freud, *"appears to be a thrust, innate to the living organism, aiming to re-establish an earlier state* which this living being had to abandon under the influence of perturbing forces coming from the outside; it seems a kind of organic elasticity or, if you will, the manifestation of the inertia characteristic of organic life."[31] All the drives prove to be conservative, which manifests their most intimate character; acquired "historically," to use Freud's term, they tend to restore a preceding state.

In his representation of an initial mythical state of the elementary organism, by nature inert, Freud emits the hypothesis that the phenomena of organic development must be attributed to external

---

[31] S. Freud, *Jenseits des Lustprinzips* (1920), *Gesammelte Werke XIII* (Frankfurt am Main: S. Fischer Verlag, 1987), 38.

factors. With the definition of the drive as manifestation of the inertia characteristic of organic life, "the external," with the perturbing forces that come from it, confirms its aspect as a real, as radically Other, of which the traumatic impact implies a form of violence; by provoking a change, it carries an inscription that ceaselessly insists. Not only does Freud maintain the notion of trauma, he places it at the center of the idea of the living. The encounter with an overwhelming and unassimilable real is at the same time a motor of life and an opportunity, in repetition, for the drive's inertia.

From the inertia intrinsic to the drive, the paradox of life is drawn: namely, the fact that the living organism rebels with extreme energy against events—dangers, for instance—"that could help it more rapidly attain its life goal"; and, Freud adds, the fact is that "the organism wishes to die only in its own fashion."[32] The drive is thus revealed as fundamentally a death drive: it represents "in itself the share of death in sexed life."[33]

Inscription, Repetition

According to the model of the psychic apparatus described by Freud in his letter to Fliess of December 6, 1896, made up of successive registers, the first register (defined by the *Wahrnehmungen*, neuronal impressions or perceptions) corresponds to the encounter with the real. Following the inscription of traces of perception (*Wahrnehmungszeichen*), the constitution of a first ciphering successive to the primary repression that struck the real, is a second act, the effect of the creation of the *nihilo*, of the void that allows the first imprint to be registered. Freud names *Das Ding* the element originally isolated by the subject in his experience of the real as *Nebenmensch*, foreign in and of itself (*Fremde*), and, by its nature, outside signification. *Das Ding*, Lacan stresses, is "the first exterior; it is that around which is oriented the subject's entire journey ... the Freudian world, in other words, that of our experience, entails that it is this object, *das Ding*,

---

[32] S. Freud, *Beyond the Pleasure Principle* (1920), *The Standard Edition of the Complete Psychological Works of Sigmund Freud XVIII* (London: Hogarth, 1955), 39.

[33] J. Lacan, *Le Séminaire livre XI: Les quatre concepts fondamentaux de la psychanalyse*, op. cit., 187.

as the subject's absolute Other, that needs to be recovered. At best it is found as regret. It is not what is recovered, but its pleasure coordinates are."[34]

Lacan stresses Freud's need to separate perception and consciousness through a particular time, the time when the *Wahrnehmungszeichen* are articulated in simultaneity; he also notes that the term *Wahrnehmungszeichen* is what Freud found that was "closest to the signifier at a time when Saussure had not yet updated it."[35] The register of the *Unbewusste* is that of deciphering: "Now, what Freud articulates as primary process in the unconscious ... is not something that is ciphering but deciphering. Namely: *Jouissance* itself."[36] The work of the unconscious structured like a language, of this network of metaphoric and metonymic relations that characterize the nature of psychic associations—condensation and displacement, as Freud calls them—is a work of deciphering. In its formations—dreams, slips of the tongue, wordplay, or the symptom—the unconscious proceeds "by interpretations."[37]

The insistence of the signifier that cadences the return of traumatic experiences involves the encounter with an unassimilable real, which cannot be symbolized (and which, according to Freud, needs to be bound and elaborated); it brings with it the persistence of the *jouissance* that belongs to it, given that it is *jouissance* itself that necessitates repetition. But, as Lacan notes, repetition does not mean that what is finished is started over again, as in the case of physiological functions like digestion. The repetition is of a trait that "commemorates an irruption of *jouissance*."[38] This trait, the simplest kind of mark, of writing element, is also "the origin of the signifier"; and it is to the extent that the signifier represents a subject for another signifier that the repetition will be a repetition aiming for *jouissance*.[39]

---

[34] J. Lacan, *Le Séminaire livre VII: L'éthique de la psychanalyse* (Paris: Éditions du Seuil, 1986), 65.

[35] J. Lacan, *D'un discours qui ne serait pas du semblant*, "Lituraterre," Leçon VII, 12 mai 1971.

[36] J. Lacan, *Télévision* (Paris: Éditions du Seuil, 1974), 35.

[37] J. Lacan, *Le Séminaire livre XI: Les quatre concepts fondamentaux de la psychanalyse*, op. cit., 118.

[38] J. Lacan, *Le Séminaire livre XVII: L'envers de la psychanalyse*, op. cit., 89.

[39] *Ibid.*, 52.

Bolstered by the insistence of primitive inscriptions of satisfaction, the surge of the drive involves repetition. If one has *Wunsch,* if one's apparatus has a motor, the motor of life, it is because the original object is structurally lost and causes the messianic movement of desire, as Freud had stressed by formulating the hypothesis of the *Befriedigungserlebnis.* The return of *jouissance* entails a loss, an entropy. In Freudian terms, there will be a structural difference between the quantity of pleasure sought in repetition and the pleasure actually obtained, always other and deficient compared to the original *jouissance* which set in motion the repetition. The repetition, which always seeks something new to try to recover what was, entails the repetition of a difference, entails a new inscription. It is structuring the subject, effect of the signifier.

Phantasieren, Fantasm

Fantasy faces the real. This is what Freud indicates in the link between sexuality and fantasy, between the advent of *jouissance* and its deciphering. While *das Ding* is the real toward which the subject of the drive tends, there is no way to approach the real except through fantasy.

Freud attributes a structural role to *Phantasieren.* As a group of signs conveying the fulfillment of desire (*Befriedigungserlebnis*), it channels the drive's satisfaction; as an answer to the confrontation with the inconceivable (*Urphantasien*), it has a liminal function between the symbolic and the real. The reservoir quality of the pleasure principle within the reality principle, peculiar to (pre)conscious reverie, grows with the redefinition of the libidinal economy introduced by *Beyond the Pleasure Principle.* As reservoir of the primary processes, fantasy is the intermediary of a satisfaction that reflects the fusion of both libido and death drives. Imaginary framework of the drive's satisfaction in symptoms or of desire in daydreams, fantasy is a pivot between trauma, *jouissance*, and subjectivization; it is the support and confirmation of subjective recognition. It articulates the relationship of the subject to the object of desire, as well as the relationship between psychic reality and external reality.

Lacan stresses the functional value of fantasy in the Freudian corpus and its essential status for the speaking being (*parlêtre*). In so doing, he brings a completely new contribution to the notion of fantasy by expressing it, as is well known, in an original logical formulation: $ \$ <> a $, the *fantasm*.[40] The fantasm is an imaginary caught in a signifying function, which was implicit in the Freudian discovery. The algorithm of the fantasm—which, as Lacan notes, "is designed to allow for a hundred and one different readings"—shows the different modalities of the logical relationship between subject and object.[41] The subject appears there divided by its relation to the object and the object *a* appears according to the functions that define it: that of the cause of desire and that of the *plus-de-jouir*, according to the desire that causes and the economy that regulates.[42] The object *a* is as much what divides the subject as what unifies it.

Of the twenty and one hundred readings suggested by Lacan, we shall limit ourselves to a few elements essential to approaching the world scene. While the fantasm serves as a screen for the real, its function is a critical one in the relation of the subject to the world. On the scene of the world the subject speaks; s/he is a speaking being, which means that his or her approach to reality is subordinate to the laws of language. The characteristic of natural language is its *trinary* structure: "I" am speaking to "you" about "s/he," "it," or "they," bringing to presence what is absent (the parents who passed away, the ancestors, but also your boss, your partner, our political leaders, our future, and so on and so forth), which allows for the unfolding of the symbolic register, capable of producing abstractions and metaphors, of join-

---

[40] We choose to translate the French term *'fantasme'* used by Lacan with an archaic spelling of the English word 'phantasm,' *fantasm*, used in Middle English (1175-1225) and derived from the Latin *'phantasma.'* In doing so, we want to indicate the particularity of this concept as opposed to the one of 'phantasm,' the primary meaning of which is that of 'ghost,' and the common post-Freudian usage of the notion of 'fantasy' in the English psychoanalytic community. It is remarkable that when Lacan introduced the notion of *'fantasme,'* he selected a word that was not in current use. According to the dictionaries (Larousse, Petit Robert) the term *'fantasme'* became widespread in the French language during the twentieth Century, borrowing from psychoanalytic vocabulary. Lacan took an old French word to designate a new concept. The fact that it leant itself to spreading 'naturally' to the spoken language seems to give it even greater pertinence.

[41] J. Lacan, "The Subversion of the Subject and the Dialectic of Desire in the Freudian Unconscious," *Ecrits: The First Complete Edition in English*, trans. B. Fink, op. cit., 961.

[42] We leave the term *plus-de-jouir* in the original French, as it cannot be appropriately translated into English. The French expression means both 'more *jouissance*' and 'no more *jouissance*.'

ing what is distant, of creating visions and paradoxes. In the act of speech, in addressing myself to you, a place Other is established that can guarantee the foundation and the truth of our speech, a place that grounds it. Lacan says about this place that it is a code that contains a multiplicity of signifying combinations, the place of the signifying treasure, "which commands everything that can be made present of the subject."[43]

From the mother or from the caretaker in charge of the first needs and the first demands, the newborn receives the first sign of his relationship with the Other, the *unary trait*, as Lacan calls it, that marks the weight of what is said in the parental sphere.[44] These utterances establish the child's first identifications, the basis of the ego ideal. Beyond need, for which demand acts as an intermediary and which is propelled by desire, the child's discourse asks questions about the things of the world; it names them. It is a discourse that questions the very nature of discourse as well as its function in the place of the Other, a place from which the subject situates herself or himself as subject of speech.

The fantasm arises in the child's life in response to the enigmatic desire of the original caretaker, on which the child's life and first identifications depend: she or he says this to me, but what does s/he really want? What kind of warranty do I have of his/her love and recognition? The child encounters an uncertainty, a lack of guarantee. In the intervals of the adult's speech the question arises; the enigma of its desire pierces what doesn't fit in the discourse. The Other is desiring, therefore lacking something, an acknowledgment that entails a trauma, a *trou-matisme*.[45] If the first response to this unknown is the fantasm, this is because the fantasm provides an answer, a logical construction, that summons up an object to help rescue the subject's very being and that infuses reality with desire.

---

[43] J. Lacan, *Le Séminaire livre X: Les quatre concepts fondamentaux de la psychanalyse*, op. cit., 185.
[44] "*Trait unaire*." The unary trait is the trait of identification as trait of difference. Lacan appropriates Freud's expression *ein einziger Zug* (in chapter VIII on identification in *Group Psychology and the Analysis of the Ego*), and translates it as *trait unaire*, further developing the concept.
[45] '*Troumatisme*' is a neologism and pun created by Lacan. This portmanteau word includes 'trauma' and '*trou*,' hole. Lacan uses it to indicate the traumatic encounter with the castration in the Other.

There is nothing, in the realm of speech, that guarantees or authenticates in any way what the Other is saying and the signifying chain; there is no Other of the Other, no Other that guarantees the Other. At the moment the subject "vanishes before the deficiency of the signifier that answers for his place on the level of the Other," s/he finds support in the objects s/he extracts from her or his own substance.[46]

Fading

The divide between the subject of the enunciation and the subject of the statement is characteristic of the act of speech; the saying does not coincide with the said: "That we say remains forgotten behind what is said in what is heard."[47]

The first person is always the last to appear in grammatical usage. At the beginning the child refers to herself by using the third person, "Georgia is hungry." Then she will declare without hesitating that she has "three sisters: Lucy, Jan, and me," which shows that when she speaks the subject tends above all to count herself, as Lacan notes.[48] If it takes time for her to learn the form "We are three sisters," it is because its acquisition involves the recognition of the distinction between the subject of the enunciation and the subject of the statement. The form "*It's me*" through which, for example, we answer the phone or the intercom, ensuring the validity of our enunciation on the referent "voice," declares with simplicity the way the subject perceives and designates himself and herself: namely, in the third person. In language there is no identity other than the apparent one between the two A's in the formula "$A=A$"; from the point of view of the signifying articulation, the first A doesn't coincide with the second, as seen in statements of the type "a dream is a dream" or "my child is my child," that pass, according to the contest of the speakers, from the register of the real to that of the imaginary or the symbolic. What appears as a

---

[46] J. Lacan, *Le Séminaire livre VI: Le désir et son interprétation*, op. cit., 446.

[47] J. Lacan, "Qu'on dise reste oublié derrière ce qui se dit dans ce qui s'entend," *L'étourdit*, in *Scilicet* 4 (Paris: Éditions du Seuil, 1973), 5.

[48] J. Lacan, *Le Séminaire livre VI: Le désir et son interprétation*, op. cit., 102.

tautology on the logical level is a predicate in the domain of speech; it introduces a new signifier and difference.

At the very moment when the act of speech grants the subject a pronoun with which to designate herself or himself, it discards him or her as subject of the enunciation. The subject cannot designate itself in a signifier without simultaneously disappearing to appear elsewhere, in another signifier, a phenomenon Lacan calls *fading*. The relationship of the speaking being with the signifier *prevents* the reduction to the same in the act of speaking; the signifier is pure difference: wherever it is present, difference is manifested. It refers to another signifier, it is never alone; it produces a signification in a retroactive way, when punctuation invests what is said with effects of meaning, interrupting the signifying chain. The signifying structure is organized around the function of the cut, which is expressed topologically as the function of an edge.

The signifier represents the subject for another signifier. It is not a sign. It is the sign of nothing if not a subject, although the subject in question is permanently displaced by the use of the signifier, other than with the designator and other than with the designated: "The subject is only ever punctual and evanescent, for it is only a subject through a signifier, and for another signifier."[49] S/he is a being whose being is always elsewhere, as the predicate shows.

The moment of subjective *fading* characteristic of the act of speech, this moment straddling enunciation and statement where the subject shines of its own evanescence, for the most part passes unnoticed. The temporal pulsation that is peculiar to it—what Lacan terms *"l'esp d'un laps,"* the space of a slip—manifests itself following a stumbling block that interrupts the course of the signifying chain.[50] So the non-coincidence between enunciation and statement appears in a fleeting way; we are surprised by what we just said. It's the *laps*, the space of a slip. When the discursive narration is disrupted by slips of the tongue, memory blanks, puns, absent words, and so forth, an unexpected and unpredictable effect of meaning can emerge, or nonsense, nevertheless loaded with a knowledge that expresses itself beyond the speaker's intentions. The interruption of logical narrative

---

[49] J. Lacan, *Le Séminaire livre XX: Encore* (Paris: Éditions du Seuil, 1975), 130.
[50] J. Lacan, "Préface à l'édition anglaise du séminaire XI," in *Autres écrits*, op. cit., 571.

exposes the subjective division. The *Verblüffung*, as Freud identifies it in his book on *Witz*, the stunning that accompanies the suspension of the discourse, is followed by an eventual illumination, a rediscovery of meaning that allows a shift in registers. The signifier of the *Verblüffung*, of stupor, can become "smuggler of the real": the encounter with the real that insists behind the signifying chain can become an affirmation that interrupts repetition.[51] Not only does it allow speech to appear beyond what we think we are saying, allow the encounter with a knowledge we did not know we knew, it also allows, through a break in the repetition, the birth of a new signifier.

It goes without saying that the attempt to express in one's own language seemingly inexpressible emotions and affects, or the passage from one language to another, favors stumbling blocks, misunderstandings, word play. These "passages" provoke the confrontation with the resistance *of* and *in* language, the confrontation with an untranslatable that is the echo of what is most intimate and inaccessible in the subjective use of language. It is the echo of the language the unconscious is made of, *lalangue*, as Lacan calls it, maternal *lalangue*, always unique and singular, a language that far outstrips what we can account for by using speech.[52] According to Lacan nothing is less certain than that the purpose of *lalangue* was originally communication; we can simply affirm that, since it implies a reply, dialogue supports a *jouissance* specific to *lalangue*, the fact that, when speaking, the unconscious enjoys. Language, distinct from *lalangue*, is a "theory" of *lalangue*, a system by which we try to approach the function of *lalangue*. But if the unconscious is "*a savoir-faire with lalangue*," the *savoir-faire* one possesses with *lalangue* goes far beyond, without question, what can be said about it using language.[53] The affects are an example of this.

---

[51] A. Didier Weill, "Passeur du réel," *Les trois temps de la loi* (Paris: Éditions du Seuil, 1995), 125.

[52] A term that Lacan wanted to make "as close as possible to the word lallation" ("Conférence de Genève sur le symptôme," op. cit.). "Lallation," from the Latin *lallare*, evokes the rocking, the "la, la, la," that puts children to sleep, as well as the production of the first sounds emitted by the child, sounds without meaning but gratifying nevertheless, the start of a progressive phonetic mastery.

[53] J. Lacan, *Le Séminaire livre XX: Encore*, op. cit., 127.

Object: Between Less and More

If desire is the motor of the apparatus, its object, Freud repeats, must be rediscovered, given that it is constituted as lost, which manifests its real, hence inaccessible, quality. Whether looked at from the point of view of psychic reality, according to Freud, or from the point of view of the *parlêtre*, according to Lacan, the object above all appears as what is lacking, a lack of *jouissance* that is located in the place of cause: "We observe desire and from this observation we induce the cause as objectified."[54] As lack, the object *a* can take the form of "four episodic substances," following the relation of the subject to the primordial Other. In the contact between the caretaker and the child, the partial drives mark the body's borders. Breast, stool, gaze, and voice are, according to Lacan, the four forms of the object of the drive, objects that are separable from the subject's body—able to be situated between the mother and the child—objects structured by a cut, as much through their relation to the body's cuts as through their relation to the signifying cut. This episodic substance does not result from the developmental phases, but rather from the relationship between demand and desire in the relation to the Other. Clinical practice shows that no object can have the function of *a* if it is not associated with other objects according to a group structure, stemming from a solidarity specific to the partial drives.[55]

As effect of the operations of alienation and separation, the object *a* is at the center of the logical combinations of subject and Other; but between the object *a* as cause and the objects of the drive, there is no symmetry. The object *plus-de-jouir*, in the episodic substances of the drive's objects, attempts to make up for the lack. The movement of

---

[54] J. Lacan, *Le Séminaire livre XXIII: Le sinthome* (Paris: Éditions de Seuil, 2005), 36.
"I produced the only conceivable idea of the object, that of the cause of desire, namely what is lacking," "Préface à l'édition anglaise du séminaire XI," in *Autres écrits*, op. cit., 573.
[55] The oral object refers to the demand to the Other, the anal object to the Other's demand, the scopic object to the desire toward the Other, and the vocal object to the desire of the Other. Lacan identifies the object *a*, which doesn't have a mirror image, to a surface created by an interior 8, with a double loop around the pointing of a cross-cap. In the Borromean knot, Lacan situates it where the three registers meet, which shows its different sides: real, imaginary, and symbolic.

life is thus tensed between cause and goal, between a structural "less" and a "more" that is unsatisfying by definition.[56]

Of the Subject in Question: The Space of an Edge

"There is no sign of the subject other than the sign of its abolition as subject," says Lacan.[57] Among the different operations represented by the algorithm that articulates the subject to the object in the formula of the fantasm, $ <> a, alienation and separation are at the base of what Lacan calls the subject's causation (*causation du sujet*). Alienation is expressed in the *vel* (the "or or" alternative) that condemns the subject to not being able to manifest itself unless divided; while on the one hand it appears as meaning produced by the signifier, on the other it is condemned to *aphanasis*, to disappearance. Lacan distinguishes three logical uses of the *vel*: the exhaustive *vel* (I go there or there); the *vel* of equivalence (I go on one side or another, its equivalent); the *vel* of alienation. In the operation that symbolic logic calls reunion,[58] the *vel* of alienation results in the fact that "whatever choice is made, the consequence is a neither one nor the other."[59]

Lacan cites certain expressions as examples: "Your money or your life!," where if you choose the money you lose both money and life, and if you choose life you lose something precious needed for life; "freedom or life!," where if you choose freedom you lose both, and if you choose life it will be without freedom; or, even more radically, "Freedom or death!," where the only freedom is that which is expressed in choosing death. In the case of the subject's being, the signifying alienation is expressed between being and sense: if we choose being, the subject eludes us, it falls into nonsense; if we choose sense, the subject can only subsist deprived "of this part of nonsense that is,

---

[56] "The true, authentic object, which is in question when we are talking about the object, is in no way grasped, transmissible, exchangeable. It is the horizon around which our fantasies gravitate. And yet it is with this that we must make objects that *are* transmissible." J. Lacan, *Le Séminaire livre VIII: Le transfert*, op. cit., 285.

[57] J. Lacan, *Le Séminaire livre VI: Le désir et son interprétation*, 7 janvier 1959 (Paris: Éditions de la Marinière/Le Champ Freudien, 2013), 130.

[58] The union of two sets entails that they share elements by superposition.

[59] J. Lacan, *Le Séminaire livre XI: Les quatre concepts fondamentaux de la psychanalyse*, op. cit., 191.

strictly speaking, what constitutes, in the making of the subject, the unconscious."[60]

Alienation expresses the subject's condition in its dependence on the signifier. It introduces what Lacan calls the *lethal factor* of choice, a factor responsible for allocations within the signifying structure and that expresses itself at the very heart of life: "This alienating 'or' is no arbitrary invention ... it is in language. This 'or' exists."[61] Alienation is at the heart of the encounter between the subject and the Other. The subject and the Other are equally beings of lack: the signifier opens a gap in the Other, prompting the enigma of his or her desire.

The second movement of subjective causation involves the operation of separation. It modifies the conjunction's logical form and provokes the emergence by intersection of two lacks:[62] the subject finds in the Other's lack a lost part of herself or himself and s/he rediscovers in her/his lack the part from which the Other is separated.[63] The subject thus separates itself from, and generates itself with, the objects *a* that enter into the dialectic of desire enacted by the drive.

In a further development of the logic of fantasm, Lacan lingers at length on the *cogito,* showing that the subject is based on a forced alienation, diametrically opposed to the Cartesian certainty of thought. Freud's Copernican revolution involves the impossibility of a return to the thought of Being. While Descartes, moving away from Aristotelian metaphysics, reduced the question of being to that of "the being of the I," Freud overturns the very being of the "thinking I." Referring to De Morgan's logic, Lacan applies the function of negation to the *cogito*: if "I think," then "I am not," and if "I am," then "I don't think," followed by the exclusive alternative: "either I don't think or I am not," the implications of which Lacan details. In the alienating alternative between being and sense, between "either I don't think or I am not," the choice "I don't think" allows being to be preserved on condition of being unable to think anything about it.

---

[60] J. Lacan, *Le Séminaire livre XI: Les quatre concepts fondamentaux de la psychanalyse*, op. cit., 192.

[61] *Ibid*.

[62] The intersection of two sets is constituted by the elements that belong to the two sets.

[63] See J.-M. Vappereau in *Le vel de la séparation*, http://jeanmichel.vappereau.free.fr/

The subject's manifestation entails the impossibility of maintaining sense as an "all": "'I know' never means anything and it's a sure bet that what one knows is false, but is sustained by consciousness, the characteristic of which is precisely to sustain this falsity," which echoes the Freudian notion of secondary elaboration.[64] The experience of the unconscious overturns the classical relationship between subject and knowledge: the unconscious is a knowledge without a subject. Seeing that the unconscious cannot say "I," it is represented by a "he" or "she": "the third person is the Other such as I define it; it is the unconscious."[65] From this place, the place of a "he" or "she," the subject speaks his or her own desire.

The subject only manifests itself as divided; it is division itself, as is illustrated by *fading* and the operations of alienation, separation, and repetition that give birth to it: "Each time we talk about something called a subject we turn her or him into a 'one.' But what we have to realize is precisely this: the one with which to designate it is lacking (*il manque l'un pour le désigner*)."[66] While the notion of fading illustrates the spatio-temporal pulsation of the subject-effect of the signifier, the cut of the Moebius strip gives the subject a topological collocation: in its essence the Moebius strip is the cut itself, is a structure of the divided subject. The subject is edge.

In relation to the "I don't think" of the alienating and constitutive choice of the subject looms the "not-I" (*pas-je*), as Lacan calls the Freudian Id (*ça*): what escapes the I (*je*) in the logical structure of discourse appears as "not-I" (*pas-je*). By logical structure we should understand grammatical structure, as the fantasm demonstrates. The fantasm is expressed by a grammatical form that excludes the "I," as in the phrase "a child is being beaten." The structure of the sentence does not require a comment, Lacan notes, "it shows itself."[67]

---

[64] J. Lacan, *Le Séminaire livre XXIV: L'insu que sait de l'une-bévue s'aile à mourre*, 15 février 1977.
[65] *Ibid*.
[66] J. Lacan, *Le Séminaire livre XIII: L'objet de la psychanalyse*, 15 décembre 1965.
[67] J. Lacan, *Le Séminaire livre XIV: La logique du fantasme*, 11 janvier 1967.

Space of the Drive

According to Freud, the drive is a constant force that follows a trajectory around the object seeking its goal, which is to say its satisfaction. It leaves from an erogenous zone of the body to return to it, given that the source of the drive is located where it finds its goal. It is in voyeurism-exhibitionism and in sadism-masochism that the drive's trajectory is best illustrated. It unfolds according to logical moments: an active form (which Freud bases on a preliminary auto-erotic phase); the positioning of an object toward which the drive turns; a replacement of the object by a subject and the consecutive reversal of the circuit with the constitution of a passive goal. Lacan specifies:

> It is important to distinguish the return in the drive circuit of what appears—but also *not to appear*—in a third moment. Namely the appearance of *ein neues Subjekt* to be understood thus not that there would already be one, the subject of the drive, that is, but that what is new is the appearance of a subject. This subject, the other strictly speaking, appears inasmuch as the drive was able to close its circular course. It is only with its appearance on the level of the other that what there is of the drive's function can be achieved.[68]

Lacan emphasizes the fact that the drive's trajectory is always a loop and that the drive's goal is none other than this return by circuit. The mouth that kisses itself, written about by Freud in his *Three Essays*, is the ideal model for this. But the fact that it is only with the appearance of the subject in the place of the other that the drive's function can be achieved points to the gemellary relationship linking subject and object. The drive's circuit draws a figure that ties together time and space: a logical time and a topological space.

In "Drives and Their Vicissitudes," Freud considers that the drive stems from a preliminary autoerotic phase. He conceives of voyeurism-exhibitionism as the contemplation of an object on one's own body. In sadomasochism, although he still considers sadism primary, Freud presents the hypothesis of a preliminary masochistic phase based on the efforts the child makes to master the use of its limbs.

---

[68] J. Lacan, *Le Séminaire livre XI: Les quatre concepts fondamentaux de la psychanalyse*, op. cit., 162.

Later on, in "The Economic Problem of Masochism," Freud establishes masochism as primary.

Thus we take note of the fact that autoeroticism, in condensed form, contains the seeds of the drive's outcome; the object found on one's own body is primary. In autoeroticism, Lacan notes, *one is* the object *a*. How does the autoerotic circuit operate? There are extrinsic properties of an object that disappear in the intrinsic analysis of it. I look at a glass that I am holding and I can describe its properties. That is an extrinsic analysis. But if I am inside the glass wall of the glass, in an intrinsic position, the glass's properties will have a very different appearance. What autoeroticism materializes is the passage from the extrinsic to the intrinsic and vice-versa. A subject can treat his or her own body as an object and consider himself or herself external to that same body. Except that, in this change of perspective, something opaque and unrepresentable occurs. The passage from the intrinsic to the extrinsic includes a vertiginous element, a real; something that cannot be grasped happens unexpectedly when, while caressing my arm with my hand, I wonder who is caressing and who is being caressed. Something of the splitting associated with the act of speaking, and the subjective evanescence associated with it, is confirmed on the real side of the drive's circuit. The circuit of the drive is expressed in a grammatical montage as a reversal; it is a topological itinerary. The subject identifies with the object, says Freud, but it is to the extent that there is identification that the subject emerges.[69]

Each time we reread "Drives and Their Vicissitudes," why do we have the impression of needing to repeat the reasoning from the beginning, to repeat Freud's path step by step in his thinking about the drive's vicissitudes? The intuitive difficulty we encounter seems to be associated with the representational opacity that ties subject and object together in the drive's reversal.

---

[69] An important clinical observation. Among other things, it allows us to understand a key aspect of the function of fantasm in the sex act. For example, the need expressed by a person to be a bottom, a position allowing him to enjoy identification with the partner and to emerge as subject. And this precisely with an act in which he affirms himself as object.

Psyche ist Ausgedehnt

The Freudian discovery of the unconscious reflects a broadening of nineteenth-century conceptions of space and time. In fact, it is in the *zeitgeist*; it hews to the succession of advances in the domains of geometry and physics that occurred between the nineteenth century and the beginning of the new century and that led to the formulation of the general theory of relativity. In the case of psychoanalysis, the movement away from the foundations of Euclidean geometry and of the dominant philosophical conceptions happens on a particular terrain—neither that of physics or geometry nor that of philosophy, but that of the talking cure—which entails a new conception of psychic causality and a progressive clarification of the relation between subject and object.

At the end of his life, Freud hypothesizes:

> Räumlichkeit mag die Projektion der Ausdehnung des psychischen Apparats sein. Keine andere Ableitung wahrscheinlich. Anstatt Kants a priori Bedingungen unseres psychischen Apparats. Psyche ist ausgedehnt, weiss nichts davon.[70]

The Standard Edition translation reads:

> Space may be the projection of the extension of the psychical apparatus. No other derivation is probable. Instead of Kant's *a priori* determinants of our psychical apparatus. Psyche is extended; knows nothing about it.[71]

The last sentence, "*Psyche ist ausgedehnt, weiss nichts davon,*" presents a weighty translation problem. Two persons can be attributed to "*weiss*": the first and third persons singular. The sentence can be read as "*Ich weiss nichts davon*" or "*Es weiss nichts davon.*" The version published by Presses Universitaires de France makes the fol-

---

[70] S. Freud, "Ergebnisse, Ideen, Probleme" (1938), *Gesammelte Werke XVII* (Frankfurt am Main: S. Fischer Verlag, 1986), 152.

[71] S. Freud, "Findings, Ideas, Problems" (1938), *Standard Edition XXIII* (London: Hogarth, 1964), 300.

lowing choice: "The psyche extends, I know nothing about this."[72] The German *"weiss nichts davon"* can indeed be commonly used to say: "I know nothing about this." But the context in which the sentence appears causes us to lean towards a *"weiss"* that refers primarily—or at the same time—to the psyche, the unconscious, and, more specifically, to the Id. The Id is 'not-I' (*pas-je*), a knowledge without subject, which clinical practice encounters in the third person. Freud's wording allows him to express two things at the same time, equally appropriate to the context in question: the 'I' doesn't know anything about this; the Id doesn't know anything about this. It is not surprising that the 'I' does not know anything about the extended psyche; that is evident from the very structure of the apparatus. That the Id knows nothing about it, on the contrary, sheds light on an aspect of the 'not I,' and implies that the psyche is the effect of its own deployment.

Synthetic, complex, and enigmatic, Freud's wording is at the same time a point of arrival after years of research and a point of departure. Let us limit ourselves to observing that, based on the model of the psychic apparatus proposed by Freud, the idea of an extended psyche coincides perfectly with the idea of a psyche defined as the effect of its own articulation: a *forward* psyche. In the Freudian model, the succession of psychic registers is deployed based on a series of signifying inscriptions, according to a forward motion that characterizes the psychic process as much as it does memory. In this sense, memory is extension.

Time Punctuated

Lacan uses a sort of theatrical production to illustrate the logic of subjective time. It is not by chance that the writing of his remarkable 1945 article "Logical Time and the Assertion of Anticipated Certainty, A New Sophism" precedes the publication of his 1949 article "The Mirror Stage as Formative of the I Function" (drafted in the late thirties): the two are bound in the study of subjective identification. The anecdote in "New Sophism" is well known. A prison warden summons three prisoners and promises to free the one who discovers the color of the

---

[72] S. Freud, *Résultats, idées, problèmes* (Paris: PUF), 288.

disc he attaches to their backs. He tells them that there are three white discs and two black ones. Each prisoner sees white discs on the others' back. After a time—which includes two significant suspended motions—the three simultaneously move toward the exit, each separately concluding that he 'is white,' what Lacan calls the perfect solution.[73] Like Freud, Lacan does not separate thought and extension. Logical time is articulated on a "logic of the act," an act that marks the emergence of the subject of assertion from the collective s/he is part of.[74] "The act," Lacan stresses, "founds the subject."[75] It is a spatio-temporal punctuation.

We shall limit ourselves to mentioning a few essential elements of logical time. Lacan points out three temporal instances: the instant of the glance, the time of comprehending, and the moment of concluding, all intrinsically bound together in the logic of the action that leads to the solution. They succeed each other according to a precise logical structure, retroacting upon each other, each of them determined by the other. Given the rule of the game (being opposite two blacks, one knows that one is white), the instant of the glance presents the situation as such (one sees two whites); this generates the intuition by which the subject measures the situation, a time for comprehending (had I been a black, he would have left without waiting) that unfolds the urgency of a moment of concluding, a judgment that results in an assertion about oneself (I'm white) and a shifting away from the position of reciprocity with the others on which the reasoning is based. But the unfolding of the logical movement is marked by two suspended motions: if he has legitimately concluded that he is a white (positing that, had he been a black, the others would not have been long in realizing they were whites and leaving) "he must abandon his conclusion as soon as he comes to it; for at the very moment in

---

[73] Everyone gives a similar answer: "I am white, and here is how I know. Since my companions were white, I thought that, had I been black, each one of them would have been able to infer the following: 'If I too were a black, the other would have necessarily realized straight away that he was white and would have left immediately; therefore I am not a black.' And both would have left together, convinced they were white. If they did nothing of the kind, I must be a white like them. At that, I made for the door to make my conclusion known." J. Lacan, "Logical Time and the Assertion of Anticipated Certainty," *Ecrits: The First Complete Edition in English*, trans. B. Fink, op. cit., 162.

[74] E. Porge, *Se compter trois: Le temps logique de Lacan* (Paris: Erès, 1989), 83.

[75] J. Lacan, *Le Séminaire livre XIV: La logique du fantasme*, 15 février 1967.

which he is stirred into action by his conclusion, he sees the others setting off with him."[76] He then doubts. This leads to a hesitation, to a temporal modulation that is an integral part of the possible solution, since this very hesitation is shared by the others (had he been a black, they should not have stopped). The second hesitation allows for the moment of concluding. The time for comprehending proves to be an essential function of the logical relationship of reciprocity.

Lacan stresses that time, and not space, is at the core of this logical movement, in opposition to the spatialized conceptions of classical logic that underlie empirical experiments. And indeed, what the suspended motions disclose is not what the prisoners see but rather what they do not see (a black disk).[77] The entire unfolding of the sophism follows a series of deductions grounded on what is not presented, on hypotheses based on logical anticipations and retractions.

The *time* of the emergence of the subject of the assertion—via the intermediary of a passage through an indefinite subject (there are three whites) and a reciprocal subject (putting oneself in the others' shoes)—is nonetheless articulated in the drive circuit, here guided by the gaze and dictated by the voice. Logically, time leans here on space. If the visual representation of the sophism of the three prisoners, which we are forced to repeat in order to find the solution, deploys a spatialization of time, its logical progression inserts time into place (in this case, a particular place, that of a prison where the freedom of the prisoners is at stake). We cannot help but take note of how much the very effectiveness of the doubting scansions depends on a movement suspended in space, and immerses logical time in the specificity of the collective relation to place.

---

[76] J. Lacan, "Logical Time and the Assertion of Anticipated Certainty," *Ecrits*, op. cit., 164.

[77] "What makes surface and time in logical time is not made through measurable time, nor by measurable [metric] and visible space, it is topological in nature." E. Porge, "L'identification: une physique sans métaphysique," in *Se compter trois: Le temps logique de Lacan*, op. cit., 48. In *Problèmes cruciaux pour la psychanalyse*, Lacan represents the topology of logical time with the Klein bottle.

The Space-Time of Identification

The mirror stage, as Lacan calls the phenomenon triggered by the captivation produced by one's own image around 8–9 months, shows how space is an essential element of subjective structuring. For the newborn, the process of learning motor skills is long and laborious. The fragmentary movements of the body are tentative at first, before becoming operational, before being able to reach an object, to grasp it or to push it away, which characterizes the baby's long dependency on those who take care of him or her. Specular identification is an anticipatory movement toward an ideal unity: to recognize oneself in the reflected image is the logical anticipation of a unity to come, is the condition for the emergence of the ego, for the emergence of the subject of the assertion, and for the articulation of the future gravitational and gestural unity.

"In any identification there is what I have called the instant of the glance, the time of comprehending, and the moment of concluding," Lacan stresses.[78] In the scene he proposes several times in order to illustrate the mirror metaphor, the child, captivated by his or her own image, turns away from it toward the adult who carries him or her, seeking the adult's assent and approval. The instant of the glance is followed by a time of comprehending. If the gaze plays a key role here, it is because its trajectory, which solidifies vision, gives to the captivating quality of the specular image the value of reality, even if only ideal, materializing the call to subjectivization coming from the adult's voice. The child awaits a sign that gives a measure of how much the specular image is, in effect, desired by the person toward whom s/he turns. The Other's gaze is internalized through a trait (*ein einziger Zug*): its symbolic introjection constitutes the basis of the ego ideal and solidifies the imaginary projection of the ideal ego. The identification that follows "depends on the possibility of reference to that primordial symbolic term that can be mono-formal, mono-semantic, *ein einziger Zug*."[79] This trait confirms and stabilizes the specular image, allowing for the narcissistic satisfaction tied to the ego ideal. As the hinge between the ego ideal and the ideal ego, it attaches the image to

---

[78] J. Lacan, *Le Séminaire livre XII: Problèmes cruciaux pour la psychanalyse*, 13 janvier 1965.

[79] J. Lacan, *Le Séminaire livre VIII: Le transfert* (Paris: Éditions du Seuil, 1991), 414.

the real of the body. Its nature shows how the process of identification involves both an introjective and a projective movement, structurally interlaced in the ego's advent. By identification, we mean the transformation produced in the subject by the assumption of the image, as underlined by Lacan. In it, imaginary, symbolic, and real are knotted together; if they weren't, there would be no identification. From a topological point of view, "the exterior (image) turns over to line the interior (of the ego)."[80]

The confirmation received from the Other sustains the logical time/space that cadences the emergence of the I; it allows for a subjectivization of space. It is a validation of the "here" and "there" that—linking the body, its image, and the Other's desire—creates a libidinal extension of the subject in space.

The anticipation specific to identification in the reflected image, the assumption of an ideal unity, is at the same time an invitation to become and an invitation to develop the motor articulation needed to handle one's own environment. The primordial "dissonance between ego and being," which marks the distance between the experience of the body and the identification with one's reflected image, introduces into the imaginary dimension a structural doubt that underlies the appearance of the 'I,' and from which the 'I' will ceaselessly suffer.[81] This doubt may appear unexpectedly and undermine the subjective image as well as its spatial extension, which means that a person's suffering regarding his or her own image can very often manifest itself as the suffering of the surrounding space, as the decomposition of his or her own environment.

The mirror attracts, seduces. It reproduces. But how does it reproduce? To be reflected in the mirror involves the passage from a perceptive experience of space via the body to its image reflected on a flat surface; it involves the passage from an indeterminate pluri-dimensional space to a bi-dimensional surface. The cliché according to which the human image in the mirror is symmetrically reversed turns out not to be correct; it signals the confusion to which the passage between different spatial dimensions gives rise on the intuitive level.

---

[80] E. Porge, "L'identification: une physique sans métaphysique," op. cit., 40.

[81] J. Lacan, "Presentation on Psychical Causality," in *Ecrits: The First Complete Edition in English*, trans. B. Fink, op. cit., 152. "La discordance primordiale entre le Moi et l'être," "Propos sur la causalité psychique," *Ecrits*, op. cit., 187.

In the experience of specular identification, a dimension is inverted: "It is marked as difference but it is not written, it cannot be assigned without reducing the structure in one of the coordinates, it remains forbidden. The ambiguity produced is real, impossible to resolve as denotation or univocity, but defined by writing."[82] The non-equivalence of dimension, the passage from a plural dimension to a bi-dimensional space and the return, reiterates the presence of a point of opacity on the level of identification. This opacity already belongs to the relationship between intrinsic and extrinsic specific to the drive circuit that underlies the operation of identification. It reiterates the inclusion of the real, of the unrepresentable, in the experience of the body and in the establishment of subjective space. The fact that there is a leftover in the operation of identification, as Lacan points out, that everything is not reflected in the specular image, shows that auto-eroticism is at the heart of this operation. The object exempt from the mirror includes the writing of a lack (*-phi*), a flaw in the ideal image.

The experience of space remains marked by the passage of dimensions that underlie the organization of the subject's place. Something of the order of the incommensurable remains structurally and secretly included in the imaginary commensurability of the representable dimensions that guide the subject's relation to the world.

A Place with Several Dimensions

The spatio-temporal logic that supports identification is topological; however, this process unfolds within the experience of the space we perceive. What can be said about this experience and its different dimensions? We are in the habit of thinking that the space in which we live is three-dimensional. Now, the three dimensions that underlie our intuitive perception are "probably the result of a long learning process that began in early childhood," as Marc Lachièze-Rey puts it, which brings up the question of what kind of learning process is involved and

---

[82] "Elle est marquée en tant que différence mais elle n'est pas écrite, elle ne peut être assignée sans réduire la structure dans une des coordonnées, elle reste interdite. L'équivoque produite est réelle, impossible à résoudre au sens de la désignation et de l'univocité, mais cernée par l'écriture." J.M. Vappereau, "Afin de préciser le narcissisme," on the site: jeanmichel.vappereau.free.fr

where it comes from.[83] According to Jean-Pierre Cléro, the idea that we live in a Euclidian space is a prejudice: "Euclidian space is a reductive fantasy affecting perceptive space."[84] And Erik Porge concludes: "we are not in geometrical space but we apprehend it as a fiction from the vantage point of the psyche's topological structure."[85]

The ego thinks it is moving in a three-dimensional space "*in comformity with its form*," a form that is the result of the specular operation of identification. "In this three-dimensional kingdom, absence and presence are organized dualistically: what is in front is not behind, what is above is not below, what is left is not right."[86] Is it the passage from a multi-dimensional space to a two-dimensional surface and its return that promotes the attribution to the body of a three-dimensional reality? Do the group articulation of drive objects and their relationship to the upright posture (with gravitational symmetry, oriented gestures, and the way in which the body's protruding elements—the nose, for instance—are reflected on a flat surface) reinforce the idea of a front, of a back, of an up, and of a down that orients the subject of language in the space in which s/he moves?

The idea that the space into which we are plunged is three-dimensional is a belief that is useful for orienting ourselves in that space, for inhabiting it, building it, describing it. We are the ones who define space through writing. To describe the position of an object in a three-dimensional space, to write it, we need three numbers, which define the number of dimensions. The simplest definition of dimension is formulated in relation to its "degree of freedom," a notion that, in mechanics, includes the possibility of movement in space: an object can move by changing one of its numbers, and this determines its position and changes of position.

The imaginary's vocation for figuration results in the reduction of the multi-dimensional space in which we live. The imaginary is rooted in the reference to the body, which afflicts the speaking being with

---

[83] M. Lachièze-Rey, *Au-delà de l'Espace et du temps: La nouvelle physique* (Paris: Éditions le Pommier, 2008), 21.

[84] J.P. Cléro, *Les raisons de la fiction: Les philosophes et les mathématiques* (Paris: Armand Colin, 2004), 385.

[85] E. Porge, "L'identification: une physique sans métaphysique," in *Se compter trois: Le temps logique de Lacan*, op. cit., 43.

[86] A. Didier-Weill, *Un mystère plus loin que l'inconscient* (Paris: Aubier, 2010), 37–38.

mental debility, as Lacan calls the vocation for meaning and figuration that affects humans.

"There are three dimensions of space inhabited by the speaking being, and these three di(t)mensions (*dit-mensions*),[87] such as I write them, are called the Imaginary, the Symbolic, and the Real."[88] Because they are three, "perceivable space ends up being reduced to this minimum of three dimensions."[89]

---

[87] The expression *dit-mensions* is a neologism created by Lacan with the words '*dire*' and '*dimension*' ('to say' and 'dimension,' literally 'said dimensions'). Once again, Lacan stresses the function of language in the subject's relation to reality, a reality that is constituted by the imaginary, the symbolic, and the real. In these pages we will refer to it as *di(t)mensions*.

[88] J. Lacan, *Le Séminaire livre XXI: Les non-dupes errent*, 13 novembre 1973.

[89] J. Lacan, *Le Séminaire livre XXII: R.S.I.*, 10 décembre 1974. Referring to the Borromean knot, Lacan stresses that "inasmuch as it is supported by the number three, it belongs to the imaginary register." At the same time, he insists on the real character of the knot, by virtue of the fact that the three dimensions (*dit-mensions*) are tied there in a real manner. By virtue of its writing and its function as a model, the knot is imaginary; but in so far as the three consistencies really hold together these three rings are founded in the real. *Ibid.*, 17 décembre 1974.

THE PLACE IN THE SCENE

The Place

The subject is implicated in the world that concerns him or her. Not only is the subject implicated in the object—the observer in the data s/he studies, the researcher in the object examined, the spectator in the spectacle—but the subject emerges as effect of a transferential relationship with what is other.

The advent of the subject coincides with the constitution of the milieu that is its own. We call *place* the particular space that belongs to a given subject, his or her singular relationship with the world s/he inhabits, the creation of "his" or "her" world on the world scene. The drive objects relating to demand and desire situate the subject, locate its sphere of action, draw the coordinates of its extension. While the appropriation of space corresponds to the way the subject orients himself or herself in the signifying structure, the extension of the subjective sphere is a libidinal extension. Wherever the perception of the things that surround us comes from; wherever the gaze extends; wherever silence and sound are perceived; wherever we are led by our steps, or motion, or thought, or daydream, our world is libidinal.

"We are the children of our landscape."[90] The landscape is locale, is earth, extension, sky; but it is also what fills it, composes it; it is at once what contains these forms and the forms themselves. Our landscape is our window on the world, from which we emerge as subjects of language. We are simultaneously its products and its producers. We carry it within us and unfold it outside of us. We are inside it.

---

[90] L. Durrell, *Justine* (New York: Penguin, 1991), 41.

Lalangue, the Call

"At the beginning, there is the Other and nothing else. It is without limits, it is the air we breathe, that forces the lungs to open at the time of the first cry."[91] Lacan posits the existence of an exterior prior to any interiorization. Originally, we are not missing the outside world, Lacan says, but ourselves. The primary relationship of being with the world is transformed and delimited in the libidinal articulation of place.

The landscape of the living has always been a sonorous reality; it is already a sonorous reality in the womb and at the moment of conception. There exists a sound of the body, the sound of the physiological rhythm, of the heartbeat or the breath. The body produces sound and is swimming in the sound of the world.

The world of sound is inhabited by the prosody of speech. From the outset, the infant is bathed in *lalangue*. The mother's language, which accompanies caring for the baby, is a call, an invitation, an orientation in the living landscape. Thanks to it the landscape expresses a direction, begins to acquire a contour. And if the world of sound acquires spatial coordinates, it is because the call provokes a *listening* in the world of the audible.

From the waters of the maternal language in which the baby bathes, there remain scattered and discreet elements, heard elements that permeate the living substance—and which will become the matter the unconscious is made of—the *moteriality* of the unconscious, as Lacan calls it by means of an expression that connects 'word' (*mot*) and 'matter': "The unconscious is the way in which the subject ... was permeated by language."[92]

There exists a widespread prejudice: the conviction that, since learning the language happens late and with difficulty—together with the child's neurophysiological development—language is by nature something external and separate from the body, something "added" and "secondary." In fact, language permeates the living substance as soon as it appears in the world, something that those who reduce the human being to pure organic materiality seem to forget. The human world has always been one of language, and this long before the child

---

[91] C. Millot, *O solitude* (Paris: Éditions Gallimard, 2011), 143.

[92] J. Lacan, "Conférence de Genève sur le symptôme," *Le bloc-notes de la psychanalyse* 5 (Paris: Georg, 1985), 5–23.

is able to use the language from which s/he has been fashioned. If this were not so, the child would never be able to begin to speak, as certain cases of early isolation have shown. "The baby is 'spoken' before speaking himself," as Catherine Vanier points out:

> S/he is talked about before, during, and after birth. Later on, s/he will acquire the language according to a process that seems genetically programmed. But s/he will only be able to speak if s/he hears speech. It is easy to notice the baby's interest in speech when you address him or her. Even if s/he is only a few hours old, s/he is present and attentive, and most of the time s/he opens his or her mouth wide, as if to swallow the voice that leans over him or her. "S/he drinks our words like milk," to quote an old saying.[93]

This is what constitutes the human being's particularity: an encounter between body and speech that is the incarnation of *jouissance*, that shapes an unconscious knowledge and provokes all kinds of affects that go far beyond what the speaker is able to express, but which accompany his or her speech. The affect thereby acquires the status of "epistemic witness" to an unconscious knowledge that causes it, but remains inaccessible, an incarnate knowledge—the product of a relationship with the mother and the first parental figures—that always turns out to be particular.[94] While language universally metabolizes into human substance, this metabolization is always singular, determined by a specific *lalangue*, by the circumstances of the history, milieu, and culture in which the exchange takes place with the caregiver. *Lalangue* gathers the acoustic remains "of a group's handling of its unconscious experience."[95]

When the body encounters speech the living substance is subjectified, the body is corporified in a signifying manner, and it loses its purely organic quality. In the *parlêtre* the manifestation of the body

---

[93] C. Vanier, *Naître prématuré: Le bébé, son médecin, et son psychanalyste* (Paris: Bayard Éditions), 195.

[94] "Affect, inasmuch as it is enigmatic, acquires the status of epistemic witness. It certainly does not guarantee a knowledge, but it produces the sign that an unknown knowledge is there, causing it. We are in the register of proof by affect." C. Soler, *Lacan: l'inconscient réinventé* (Paris: Presses Universitaires de France, 2009), 31.

[95] J. Lacan, "La troisième," novembre 1974, *Lettres de l'Ecole Freudienne*, Bulletin intérieur de l'Ecole Freudienne de Paris 16, 189.

is a manifestation of the body/speech; the symptom is always the renewed expression of their encounter. While affects are effects of *lalangue*, the specificity of the human being—of his or her perceptions, of his or her emotions—is congenital to the innate encounter between body and speech. The logic of *jouissance* is tied to the way in which *jouissance* inhabits language: "*Lalangue,* any element of *lalangue,* is, from the perspective of *phallic jouissance,* a shoot of *jouissance*. And it is in this that it spreads its roots so deep in the body."[96]

The remains of the a-structural sound continuum, picked up from the melody produced by the parental Other, are sonorous units coming from what is heard, units outside the signifying chain and outside meaning.[97] *Lalangue* is not a language, it does not constitute a whole.

> The fact that a child says *maybe, not yet,* before he or she is able to really construct a sentence, proves that s/he contains something, a sieve through which things pass, through which the waters of language end up leaving something behind, some detritus with which s/he plays, with which s/he has to make do. This is what all this non-reflexive activity leaves him or her: debris, to which, later on, because s/he is premature, will be added the problems of what will frighten him or her, and thanks to which s/he will combine, so to speak, this sexual reality and language.[98]

Language is no doubt made up of *lalangue,* states Lacan. But if the unconscious is structured like a language, it is an always hypothetical language in light of what sustains it, namely *lalangue.*

The Space of Transmission

Freud and Lacan both stress the fact that the transferential relationship of the subject to alterity necessarily involves transmission. Strangely, however, the idea that there can exist between generations a type of symbolic transmission, related to the domain of desire, that

---

[96] J. Lacan, *Le Séminaire livre XXI: Les non-dupes errent*, 11 juin 1974.
[97] See C. Soler, *Lacan: l'inconscient réinventé*, op. cit., 34.
[98] J. Lacan, "Conférence de Genève sur le symptôme," op. cit.

is added onto the genetic transmission codified in matter provokes all kinds of resistance and incredulity. Why so much noise? Is this reaction rooted, once again, in the belief in an intrinsic separation between *res cogitans* and *res extensa*?

The fact that the landscape that awaits the living being is a dimension of speech, even before s/he makes his/her appearance, involves diverse types of transmission from the outset. Above all there is a symbolic transmission passed on through parental discourse: from the moment of conception the human offspring is involved in a discourse made up of expectations, both positive and negative, conveyed by signifiers that appeal to his/her subjectivity and that will become the baggage of a received knowledge with which s/he will have to cope. Whether this discourse is expressed by words or by silence does not change anything of the fact that it is being transmitted; and, despite the amazement of parents and educators, the fact that something is unsaid does not lessen its shattering impact on the subject, since it is fully present precisely *because it is unsaid*, and, as such, it is material apt to be transmitted and fantasized about. Faced with the adult's enigmatic desire, what is unsaid is a privileged locale for the production of fantasy.

But transmission is also passed on through the real of *jouissance*, which accompanies the incarnation of *lalangue*. Coming from the Other, *lalangue* carries the traces of the *jouissance* of the caretakers; incarnate, it conveys scraps of *jouissance* between generations. And the pleasure taken in using language, the pleasure of everyday bla-bla-bla, produces a *jouissance* that keeps circulating between subject and Other.

The "body of the symbolic," as Lacan calls it ("which should be understood as no metaphor") is metabolized in the organic, giving shape to the subjective body.[99] Lacan calls upon the notion of the 'incorporeal' developed by stoicism. The stoical theory of "the sayable" (*lekton*) introduces a new element in the relationship between concept and object. Whereas for Aristotle the thing signified by the word is the thought, and through the thought the object, for the Stoics there

---

[99] "The first body makes the second one by incorporating itself. Whence the incorporeal that remains marking the first, from the time after its incorporation." "Le premier corps fait le second de s'y incorporer. D'où l'incorporel qui reste marquer le premier, du temps d'après son incorporation." J. Lacan, "Radiophonie," *Autres Ecrits*, op. cit., 409.

exists, as Ammonius explains, "an intermediary between the thought and the thing, which they call the sayable."[100] This intermediary is, in itself, incorporeal, since it differs as much from thought as from sound, both of which are considered 'bodies' in stoic philosophy (a notion of 'body' to which Lacan pays tribute with the expression "body of the symbolic"). Since there is no intrinsic relationship between the word and the thing, the fact that something is signified by a word must therefore be added to it as an 'incorporeal attribute.'

The stoic argument offers as an example the meeting between a Greek and a barbarian who hear the same Greek word. Both will have the representation of the thing the word designates, but the Greek will understand and the barbarian will not: "What other reality is there, then, beside the sound on the one hand and the object on the other? None. The object and the sound remain the same. But the object has for the Greek, I won't say a property (because its essence remains the same in both cases) but an attribute that it does not have for the barbarian, namely that of being signified by the word. It is this attribute of the object that the Stoics call a sayable."[101]

The reference to the incorporeal, to the indispensable attribute for there to be meaning, allows a differentiation between sense and signification.[102] Whereas sense is something on the order of what is translatable in the transposition of content from one discourse to another, from one language to another, signification is the fruit of live discourse, of an act of speech that takes place in a precise context within the social bond and, as such, is 'incorporeal.' It indicates the space of the *untranslatable*, a decisive and irreducible presence, which, to be heard or appreciated (in the case, for instance, of wit), involves a series of transpositions, of forms of identification in a foreign or unknown social bond, and involves, in any case, *a loss of meaning*, as well as the production of *additional* meanings in the context of the target language, which are themselves not necessarily translatable later. The incorporeal accompanies the transformation of the social bond within

---

[100] Quoted by E. Bréhier, *La théorie des incorporels dans l'ancient stoicisme* (Paris: Librairie Philosophique J. Vrin, 1997), 15.

[101] *Ibid.*, 14.

[102] As Jean-Michel Vappereau noted in his presentation "The Two Moments Prior to Narcissism: Trauma and Incorporation" at Après-Coup Psychoanalytic Association, New York, March 24–25, 2012.

the same culture and the transformation of meanings during different periods of time. From one era to another, or simply from one generation to another, a witticism can become incomprehensible within the same culture. This reflects the constant mutation of languages, their characteristic "hallowed growth," as Benjamin calls it.[103]

Underlying the gap between *lalangue* and language, as well as the gap between different languages, the untranslatable signals the loss intrinsic to the act of speech. It is obvious that the act of translating from one language to another greatly highlights the incorporeal and accentuates its resistance. However, it is precisely the encounter with the untranslatable, with what seems to be impossible to convey, that becomes an opportunity for invention. The space of the untranslatable turns out to be crucial for transmission: "Failed therefore, but by this very fact succeeding in light of an error, or to put it better: of a straying."[104] The straying conveys transmission. And while the untranslatable is at the center of the act of speaking, transmission is seeded in its stead.

Benjamin notes that kinship is not necessarily accompanied by resemblance, as much in the domain of languages as in that of families. Resemblance implies a displacement. Transmission is not on the order of the similar: "What you inherited from your ancestors, re-conquer it if you want to truly possess it" (*Was du ererbt von deinen Vätern hast, Erwirb es, um es zu besitzen.*)[105] It is in the verb *erwerben* "to re-conquer," "acquire," "take possession," that we appreciate the importance of a return to the past, to the letter, to the study of its meaning-effects in a given context. This includes the need to know one's own history, to understand one's own culture, while taking into account the untranslatability peculiar to it. But it is through this *erwerben* that we also measure the importance of the fact that this work of acknowledgement and appropriation involves an entry of the current into the past, making acquisition an enacted and acting transformation. This shows that transmission is by nature transformation, involving, of

---

[103] W. Benjamin, "The Task of the Translator," in *Selected Writings I, 1913–1926* (Cambridge, MA: Belknap, 2004), 275.

[104] "Raté donc, mais par là-même réussi au regard d'une erreur, ou pour mieux dire: d'un errement." J. Lacan, *Télévision*, op. cit., 9.

[105] Goethe, *Faust*, quoted by Freud, *Totem und Tabu, Gesammelte Werke IX* (Frankfurt am Main: S. Fischer Verlag, 1996).

course, entering the domain of the incommunicable and encountering the inexplicable, the ingredients for the production of new meanings. It is this passage into the aspheric zone of the untranslatable, of the incorporeal sheltered by the world of sense and nonsense, that allows for transmission to take place.

While to translate (from the Latin *transducere*) is to lead through, a crossing in which we are accompanied toward new shores in a different landscape, to transmit (from the Latin *transmittere*: composed of *trans*, beyond, and *mittere*, to send) is, above all, to transfer (from one person to another, from one space to another, from one era to another), where the accent is put on the passage that conveys the transmission, the delivery, the diffusion.

In the Place: The Object Voice and the Object Gaze

The object *a* cannot be grasped, transmitted, or exchanged; constitutive of the speaking being's very structure, the object *a* is "what is missing." As such, it is on the horizon of all the things around which the fantasm gravitates on the world scene.[106]

When speaking of the subjective place, we should recognize the presence of the object *a*. Its episodic forms (oral, anal, scopic, and vocal) are interlinked in a synchronic group structure, articulated by the inversions of demand and desire in the relationship between subject and Other. The libidinal reality of the place, its *di(t)mension*, is traversed by the network of connections of the different episodic sides of *a*.

The voice, as object *a* related to the desire of the Other, and the gaze, as object *a* related to the desire towards the Other, arise from the domain of the audible and the visible. Although silent and invisible, their presence is central to the subjective landscape.

Originally, Lacan isolates the voice object from the domain of speech:

> In the fully developed signifier that is speech, there is always a passage, in other words something that is beyond each of the articulated el-

---

[106] J. Lacan, "Préface à l'édition anglaise du *Séminaire XI*," *Autres Ecrits*, op. cit., 573.

ements, and which stems from their fleeting, evanescent nature. It is this passage from one to the other that makes up the crux of what we call the signifying chain. As evanescent, this passage is the very thing that gives voice—I don't even say that it becomes a signifying articulation, because it may be that the articulation remains enigmatic, but what sustains the passage is voice.[107]

The voice sustains the passage of the elements articulated in the signifying chain; evanescent, *it is* this very passage. As object *a*, it provides the cadence of the circuit of the invocatory drive deployed in the Other's domain through speech, in the universe of *lalangue*. Like the other drive objects, the voice is structured by the cut associated with a bodily orifice. It has a particularity, however. The three logical moments of the drive trajectory involve a topological itinerary, from the intrinsic to the extrinsic and vice versa. Lacan illustrates this itinerary with verbal conjugation: in the case of the oral drive, to eat, to be eaten, to make oneself eaten; in the case of the anal drive, to shit, to be shat, to get shat; in the case of the scopic drive, to see, to be seen, and to make oneself seen.[108] The verbal illustrations in question are the active, the passive, and what I would define as a *reflexive through procuration*, a form that signals what is most intimate—*ex-timate*—in the drive itinerary and its realization. It is a reflexive form that needs the other in order to be realized and that topologically ties the domain of the subject to the domain of the Other.

This is also what occurs in the case of the invocatory drive—to hear, to be heard, to make oneself heard—except that here the organs involved are two (mouth and ears) and "the ears are in the sphere of the unconscious the only orifice that cannot be closed."[109] Whereas the making oneself seen implies a circuit that returns to the subject, the making oneself heard entails a supplementary twist, a going toward the other anew. Hearing and speech are the two sides of a Möbius strip.

---

[107] J. Lacan, *Le Séminaire livre V: Les formations de l'inconscient* (Paris: Éditions du Seuil, 1998), 343.

[108] In French: manger, être mangé, se faire manger; chier, être chié, se faire chier; voir, être vu, se faire voir.

[109] J. Lacan, *Le Séminaire livre XI: Les quatre concepts fondamentaux de la psychanalyse*, op. cit., 178.

There is a link between hearing and speech that is not external, in the sense of hearing yourself speak, but that happens at the level of the phenomenon of language itself. It is at the level where the signifier brings about signification, and not at the sensory level of the phenomenon, that hearing and speech are like two sides of the same coin.[110]

The voice as object *a* makes no sound, is not audible: "It is what falls from speech, which is to say literally an emptiness, a silence, which could be pure silence, an emptiness at the heart of any object, that of the object *a*, a hole, that is."[111] In the original exchange with the caregiver, it emerges in the interval of the adult's speech, in the scansion between signifiers where the question of the other's desire appears. The child receives a *"You are"* that is preliminary to any *"Who am I?"* Lacan situates the primordial separation from the voice in the mythical moment when the subject submits to an order that does not yet mean anything to him/her, the internalization of which sediments demand. In the sphere of the Other, not everything necessarily has meaning; however, "the first words spoken decree, legislate, aphorize, and are an oracle; they give the real other its obscure authority," tracing a structural link between voice and superego.[112] But if the superego's purpose is the instauration of an Other completed by the voice, the voice structurally de-completes the Other, expressing its implicit lack of guarantees.

The scansion of speech, its emission, "creates the voice as object *a*."[113] As scansion, it has a temporal value, "connected to the time I take to say things."[114] In speech, the scansion allows meaning effects to emerge retroactively. However, the difference between enunciation and statement favors ambiguity and misunderstandings. It is the dimension of writing, rather, that allows us to distinguish the ambiguity of the signifier and to recognize what is spoken from is written: beau

---

[110] J. Lacan, *Le Séminaire livre III: Les psychoses*, 8 février 1956, 155.

[111] A. Vanier, "La musique, c'est le bruit qui pense," *Insistance: Art Psychanalyse Politique* 6 (Paris: Erès, 2011), 17.

[112] J. Lacan, "The Subversion of the Subject and the Dialectic of Desire in the Freudian Unconscious," *Ecrits: The First Complete Edition in English*, trans. Bruce Fink, op. cit., 684.

[113] E. Porge, "Les voix, la voix," *Essaim* 26 (2011), 20.

[114] J. Lacan, *Le Séminaire livre XXI: Les non-dupes errent*, 9 avril 1974.

from bow, two from to, one from won, and so on. As function of the written, the voice sustains legibility in the world of speech.

Like the object voice, the gaze as object *a* inhabits the subjective place and silently supports its structure. Of the verbal forms belonging to the circuit of the scopic drive, the passive (being seen) plays a central role, common in everyone's experience. From the beginning every newborn is subjected to the gaze of others who take care of him/her. "*Io sono sempre vista*," "I am always seen, *a vista*," is a saying that expresses the condition of the subject of vision; we can grasp here the persistence of the gaze to which one is subjected, as well as the way this persistence can reduce one to being both an object and a landscape. The gaze can turn, therefore, into surveillance, intrusion, or persecution, which brings about its maleficent quality.

In the scopic drive's circuit, the first logical moment is the active one, to look. The gaze breaks away from our own seeing; however, it remains exterior to us, we are subjected to it. Like children or ostriches, we can believe that by closing our eyes it is possible to leave, to escape it. Yet, when internalized, it still has this characteristic of the 'outside.'

The world is *omni-voyeur*, but the gaze cannot be isolated from it. As object *a*, it is what is lacking; it is what, invisible, breaks away from the visible as unrepresentable, which does not diminish its presence and function.

Sound Architecture

We move through a world of sounds while making sounds. The voice dwells in sound; the voice subjectivizes. The child appropriates some of the sound that s/he harbors. S/he discovers the modular quality of the voice as instrument. Before the acquisition of linguistic articulation, which is accompanied by a particular fragmentation of the sound prosody, the child has a phonetic capacity some linguists define as unlimited. Jakobson observes that, at the peak of babbling, the child is able to make all the sounds found in human languages.[115] And s/he exercises this power in his/her experiencing of the world, to which the

---

[115] R. Jacobson, *Child Language, Aphasia, and Phonological Universals* (The Hague: Mouton, 1968).

voice belongs. It is interesting to note that, during the period prior to gross motor development, when it is impossible for him/her to have oriented movements, the child has the ability to utter a great variety of sounds. Might these sounds amount to actions?

In fact, sound accompanies the gaze and light; it gives volume to the world scene. But if the world acquires spatial coordinates, it is because the call coming from the Other has inserted listening into the universe of the audible. The voice is an instrument of spatial dimensionality; it emerges from a here in order to spread out and return to the body, after having travelled through the surrounding volume. From alterity, it returns to the subject, conferring a dimension to the milieu. It is possible to think of sound as having a tactile value, of sound activity being a logical anticipation of gestural activity.

What the baby experiments with, as much in the articulation of sound as in its production, is its efficacy. This experimentation permeates his/her relationship with the world and with the Other and takes the shape of a creative activity, an activity which, tied to the gaze, to the proximity and the distance of the objects of the drive, organizes the place. It isn't by chance that this activity produces an apparent satisfaction. This brings to mind the Bauhaus motto: "Architecture is the goal of all creative activity."[116] By using the body's sonority, its power, by experimenting with the voice following the gaze, the very young child is an architect.

The sound variations s/he is able to produce are destined to disappear. The acquisition of language involves a phonetic amnesia, a progressive and partial atrophy of this ability. The apprenticeship of the native language involves leaving behind the original sounds made by the voice, producing a sequential cutting up of the verbal flux, a cutting that introduces an initial *legibility* to the world of sound.

From the moment the infant articulates the first demands, s/he acquires his/her own voice and abandons the space where s/he was only spoken. S/he benefits from the speech coming from the world to articulate signifiers outside the received discourse and lay out the elements of his/her own place. Leaving behind the plural series of sounds seems to be the condition required to master the finite system of con-

---

[116] W. Gropius, *Manifest des Staatlichen Bauhauses in Weimar* (Weimar: Staatliches Bauhaus, 1919).

sonants and vowels that characterize each language.[117] The acquisition of the native language takes us away from the sounds that make it up and that cut up from the world of prosody the segmentations specific to it, carriers of a musicality and a rhythm henceforth discernable only (or almost) when listening to a foreign language. While "speech silences the voice," speech emerges from the field progressively constructed by the child's use of sound.[118]

Going back to Troubetskoï's observations on the abnormal phonological elements of a language (those that don't belong to its phonetic system), Heller-Roazen points out that the child's original sound potential resurfaces in certain series of sounds—such as exclamations, sounds imitating animals or mechanical noises—which do not belong to a particular idiom.[119] The latent sound expression that reappears as the effect of surprise, as the effect of an interruption of the signifying chain, shows that the sound support the language moves away from—an echo of *lalangue*—becomes a grip for the subject of language in the moment when s/he is on the verge of disappearing, in the anticipation of a new signifier, on the edge of meaning.

Locus Amoenus et Gaudens

The sound experimentation by means of which the child feels out the coordinates of the world scene, of the space that belongs to him/her, often takes the shape of a ludic activity. The obvious satisfaction that accompanies it associates play and creativity. According to Winnicott, the ludic space establishes an intermediate area between mother and child, where internal reality and external life contribute to the subject's experiencing; in the transitional space *between* subject and object, the child *creates* the thing the world gives him.[120] But the

---

[117] D. Heller-Roazen, "The Apex of Babble," in *Echolalias: On the Forgetting of Language* (New York: Zone Books, 2005).
[118] J.M. Vives, "Pour introduire la question de la pulsion invocante," dans *Les enjeux de la voix en psychanalyse dans et hors la cure* (Presses Universitaires de Grenoble), 13.
[119] D. Heller-Roazen, *Echolalias: On the Forgetting of Language*, op. cit., 18.
[120] D. Winnicott, "Transitional Object and Transitional Phenomena" (1951), *Playing and Reality* (London: Tavistock, 1971); "The Deprived Child and How He Can Be Compensated for Loss of Family Life," *The Family and Individual Development* (London: Tavistock, 1964).

satisfaction that accompanies experimentation and play with sound raises the question of the *jouissance* belonging to their practice: its libidinal nature has its roots in the coalescence between sexual reality and language. While the dimension of play acquires a specific signifying value connected to speech, it uses language to pull the strings of *lalangue* and find satisfaction. The ludic space is a space of *jouissance*.

Ludic activity and language are bound together in that classic model of entry into language that is the *fort/da* game described by Freud in *Beyond the Pleasure Principle*, a model of the first signifying opposition—oo/aa—that accompanies the repeated gesture of the child, who throws the reel far from him in order to then pull it back to him. Lacan observes that the thrown reel does not represent the absent mother, but "a little something of the subject that falls away all the while being his, still held," a self-mutilation allowing the signifying order to be shaped.[121] If the signifier is the first mark of the subject, it is in the object's place that, according to Lacan, we must find the subject.

Among the innumerable implications of the *fort/da* game, one cannot help but note that the alternation oo/aa-aa/oo, used in the game, associates signifying opposition and spatial difference. Signifying discontinuity is at once a temporal and spatial discontinuity.

Playing with Words: Economy and Extension

Freud examined several times the intrinsic satisfaction children derive from playing with words, treating "words like things." He develops a theory about this, based on his conception of the psychic apparatus governed by the pleasure principle.

As thing-representations, the memory traces of perceptions are considered over-invested through their link with the word-representations, an over-investment that makes possible the development of the secondary process, which organizes the pre-conscious. With the suspension of the reality principle, the apparatus' function—that of

---

[121] J. Lacan, *Le Séminaire livre XI: Les quatre concepts fondamentaux de la psychanalyse*, op. cit., 60. Originally, Lacan identifies the *fort/da* reel with the Winnicottian transitional object. However, the importance given to the signifying order, which attributes to the object an operational value in the articulation between drive and language, shows how Lacan both relies on Winnicott's concept and moves away from it.

discharging excitation—gives in to the temptation of the shortest path, of the path of least resistance. This regressive tendency may manifest itself in dream formations, in daydreaming, in certain kinds of play, or, generally, in a weakening of the psychic function of attention (which governs the reality principle). It expresses the apparatus' function of returning to a kind of original perceptive concreteness, following the movement traced by desire toward hallucinatory fulfillment.

Among the modes of play, playing with words illustrates this tendency particularly well: supported by the materiality of language, by sound—by the echo of *lalangue*—verbal elements are considered to be redirected to the memory traces of which they are the qualitative residue and to recover their original concreteness. They seem to acquire in this manner those particular qualities Ferenczi defined as belonging to obscene words, pointing out in them the mixture of verbal images and motor elements. Following the Freudian model of the psychic apparatus, Ferenczi concludes that the concreteness specific to obscene words is a quality that "*all* words must have possessed."[122]

Freud stresses the *jouissance* associated with the use of language: he considers the techniques used in the production of play *with* words and of *wordplay* as the very sources from which the apparatus derives pleasure from its own psychic processes. This is also the case in the pleasure of the already known (*Wiederfinden des Bekannten*), in the pleasure of rediscovery and evocation, as children's insistence on being told the same story again and again illustrates, transforming the narrative into a game. Rhyme, alliteration, and assonance all allow for discovering a signifier that uses novelty to feed repetition. The real secret of ludic activity "is the more radical diversity that constitutes repetition."[123]

This seems to also be the case for the pleasure of the absurd (*Lust am Unsinn*), fruit of the lifting of the censorship that governs secondary elaboration and rational thought. When inhibition and censorship are suspended—for example, through alcohol or other substances—the tendency of the apparatus is to derive pleasure from lin-

---

[122] S. Ferenczi, "Le parole oscene: saggio sulla psicologia della fase di latenza" (1911), in *Sandor Ferenczi: Fondamenti di psicoanalisi, Parte Prima: teoria, Vol. I* (Rimini: Guaraldi Editore, 1972), 127.

[123] J. Lacan, *Le Séminaire livre XI: Les quatre concepts fondamentaux de la psychanalyse*, op. cit., 60.

guistic material, to follow "acoustic representation of the word to the detriment of its meaning," the "'external' associations rather than the 'internal' associations of verbal representation," approaching in this way the formations of the unconscious and the *jouissance* that inhabits them.[124] The main characteristic of the *Lustprinzip* is that it satisfies itself "by blablabla."[125]

Making Space

According to Tibetan lama Sogyal Rimpoce, humor consists in making space where there is no space.[126] I don't know what this definition refers to in Tibetan philosophy, but for someone who hears it from the vantage point of a very different thought tradition, it resonates a great deal.

Humor is raising, lightening, diminishing. It suffices to think of the relief it brings to situations that are tense, awkward, tiring, or simply situations of daily alienation. And this isn't all: according to an article in the *New York Times*, it seems that the laughter provoked by witticisms and jokes causes weight loss and increases productivity: for this reason, certain companies in the United States are considering hiring professional comedians to entertain their workers, thus demonstrating their willingness to confront the problem of physical and mental health in a productive manner. It remains to be seen whether the companies in question see the humor in this. To lose weight thanks to laughter is certainly a way of making space; increasing production seems more like the opposite.

As for finding space where it is lacking, *Witz* is exemplary: according to Freud, the work that allows its formation (*Witzarbeit*) is finely woven in the different registers of the apparatus with an amazing and indefatigable rigor that gives rise to a sudden and brand new pro-

---

[124] S. Freud, *Der Witz und seine Beziehung zum Unbewußten*, op. cit., 134.

[125] J. Lacan, *Le Séminaire livre XX: Encore*, op. cit., 53.

[126] This definition was formulated during a conference in Lausanne in August of 2009, during the days dedicated to the teachings of the Dalai Lama. I thank Giulia Niccolai, Italian poet and Tibetan monk, for the reference. G. Niccolai quotes it in "I Ballerini," *Balleriniana* (Ravenna: Danilo Montanari Editore, 2010), 372.

duction; production—as in theatrical production—is the right word, seeing as it is the fruit of a complex and imperceptible coordination.

Freud enumerates the facets of this work: it uses the pleasure of subtlety as a preliminary pleasure in the service of new tendencies and engenders new pleasure by ridding itself of repressions. The work begins with play (*Spiel*) to derive pleasure from the free use of words and thoughts; as soon as reason forbids it, because of its lack of meaning, it turns into a joke (*Scherz*), so as to give itself the pleasure of the absurd; it then becomes wordplay (*Witz*) to avoid criticism and align itself with the great tendencies that struggle against repression and thereby free up internal inhibitions. This is the work of a good jockey, who overcomes one obstacle after another—reason, critical judgment, repression—and firmly retains the first sources of pleasure. It is the work itself that turns into pleasure; it isn't the result, the content, that counts, Freud says. If *Witz* must succeed, it is simply in order to preserve the pleasure engendered by the work of which it is the fruit.

This subtle work fishes in the waters of language so as to catapult itself into the new. The new in question is the production of an unsuspected space. At the same time, the fall of inhibition and of censorship, regulated by critical reason, results in an emptying of meaning, in a rarefaction.

In *l'esp d'un laps*, the *Verblüffung* dis-aggregates the cohesion of repetition in the signifying chain, the coherence of narrative logic, and suddenly shows the discordance between enunciation and statement, the thread by which the subject of language is suspended. Laughter in the *Witz* is the effect of two different moments: the first is the experience of the new, of the unexpected, which one doesn't necessarily "get"; the second is the illuminating experience of laughter. "The first is the experience of the real, of the 'no sense,'" and the second is the experience of the symbolic, of the "step-toward-the-direction-of-desire," (*pas-vers-le-sens-du-désir*) as Alain Didier-Weill puts it.[127]

Illumination follows stupor: an unexpected meaning is found that unleashes the comical effect. And if the signifying suspension falls back into sense, there was a cut between suspension and illumination in the repetition and the appearance of a new signifier. Surprise trans-

---

[127] A. Didier-Weill, *Un mystère plus loin que l'inconscient* (Paris: Aubier, 2010), 106–107.

forms the encounter with the unintelligible into an opportunity for revelation.

According to Freud, the production of *Witz* is a social process. To analyze it, three people have to be counted: the one who says it, the person it is about, and a third person (*dritte Person*), who is the intended recipient of the witticism, the intention always being the production of pleasure. It "buys," to use Freud's expression, its pleasure without spending, it receives it "as a gift."[128] By means of the other in the position of third person, *little sense (peu-de-sens)* turns into a *step of sense*, a *no sense (pas-de-sens)*, and acquires the properties of the metaphor.[129] This act in three parts highlights the "ternary organization constitutive of the subject itself."[130] It reveals the number of places through which the subject passes so that, when s/he addresses the Other in the act of speech, s/he is able to communicate the new as wit. The new involves a displacement, that of the subject and the collective that produces it. We find ourselves elsewhere. The space "does seem to belong to the unconscious structured like a language."[131]

Moving, Walking

In *Gesture and Speech,* André Leroi-Gourant shows how the standing position constitutes the border between the human species and other species. Locomotion appears to be the determining factor of biological evolution; the standing position involves a particular mechanical organization of the spine in relation to the limbs, the suspension of the cranium, and the freeing of the hands. While the foot is the only organ devoted to locomotion, the hand's vocation is making, fabrication, technique. As Gregory of Nyssa declares, man would not have been able to speak if the hand had not shouldered the heavy task

---

[128] S. Freud, *Der Witz und seine Beziehung zum Unbewußten*, op. cit., 174.

[129] "To take an element where it is and to substitute another one in its place, I would say almost any one, introduces that beyond of need in relation to any formulated desire, which is what is always behind metaphor. What is the witticism doing there? It points to nothing less than the very dimension of the *pas* [*pas* meaning both 'step' and 'not'] strictly speaking. It is the *pas*, so to speak, in its form. It is the *pas* emptied of any kind of need." J. Lacan, *Le Séminaire livre V: Les formations de l'inconscient*, op. cit., 101.

[130] E. Porge, *Transmettre la clinique*, op. cit., 158.

[131] J. Lacan, *Le Séminaire livre XX: Encore*, op. cit., 122.

of meeting bodily needs, thereby leaving the lips free to speak. The production of tools coincides with the appearance of man, the tool being a veritable "secretion" of the brain and the body, a production of intelligence integrated into function.[132]

The spine, the face, and the hand are indissolubly linked: man is the only living species in which a vast neurological connection exists between the facial pole and the manual pole, without the anterior limbs being involved in locomotion. Leroi-Gourant examines at length the structure of vertebrate brains and the particularities of the human brain, noting that, along the Roland canal, on the ascending frontal circumvolutions of the primary motor cortex, the neuron groups that control the face, the fingers, the upper limbs, the trunk, and the lower limbs, can be clearly distinguished, where the quantity of neurons devoted to each part of the body is proportional to the minutiae of the demands. In the human brain no less than 80% of the cortex in question is devoted to the motor control of the head and the upper limbs, and, in this cortex, the lips, the larynx, the pharynx, and the fingers alone make up half of the entire surface.

The language apparatus and the manual apparatus that developed from the standing position are structurally interconnected. If technicity can be considered a zoological fact that can be ascribed to specific characteristics, if paleontology can suppose a synchronic evolution of the skeleton and tools, it starts with the relationship between language and the hand. Bridging language and handedness, writing presents itself as witness of their connection.

Skeletal/motor prematurity increases the effort required by the human offspring to reach the standing position, the expression of belonging to the species. But the success of this effort does not exclusively depend on physiological development. In the absence of cerebral or neuro-vegetative lesions, it corresponds to the way the symbolic, imaginary, and real are tied together in the process of identification, a process that matches the evolution of the subjective use of language to the evolution of the mastery of motor skills. Language and motor function are structurally interconnected therein.

---

[132] A. Leroi-Gourant, *Gesture and Speech*, trans. A. Bostock Berger (Cambridge, MA: MIT Press, 1994).

The effort to achieve the standing position reflects the wish to be rid of the burden of the early lack of coordination and the congenital dependency on the other. It is the drive towards walking, towards exploration; it allows for the expansion of space and the opening of the subjective sphere of action.

Walking, Horizon

In their book *Freud en Italie: Psychanalyse du voyage*, Antonietta and Gérard Haddad put forth the concept of a particular drive: the *viatoric* drive, the drive of walking and travel. "What would its parameters be? The push comes from the enigmatic call of Elsewhere, of the Unknown, of the Other, which man perceives by virtue of being constantly prodded by the signifier and speech."[133] Its object would be space, which the drive cuts into loops; the source organ would be the ball of the foot, with its variable contact with the ground, reminiscent of the open-closed alternation of a sphincter, closed when the foot lands back on the ground, open when it leaves to make a step. In relation to the demand addressed to the Other or received from the Other, the viatoric drive would involve the articulation of these two interconnected registers. Abraham's case is a good illustration of it: Abraham leaves of his own volition, but on the way he receives the divine order to be on his way. "Would Yahweh have addressed Abraham if the latter had not already been on his way?"[134]

The concept of a viatoric drive has the advantage of taking into account an essential dimension of the world of the drive, that of space:

> This space certainly encompasses accidents, singular points, such as the nipple of a breast or a stain that calls attention. These accidents are in fact the territory of Freudo-Lacanian drives. But what about indefinite and infinite space, vanishing point of the horizon, empty immensity of the desert or the ocean? This kind of space is not covered by the usual concept of drive. The viatoric drive fills this gap, it introduces into the psychic sphere the category of space as the first and privileged figure of

---

[133] A. and G. Haddad, *Freud en Italie: Psychanalyse du voyage* (Paris: Hachette Littératures, Éditions Albin Michel, 1995), 25.
[134] *Ibid.*, 26.

the big Other, it allows the subject to inhabit and move within the infinity of this space without getting lost.[135]

The Haddads' innovation has the great merit of stressing the human desire to walk and of examining the subjective relation to space, to the call of what appears limited or unlimited, which allows highlighting the central role travel plays in myth. We might, however, wonder to what extent the introduction of a viatoric drive, in addition to the drives enumerated by Freud and Lacan, is in and of itself necessary. Isn't the desire to walk already inscribed in the coordinates of a place where the Other's call has traced directions? Isn't it implicit in the connection between scopic and invocatory circuits, where the body moves in response to a listening that subjectivizes it? In the *dits-mensions* of space/time inhabited by the speaker, the structural relationship between foot, mouth, and hand responds to the drive dialectic between subject and Other, which produces the place. The space to wander through, to leave, to explore, the time required to cross it or to imagine crossing it, don't they already amount to the product of a logical operation of alienation and of separation from the sphere of the Other?

The drive, Lacan says, "is the echo in the body of the fact that there is speech."[136] The relation to space is the effect of the way the subject asserts himself/herself and finds his/her bearings in the place that belongs to him or her. The very notion of distance—that, for example, necessary to reach you, or to see the other side of the world—involves the solidarity peculiar to the group structure of objects of the drive. The Haddads mention the attraction exercised by the enigmatic call of the Elsewhere, of the Unknown, of the Other, prodded by the signifier. In fact, this Elsewhere is the companion of the subject of language. Its call exposes the coordinates of the subjective place, demonstrating that what appears to be Other, Elsewhere, and Unknown expresses in fact what is most intimate, most *ex-timate*, to the subject.

As far as it may be, the horizon presents a limit; when it has been reached, the landscape will still have its horizon. The very notion of landscape contains the horizon, the line up to which the gaze may go or the ear hear, whether it is a familiar landscape or one that is radi-

---

[135] *Ibid.*, 27–28.
[136] J. Lacan, *Le Séminaire livre XXIII: Le sinthome* (Paris: Éditions du Seuil, 2005), 17.

cally new, just discovered or imagined. The horizon is always a point of light, of a light that is the encounter between scopic and invocatory drives.

The limit is intrinsic to the scene of the world; it is what causes the world to be scene. The sense of the limitless, therefore, may not refer to a beyond of the limit. When it emerges, it summons instead, "in the empty immensity of the desert or the ocean," the echo of a time that precedes the landscape; it summons a non-place, a before-the-limit. Catherine Millot defines it as the echo of a "pre-world."[137] We could define it as a "pre-landscape," where the frontier between ego and world has yet to be established, the echo of an exterior before any interiorization, preliminary to the ego's formation.

But, to be evoked, this echo requires a border: it is from within the landscape that it makes itself heard, inside the parameters of the subjective place on the world scene. Where the advent of subjectivization has not occurred—as in autism or in other forms of the absence of the binding of the real, symbolic, and imaginary registers—just as there is no world scene, there is no sense of the unlimited. Isn't the unlimited a concept and a feeling that necessarily occurs *a posteriori*? When the unlimited is a call, if it expresses itself as a desire for an absence of borders, it comes from a border. It isn't space, in the unlimited, that calls, but rather the call that invokes the open space from which the subject of language suffers and to which s/he aspires.

Territory, Hands, Feet

During the Paleolithic era, during the later Neolithic era, and in eras closer to ours, up to today, handprints appear in various manifestations of rock art. In his cataloguing of the visual expressions of tribal and prehistoric art, the archaeologist and ethnologist Emmanuel Anati classifies handprints as belonging to ideograms. According to him, three types of grammatically distinct signs should be considered in rock art: pictograms, in which real or imaginary objects can be recognized; ideograms, characterized by constant and synthetic repetitive signs, indications of conventional concepts meant to transmit ideas;

---

[137] C. Millot, *O solitude*, op. cit., 151.

and psychograms, signs expressing sensations or perceptions.[138] Ideograms are subdivided into the anatomical, as is the case for handprints (or for phallic or vulvar signs), the conceptual (crosses, discs, or serpentines), and the numerical (groups of points and lines), according to a functional subdivision that does not necessarily reflect a textual meaning. The goal of anatomical ideograms is ostensibly to represent the real or symbolic functions of the parts of the human body.

The handprints, whether negative or positive or the vulvar, phallic, cruciform, in the shape of a stick, and arboriforms symbols that we find in Paleolithic art in Europe, we also find in Tanzania and in Australia in similar associations and contexts. It is unthinkable that these recurrent phenomena are the result of direct contact, but we can put forth the hypothesis that they stem from a shared conceptual matrix, which, probably, leads us to the archetypes of the Sapiens in its formative period.[139]

The question is complex and enigmatic, and the conjectures are numerous. Using a structural analysis of prehistoric visual art that allows him to recognize the constants of iconographic grammar and syntax, Anati advances the hypothesis of a common visual language, of a universal symbolism or primordial language that is the essence of the *Homo sapiens*. The human race has existed on the planet for five or six million years, but art as a widespread cultural phenomenon only represents 1% of the era of mankind. It seems to correspond to the advent of *Homo sapiens*, whose presence, starting 40,000 years ago, is associated with types of rock art, first on the African and Asian continents, then in Europe, in America, and finally in Australia. During the millennia that preceded its appearance, there were already "the first attempts to carve signs with a numerical value, and even before this, attempts to produce instruments with harmonious and symmetrical

---

[138] E. Anati, *La struttura elementare dell'arte*, in *Studi Camuni XXII* (Capo di Ponte: Edizioni del Centro, 2002), 39–48.

[139] *Ibid.*, 74. According to Anati, the art of the Archaic Hunters displays a universal character, whereas the art of the Evolved Hunters already displays more frequent local characteristics: "The Tower of Babel begins when the era of hunting and gathering ends. The beginnings of this intense diversification, in one corner or other of the globe, goes back 12,000 years. In some marginal or peripheral areas, it is currently taking place." *Ibid.*

shapes."[140] That *Homo faber* (the designation that includes the long line of Anthropoids from which *Homo sapiens* emerged) opens the way for *Homo sapiens* is no surprise, seeing as how the advent of humankind coincides with the upright posture, the freeing of the hand, the invention of the tool, and the articulation of language. *Homo faber* remains "incorporated" in *Homo sapiens,* to use Haddad's expression.[141] On the coincidence between the appearance on earth of both *Homo sapiens* and art, Leroi-Gourant has a clear opinion: figurative art cannot be separate from language; it is the fruit of the articulation of the spoken and written pair. According to Anati, visual language is not only the first step toward writing; it is *de facto* writing.

We shall leave the fascinating and thorny debate about an eventual universal visual symbolism to the ethnologists and archaeologists. An observation of Anati's is still worth noting: "During all the historical periods and in the majority of tribal societies, visual art refers directly or indirectly to three fundamental themes: sex, food, and territory."[142] On the basis of a comparative study of tribal and prehistoric art, Anati claims that certain recurring ideograms—such as the rectangle and the square—signify land, place, or territory in the majority of ideographic systems and in the principal zones of prehistoric rock art in Euro-Asiatic and American regions.

It is interesting to consider that *Homo sapiens*' first visual testimony, like that of illiterate tribal cultures to this very day, refers to the relationship of the subject and the social corpus with the place, not only with the particular site of their inscription, but with the very idea of territory in its ideogrammatic representation. As Anati notes, to understand the value of rock art one has to remember that it is kept *in situ*, where man produced it.

Extraordinary archives of the history of illiterate man, the rock paintings testify to his/her geographical, cultural, and social milieu, as well as to the particularity of his/her relation to territory. Whether it involves the visual art of the archaic hunters, that of the evolved hunters, or that of the shepherd-breeders, the reference to place reflects its intrinsically drive-related nature: a piece of the universe is transformed

---

[140] E. Anati, *Il museo immaginario della preistoria: L'arte rupestre nel mondo* (Milano: Jaca Book, 1995), 14.

[141] G. Haddad, *Tripalium: Pourquoi le travail est devenu une souffrance* (Paris: François Bourin Éditeur, 2013), 96.

[142] *Ibid.*, 39.

into a subjective place thanks to the space-time coordinates that human actions establish there. It is in this place that s/he lives, acts, reproduces, and dies. The fact that territory, sex, and food emerge as basic themes in rock art reflects the nature of the subject of language, whether the linking of these themes comes from authors of the works or from the observers who catalog them.

The territory includes walking, exploration, appropriation, work, transformation, stopping, installation; it harbors the activities of *Homo faber/sapiens* in his/her relation to life and death (including the relation to sublimation of which art is the expression). It is this sublimated relationship with creation that seems to distinguish the passage to *Homo sapiens,* of which we are part.

The negative and positive handprints evoke first of all the idea of presence, of witnessing. In an emblematic way, they are, above all, the signature of mankind, of the human species, of the upright posture that distinguishes it; but they are also testimony to human actions—to producing, crossing, reaching, creating—deployed in the place. It is interesting to note that while the representations of handprints are frequent at different times and in distant places, the same cannot be said of footprints; feet rarely appear.[143] This is food for thought concerning the particularity of the handprint and its function.

The hand is the silent *alter ego* of language, its representative; it transmits something beyond what language is able to represent. It is the means of artistic creation and of the recording of signifying marks. At the same time, it expresses the relationship of the foot with the territory; it tells where the foot has gone, how far it has gone, how it moves.

Hands and Place

In the early 1980s, I had the opportunity to see the Neolithic paintings (5000–4000 BCE) on the walls of the Porto Badisco caves,

---

[143] An example of prehistoric rock art incisions of two feet executed at different times was found in the oasis of Dâkhla, in Egypt. There exist different marble tables from Roman times dating from the first centuries of our era that represent footprints accompanied by epigraphs of a votive nature; several examples are found in the Archaeological Museum of Seville where they are presented as propitiatory images dedicated to the goddess Nemesis Caelestis, eventual offerings by priests or magistrates in order to seek aid in the exercise of their functions.

in Salento in the south of Italy. At the time, the descent into the underground galleries was through a very narrow rocky passageway that required crawling several meters before encountering a wider passage, where it was possible to squat and then to stand. At the rock's first natural widening, the walls, lit by flashlight, revealed handprints made in *guano*, a kind of prelude for the discovery to follow. One had the surprising impression of seeing the signal of an entrance into a new, artistically organized dimension. The prints had the power of a declaration; in a single stroke, they ushered in the category of *Homo spectator*, "the humanizing function of imaging operations."[144] They invited us to continue along our path. And indeed, the two long galleries decorated in the meanders of different karstic cavities contained one of the most important monuments of post-Paleolithic parietal painting in Europe.[145]

The handprints reappeared much farther on, in the splendid pictorial sequences that make these galleries both a unique and a unitary work of art. This time they were unfurled in a rhythmic explosion, being integral to a few masterly compositions. In the Badisco caves—but also in many other prehistoric rock art representations, in many examples of tribal art up to this day, and also in certain examples of Peruvian shrouds that go back to the first centuries of our era—the repetition of the handprint, enigmatic and seductive, seems to transmit more of a rhythm than an emphasis on form. What is at play, of course, is the rhythm of the visual unit, which necessarily refers to another unit, another sign, in order to produce emotional and representational signifying effects, giving life to the symbolizing operations of the work in its entirety. But one has the impression that the visualization of a musical rhythm is also involved: it transmits the movement of the gesture that imprints them, of the moving body, of the foot that accompanies them. It is as if a dance were being represented (propitiatory, celebratory, ritual, festive, spontaneous, and so forth) that leaves its mark in space and becomes a work of art. In evoking the *jouissance* associated with the body in space, it also evokes the subliminal nature of art, its capacity to make the invisible visible, to represent the unrepresentable.

---

[144] M. J. Mondzain, *Homo spectator* (Paris: Bayard, 2007), 23.

[145] See P. Graziosi, *Le pitture preistoriche della grotta di Porto Badisco* (Florence: Giunti Martello, 1980).

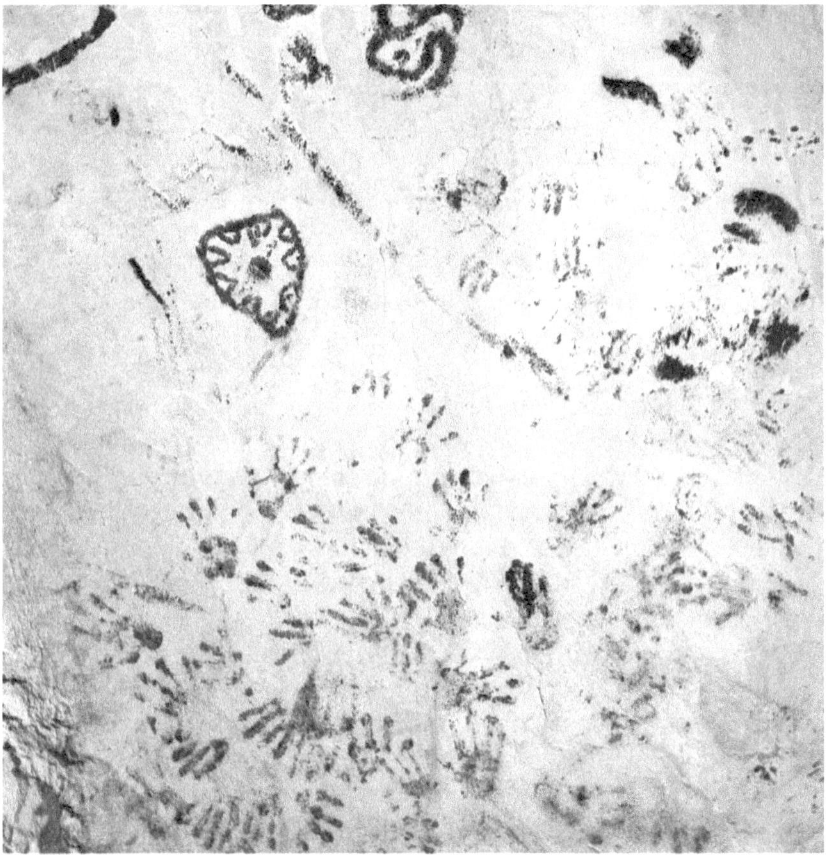

The Place in the Scene

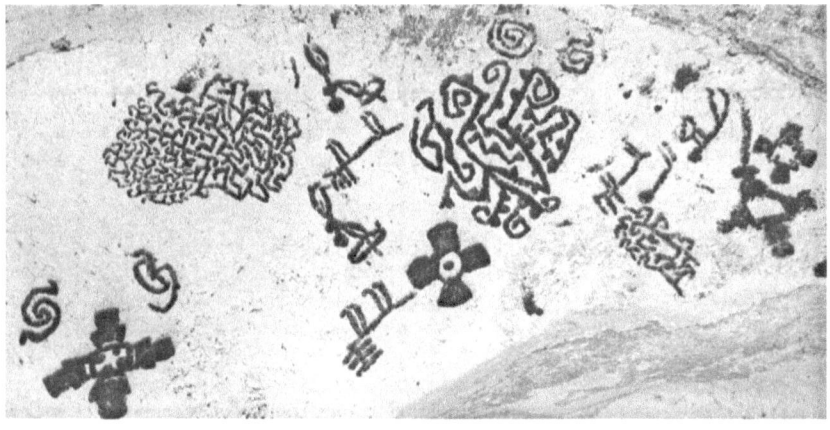

Grotta dei Cervi, Porto Badisco

The Place in the Scene

The particularity of the imprints' rhythm, their unique and universal character, makes us reflect on the function of the hand *as the representative of the representation of man* (the representative of the relationship between scopic and invocatory drives). The hand silently traces the subjective reply to the call of the Other and draws a new field for the gaze to settle on. In silence, it makes the cry, music, rhythm, *jouissance* resonate.

Positive, Negative

The controversial question of the motivations behind the handprints in positive or negative, as they are often represented in prehistory—and about which we shall leave to competent specialists the task of putting forth hypotheses—cannot but evoke for us, lay observers, a particular aspect of the relationship of the body with space. Indeed, there are two hands; they are under the eyes of the person using them, which constantly offers up the sight of the enigma of the symmetry of the body and of the "non-superimposability" of the equal. This is a problem famously addressed by Kant: the palms coincide perfectly, but the hands are not "congruent"; "I shall call a body which is exactly equal and similar to another, but which cannot be enclosed in the same limits as that other, its *incongruent counterpart*."[146] Kant finds therein the obvious proof of space as absolute, as having its own reality, which is not simply the consequence "of the positions of the parts of matter relative to each other."[147] To demonstrate this, he has recourse to a projective construct that purports to also shed light on the particularity and the characteristics of the reflected image.[148]

---

[146] I. Kant, "Concerning the Ultimate Ground of the Differentiation of Directions in Space" (1768), in *Immanuel Kant: Theoretical Philosophy 1755-1770* (Cambridge: Cambridge UP, 1992), 370.

[147] *Ibid.*, 371.

[148] "Now, in order to demonstrate the possibility of such a thing, let a body be taken consisting, not of two halves which are symmetrically arranged relatively to a single intersecting plane, but rather, say, a *human hand*. From all the points on its surface let perpendicular lines be extended to a plane surface set up opposite to it; and let these lines be extended the same distance behind the plane surface, as the points on the surface of the hand are in front of it; the ends of the lines, thus extended, constitute, when connected together, the surface of a corporeal form. That form is the incongruent counterpart of

The Place in the Scene

The question is topological in nature; it involves the transformation of an object into diverse dimensions. We shall limit ourselves here to the observation that the hand and its print involve the direct experience of the passage from the plural dimension of the body to the two-dimensional space of representation, as is the case with the reflected image. What is the relationship between the hand and the space from which it is cut out, or that it cuts out, that it perforates? Isn't the print a way of transmitting both the hand's presence and the presence of the space in which it is immersed? Its repetition reiterates the difference between the representation and the figure that is represented, as well as the point of opacity that inhabits the circuit of the drive in identification. The handprints—their positive, their negative—convey the incommensurability intrinsic to the passage between dimensions that organizes the relation of the subject to the place. They transmit the real, the non-representable, woven into the exercise of representation.

We can wonder to what extent the handprint—universal, archaic, current—condenses and metaphorizes the very question that is at the heart of representation: that of the desire to represent, the invention involved in the work of art, and the relationship among the imaginary, the real, and the symbolic that permeates it.

The Site, the Threshold

One of the peculiarities of rock art is its location: it is the expression of a specific choice and reflects a particular use of the geological characteristics of the region where it is situated, which turn the natural milieu into an opportunity for creation. Whether caves or open-air sites are involved, their access has, in any case, a function of passage between different spaces.

This choice expresses a precise relationship with the land. Among the many examples, we can linger over the great environmental prehistoric site Har Karkom, which Anati calls the oldest known natural sanctuary, at probably 40,000 years old or older. Very important

---

the first. In other words, if the hand in question is a right hand, then its counterpart is a left hand. The reflection of an object in a mirror rests upon exactly the same principles." *Ibid.*, 370.

The Place in the Scene

during the Bronze Age, it is in the Sinai on the Har Karkom mountain ("Saffron Mountain," in Hebrew; also called *Jabal Ideid* or *Djebel Ideid*, "Mountain of Celebrations" or "Mountain of Multitudes," in Arabic).[149] This site of prehistoric worship is situated along one of the major trails connecting Africa to Asia and to the rest of the world, being there since time immemorial. The landscape is surprising: there is a half-hidden valley leaning over a precipice to the east, which is dominated by two peaks to the west, which, according to Anati, evoke a vaginal shape on the one hand and a phallic shape on the other:

> It is as if the landscape of the chosen site includes the masculine and feminine principles and the principle of complementarity between Earth and Sky, between mountain and plain, and as if the sanctuary serves as a transition site between place of habitation and of hunting ground.[150]

In the central area are grouped about forty natural flint statues, with forms reminiscent of the human bust and animals. Certain flints, over three feet tall, weigh one hundred pounds, which leaves one to wonder about the effort required to transport them there. On a surface roughly 400 yards long, stones with retouched anthropomorphic and zoomorphic features were found, as well as geoglyphs and alignments of stones that demonstrate the extension and the care devoted to this majestic environmental installation. All around, there were dwellings and quarries.

As a result of its surprising position and its primordial landscape—on the edge of a precipice dominated by a limitless panorama where continents meet—Har Karkom is well suited for illustrating an essential component of the subject's relation to land: the environmental, artistic, and ritual architecture involves the inscription of an edge. In the encounter between physical reality and signifying reality, it proceeds to the creation of a threshold, which serves as transaction to a new dimension. Isn't this that we call a "place of worship": the

---

[149] Based on archaeological discoveries that seem to confirm certain passages of the Early Writings relating to the Isrealites' time in the desert, Anati thinks it is possible to identify Jabal Ideid with Mount Sinai; the religious activities there are thought to have culminated between 1950 and 1000 B.C.E. Anati dates the exodus between 1600 and 1200 BCE. E. Anati, *The Riddle of Mount Sinai: Archaeological Discoveries at Har Karkom*, in *Studi Camuni XXI* (Capo di Ponte: Edizioni del Centro, 2001).

[150] *Ibid.*, 79.

demarcation of a collective and subjective space dedicated to hearing the call coming from the Other? It traces a coastline between incommensurable registers.

Between Two: A Threshold in the Frame

The word "temple" comes from the Latin *templum*, which derives from the ancient *tem-lo*, an Indo-European root that means "to cut," related to the Greek *témenos*, "enclosure," derived from *temno*, "cut." Originally, *templum* referred to the space circumscribed in the sky by the augur in order to observe the omens. The Roman augur used his stick to carve out a space in the sky, a square or a rectangle, within which he waited for birds to appear. Depending on their flight, their appearance, and their direction, he was able to offer different divinatory interpretations.

The temple traces a frame; it is the encircling of a space devoted to a temporal event. This delimitation of a zone in the sky, and later on the ground, as a sacred place, defines the place of worship as a privileged space dedicated to addressing the Other and deciphering his/her signs. To carve out is to delimit, to circumscribe, which allows a focusing and a contemplation; at the same time, carving out is opening, opening a window wide, tracing a threshold leading to an elsewhere and invoking its presence and status.

Since antiquity, many temples have been situated on plateaus or on naturally elevated sites. Others, as is the case in India, are carved into rock. Their architecture varies by religion and era, but it always reflects the ideal modalities of organization of a space devoted to the relation to the Other. In several cases—as in Mesopotamian architecture or in the architecture of the Hindu or Buddhist religions—the temple structure reflects a complex cosmology. In the ancient Egyptian world, the temple expresses two different concepts: that of the divinity's dwelling (with a succession of portals, columns, and courtyards that correspond to the divine way of inhabiting) and that of the representation of the universe, where the architectonic elements symbolize the physical world. As the house of divinity, the temple is a private space, accessible only to a restricted priestly caste.

Originally, Greek temples had an intrinsic relationship with their natural surroundings, situated where the local divinity manifested it-

The Place in the Scene

self, for example near springs or sacred woods. Some were devoted to worship, others to the gathering and conservation of divine statues or to offerings made to the gods, and not necessarily accessible to the public. Their architecture is at once closed and open; just as the Olympian divinities interact with humans, in the temple the internal elements interact with the exterior. Full and empty, light and shadow, vertical and horizontal lines reflect a metrical relationship between the architectonic parts aiming at "symmetry and proportion," balance and harmony.[151] The arrangement of the spaces varies according to periods and dimensions, but the *naos*, the god's house where his/her simulacrum is kept, and the *pronaos*, the portico that precedes it, are always present. The temple contains the idea of a threshold: the *pronaos* plays the role of a filter between exterior and interior, between human reality and divine reality. Its role is so significant that the temple has a different name according to the number and arrangement of the columns that constitute it and surround it.[152]

In the Hebrew religion, the reference to the temple is intrinsically linked to the Temple of Jerusalem, the symbol of a people's unity. Solomon's temple—finished in the year 930 BCE—was composed of a central sanctuary, subdivided by a vestibule with an altar and a slightly raised cella (Holy of Holies) containing the Ark of the Covenant. One finds many architectonic elements of the Jerusalem temple in the temples of other religions: the demarcation, the separation between sacred and secular space, the portal through which one enters the sacred space, the altar for the offerings, or the cella. Even when temples are only accessible to priests, there exists inside a place devoted to the worship of the god. To have access to it, one has to cross a threshold.

Beginning with the second temple of Jerusalem, in all Judeo-Christian traditions, the place of worship includes this demarcation. Its forms change, but its function remains. It becomes lighter and turns into a veil, an outline, or a screen; with the iconostasis it solidifies to the point of becoming an insurmountable wall. Significantly, this threshold of demarcation is at the root of religious conflicts, of different architectonic solutions, and of evolving iconographic solu-

---

[151] M. Vitruvio Pollone, *De Architectura*, trans. Luciano Migotto (Rome: Edizioni Studio Tesi, 1990), 125.

[152] *In antis, prostylos, amphiprostylos, peripteros, pseudodipteros, dipteros, hypaetros*, trans. Luciano Migotto (Rome: Edizioni Studio Tesi, 1990), 130–133.

tions. It highlights, inside the place of worship, the inscription of a separation as symbolic as it is real, between sacred and secular, divine and human.

With Constantine's edict in 313—granting the legitimation of Christianity and the promotion of adequate places for public religious rituals—the basilica became the architectonic model for Christian worship. Used for state functions during the Roman Empire, and constituted by a long vestibule that ended in a raised apse where the public magistrate deliberated, the basilica's configuration was able to accommodate the growing number of faithful and give their place of worship, with the Emperor's approval, an official spatial genealogy.[153] Despite implicit local specificities, the plan and the liturgical organization of the first Christian churches were common to East and West in the three great centers of the Empire (Rome, Jerusalem, and Constantinople). Later, during and after the politico-religious tumult of Iconoclasm (726–843), the Eastern churches underwent several architectonic and liturgical transformations: in many cases they shrunk, the interior was subdivided, producing new units, and the inscribed cross plan became the dominant form in Byzantine churches from the middle and last period.

But the demarcation between different spaces persists. In ancient Byzantine churches, the ecclesiastics and the faithful were separated by a partition of about four feet that functioned as a screen for the choir: the transenne. It wasn't a barrier but rather a small parapet, placed between raised columns, bearing an architrave. It is interesting that, at the beginning of Christian tradition, there was no attempt to bar the faithful from viewing the clergy celebrate the sacred ritual. On the contrary, visual access was promoted by the raised sanctuary platform. The transenne was sometimes decorated with relief sculptures representing Christ, The Virgin, and the Saints.

With the deliberations of the Council of 843 in favor of the partisans of the icon, with the restoration of orthodoxy and the increasing veneration of icons, the transenne underwent a progressive transformation. In the Orthodox Church, and particularly in the Russian

---

[153] The architecture of the basilica was easily adapted to the demands of the new rituals. The first Christian churches were subdivided into three parts: the baptismal entrance, the nave for the faithful, and the raised apse of the sanctuary, also called the bema or the chancel.

churches, it became an iconostasis, a truly impenetrable partition that highlights the distinction between zones that are symbolically incompatible.[154] By means of a screen of icons facing the faithful, it refers to the beyond that it veils, to the background of divine truth alluded to by its representation.

The term transenne, of uncertain etymology, but probably deriving from the Latin *transeo* (from *transire*, to traverse, composed of *trans*, "out," and *ire*, "to go"), once meant an opening or a passage. The transenne was at the same time a passage and an obstacle: *transennae* designated the snares used to capture birds, as well as the screens in front of windows that hid the interior but allowed light to filter through. In the places of worship, the transenne retains this plurality of meanings; while it marks a separation between the divine and the human, it also supports their relationship, their exchange. It allows for the gaze and the voice to circulate, returning to the faithful from the place of the Other. Its threshold suggests the possible encounter with an incommensurable, whose presence is invoked by the priest's call, by the ritual gestures, the music, the singing. It makes the unrepresentable, the immaterial, present.

A Space for Representation

It is thought that there exists a close genealogical relationship between ritual and theater, that theater evolved from ritual. Although it seems impossible to reconstruct the theatrical manifestations of ancient cultures, we can hypothesize that, as is the case for tribal cultures we do know, certain rituals became theatrical performances (propitiatory rituals performed to celebrate the change of seasons, rituals inherent to the success of the hunt or the harvest, ceremonies of initiation and social rites of passage). Thanks to a papyrus discovered in 1928 by the German Egyptologist and philologist Kurt Heinrich Sethe, we know that, one thousand years before the advent of Greek theater, theater existed in ancient Egypt in the shape of the cult of Osiris. We

---

[154] Think of the iconostasis painted by Andrey Rublyov (c. 1408) and his school in the Dormition Cathedral (Uspeniya) of Vladimir. In the Russian church the iconostasis is often made up of a barrier that goes from floor to ceiling.

also know that dance and musical instruments accompanied the rituals of Mycenaean civilization.

In Greek, the term *théatron* means spectacle or place devoted to spectacles, from *theâsthai*, to look, to be a spectator, and *théa*, the fact of looking, sight (from the same root as *thauma*, which means admiration, marveling). The etymology therefore highlights the function of looking as well as performing, along with the marveling and transport which accompany them. The theater traces the edges of a space devoted to the actualization of the affects, summoned there thanks to the transferential relationship between artists, actors, and spectators (*théates*).

The origins of Greek theater go back to the mysteries of Eleusis, of Egyptian origin. Its first manifestations were associated with the celebration of the cult of Dionysus, with the mysteries celebrated in his honor that included personifications, masks, dithyrambic music, choral lyric, and rhythmic dances. The music, the choruses, and the dances were the very means of Dionysian transmission. Tradition attributes to Thespis, who arrived in Athens from Ikaria around the middle of the sixth century, the invention of Greek tragedy: he is said to be the first to appear as an actor separate from the chorus in 534 BCE.[155]

Tragedy grew out of the spirit of music, to reprise Nietzsche's words. According to Florence Dupont, who reveals the warping impact on Western thought of Aristotle's reading of tragedy and the loss of a philological approach to its performance, tragedy was above all a choral practice. The *aulos* was the instrument that defined it and structured the spectacle. The comprehension of the dialogues and of the fiction was based on the Dionysian chorus. The dialogues were not declaimed verses, but indeed "songs without music," veritable expansion of the chorus, and required a particular diction, a declamatory pronunciation deriving from the rhapsodist tradition. The dramatic poet was a *chorodidaskalos*, one who writes for the singing actors and chorus:

> This is therefore a complex system. The music of the *aulos* and the songs of the chorus constitute the Dionysian ritual; in the ritual, the spectators identify during the course of the tragedy with the choir, who in life

---

[155] P. Wentworth Buckham, *Theatre of the Greeks* (Cambridge: J. Smith, 1827).

are their neighbors, their family, and who, in the theater, are situated between them and the actors. To the songs of the chorus are added two other kinds of musical moments featuring the *aulos*: the melodramas sung by the actors and the *kommos*, when the actors and the choir sing and cry together. These songs are the great emotional moments in tragedy. All the parts lacking music are on the contrary distanced and more restrained; they prepare or conclude the intense moments of the spectacle. Thus a tendency among the actors, who are professionals, to excessively modulate their texts when they are speaking, and to add pathos, to make their roles more akin to the music.[156]

One of the great merits of Dupont's study is how it restores the essential aspects of tragic performance and its particular energy, reconstructing a unique theatrical space, which exists in a cultural context distant from our own, the performance quality of which is generally lost or misunderstood in the successive readings of the texts that have reached us. She gives us the measure of the value of music in tragedy and of the way it shapes the place: music engenders a synchronicity between the subject and the Other, a transferential fluidity that allows for recognition and affirmation.[157] Etymologically permeated by the different aspects of sight, theater also engages listening and action and owes to music and sound a crucial aspect of its genealogy; it stages a space where listening and seeing are structurally linked, in which the spectator has a stake thanks to the circuit of the scopic and invocatory drives. This is true as well for song without music or for language without words, as in pantomime.

In his remarks about the birth of Greek tragedy, Nietzsche stressed the implications of the encounter between the excessive spirit of Dionysian music, transmitted by the chorus, and the measured visible Apollonian forms. This sheds light on the function of the Dionysian chorus (made up of "family" and "neighbors") and of the actor as the intermediary of a transmission between an incommensurable real and the visible symbolic space through an imaginary performance.

---

[156] F. Dupont, *Aristote ou le vampire du théâtre occidental* (Paris: Aubier, Éditions Flammarion, 2007), 272.

[157] "The essence of music is to induce between the other and the subject a structural synchronicity that is also incarnate in the act of dancing and the act of singing." A. Didier-Weill, *Invocations: Dionysos, Moïse, Saint Paul et Freud* (Paris: Calmann-Lévy, 1999), 77.

Alain Didier-Weill has argued that the actor separate from the chorus is related to the *logos* and the city: Dionysus' delegate on earth, he effects "a continuity" between the chorus and the city. He lends his voice to the tragic hero, expressing the tension between irreconcilable laws, between the *phusis* of the unwritten law and the *nomos* of the *polis*. He "conveys the old into the new."[158] This is an essential role Freud attributed in particular to the epic poet, spokesperson of a historical truth in the present. But if the tragic actor plays the role of conveyor between different dimensions, this is equally the case for the actor in general. The actor's performance creates an intermediate zone, a continuity replacing what was previously discontinuous (whether the then in the now, the future in the present, the unimaginable imagined, the unheard of heard). This is exactly what characterizes the shaping of the space of representation on the world scene.

As Freud stresses, representation is related to daydreaming; it draws from the reservoir of the pleasure principle preserved in the domain of the secondary processes in order to shape the satisfaction of desire. The first expression of this fantastic/fantasmatic space is, according to Freud, the play of children, which constructs a world of its own and gives a new order to everyday things. It is an imaginary space cut out from reality, which gladly uses concrete objects to bring about a scene on the world stage, parallel to reality but true to desire. According to Freud, it is this use of the concrete that distinguishes the child's play from the daydream; it is not by chance that language has preserved the relationship between play and poetic creation, as is the case of the German word *Spiel* and the English word play.

The space of daydreaming possesses a temporal characteristic: within it, the past, the present, and the future are "threaded on the thread of desire that runs through them."[159] Fantasy oscillates between these three moments of ideation. It starts from a current impression that awakens a past desire; it attaches itself to the memory

---

[158] A. Didier-Weill, *Invocations: Dionysos, Moïse, Saint Paul et Freud*, op. cit., 71.

"The chorus and the city, which were discontinuous, are made continuous, given that what one is lacking—speech—and what the other is lacking—music—are brought into a relationship by the actor's separating stride, which we shall define as conveying the tragic flaw." *Ibid.*, 69.

[159] S. Freud, "Der Dichter und das Phantasieren," *Gesammelte Werke VII* (Frankfurt am Main: S. Fischer Verlag, 1976), 217.

of a previous experience in which the desire was satisfied; it creates a future situation that presents as an accomplishment of that desire: a space/time that reflects the articulation particular to the psychic scene and its tendency to representation.

It is this tendency that the performing space uses. According to Freud, the spectator's participation in the drama is the result of an identification that allows access to a desire (repressed most of the time), and leads to a satisfaction "based on an illusion."[160] The theater, which is thus an ethical and not only an aesthetic practice, shows itself to be essentially an art "of unveiling," an art of summoning affects, representatives of the unconscious.[161] In harmony with the process of representation, it introduces into space a time of its own, isolating the spectacle from the everyday.

Scenic time has been worked on forever, or for as long as there has been a spectacle; it is the soul of the show, it is what carves up the show's space. Performances have happened, in ancient Greece, where their length coincided with the length of an entire day; others, as in the medieval mystery plays, where the time was spread out over several consecutive days; and others yet, as in the itinerant theater, where it was cyclical. Renaissance theater produced the play in three acts, which was long the norm in our tradition, before being challenged by numerous experimental forms from the nineteenth century on. It remains that the temporality of performance does not coincide with the duration measured in real time: the time introduced by the spectacle is logical, it stages the logic of the action. It summons plural registers: the affective, the chronological, the historical. It thus restores a precipitate of the spatio-temporal dimensions in which the subject of language is immersed. Going back to the notion of perpendicular time studied by Stephen Hawking in quantum mechanics, Pierre Katuszewski observes that in performance "perpendicular time induces a particular space where the human timeline that goes from the past to the future no longer exists, since both are merged; it is a space where time is reversible and where ordinary memory, which is constituted through reference to the past, disappears to make place for

---

[160] S. Freud, "Psychopathic Stage Characters" (1905), *Standard Edition VII*, op. cit., 306.
[161] See J.M. Vives, "La catharsis, d'Aristote à Lacan en passant par Freud: une approche théâtrale des enjeux éthiques en psychanalyse," *Recherche en psychanalyse: Les origines grecques de la psychanalyse* 9 (2010), 22-35.

a memory of the past as well as of the future. Everything that can happen is already there."[162] As imaginary as we wish to define it, perpendicular time transmits the real that weaves the *dit-mensions* of the subject on the world scene. It summons the thread of desire that ties them together, of which the space of performance becomes the conveyer.

The space/time of performance has the characteristic of being unique and transitory. Its ephemeral quality is attuned to the uniqueness of the performance (and the singularity of all those who make its production possible) as well as to the uniqueness of the subjective position of the spectator who participates in it. In this sense, a successful performance is a punctual revelation, a discrete transformation.

Whether the sublime spaces of Greek theater are concerned, or the visionary classicism of Renaissance theater, or the illusions of Baroque scenic experimentation, or the Elizabethan playhouses, or the grandiose operas of the eighteenth century, the history of the theater shows the plurality of spaces devoted to performance: from the imaginary space carved out by the actor's gestures on the public square or on itinerant caravans to the most sophisticated architectures. Whatever the arrangement, the technical simplicity or sophistication, the instrumental and scenic design abilities, the physical space supports the shaping of an imaginary dimension, able to summon the symbolic and the real.

Dance and the Dit-mensions

In *The Origin of Dance*, Pascal Quignard puts forth the idea of a "dance-before-dance," of an original dimension of dance peculiar to the fetus' state of flux during its intra-uterine existence, a state interrupted at birth by the expulsion from the mother's body and the fall into a universe composed of new elements: air, light, sound, gravity.

---

[162] P. Katuszewski, *Ceci n'est pas un fantôme: Essai sur les personnages de fantômes dans le théâtre antique et contemporain* (Paris: Éditions Kimé, 2011), 27. While ordinary time is represented as a horizontal line, imaginary time, which would be perpendicular to this line, is a way of treating the dimension of time as though it were a dimension of space, and thus to resolve certain problems of quantum physics. See S. Hawking, *Black Holes and Baby Universes and Other Essays* (New York: Bantam Dell, 1994).

The Place in the Scene

There are therefore two dances, "as there are two kingdoms": "The first dance precedes birth, when it falls. The second dance reproduces, plays, mimes, transposes, translates as best it can, in the air, the lost swim in the amniotic fluid, the lost expansiveness in the lost pocket, upstream from the distress of birth."[163] It's an idea that makes us wonder, a mythic construct that has the merit of restoring something of this impression of rediscovering, of reconquering lightness, that accompanies the act of dancing.

The desire to dance gives the impression of a desire to be free from the constraints of the body in the place: there is a suspension of the usual gestures, the production of movements at once unexpected and natural, which manifests a familiarity with a gestural knowledge both intimate and yet distant. Dance introduces a bodily elsewhere that reminds us that the place possesses plural dimensions. Alain Didier-Weill claims that, unlike the man guided in his/her path by a destination, the dancer is guided by an invisible point, not subject to a particular direction. He calls "Aleph point" the silent call-point the dancer answers, which frees him or her "from the limits of the (space-time) laws and from the law of gravity."[164] This is viewed as the expression of a knowledge in the real, the effect of the particularity of the signifier being transmitted as "rhythmic scansion," a silent scansion perceptible in a non-sensorial manner. Think, for instance, of the deaf who dance.

The scansion involves a discontinuity, a signifying cut introduced in the real. As the clinic shows, it is often through the recognition of rhythm, through an initial and surprising attention given over to it, that a breach opens in the isolated world of the autistic child, and that a first contact takes place with something that is other. Isn't the discontinuity that characterizes such a scansion the precondition for the acquisition of language? Rather than an echo of a lost kingdom, of a lost biological continuity, as Pascal Quignard proposes, the rhythm inhabited by dance may be an echo of the scansion that incarnated the signifier, that inscribed the elements of the psychic scene and of the world as scene. It invites the body to let go, to move in unison with the dimensions that belong to it.

---

[163] P. Quignard, *L'Origine de la danse* (Paris: Galilée, 2013), 38-39.
[164] A. Didier-Weill, *Un mystère plus loin que l'inconscient* (Paris: Aubier, 2010), 60.

We are strangers to the body we inhabit; we are that body, we use it. But where we are, we don't think of it, which reveals the schism that is peculiar to us, the register of the impossible in the ex-timacy that is ours. To be concerned with one's image or to think about one's body is to travel in the dimensions of the imaginary and the symbolic, far from the real of the body that we are. When this real is expressed, by a disease, for instance, or an accident, a wound or a mutilation, it's as though we suddenly remembered having "the" body. During periods of physiological transformation, like puberty or old age, this fact becomes most obvious. The real of the body is often manifested as unwelcome: it is weight, pain, limitation; sometimes it brings about horror.

Contrary to what happens when dancing spontaneously, learning figurative dance—or other gymnastic activities that require a gestural education—is slow and laborious; it involves an often frustrating discipline—intolerable for some—that evokes in the present the misery of motor incapacity preceding gravitational autonomy, and the sensation of inadequacy, of resistance, that arises when faced with the body's real. Gesture after gesture, the gap that exists between the image of and the subjective experience of the body is revealed, the gulf between ideal and real, which gives gestural mastery, once it is achieved, all the satisfaction of a conquest.

The Abyss and Enthusiasm

In Charlie Chaplin's *Modern Times*, Tramp, a worker on an assembly line, arrested several times for a variety of incidents, is persuaded by the orphan Gamine to get a job as a night watchman in a department store. Once he has received his instructions, everyone leaves and Tramp smuggles Gamine into the store. He immediately brings her to the restaurant area to satisfy her hunger. Alone in this consumer wonderland, they explore the toy department on the fourth floor, where they find roller skates. Tramp puts them on and, in order to show his extraordinary skill, he wears a blindfold and executes a masterful dance. A big sign on which "*Danger*" is written goes unnoticed: the railing on the fourth floor where Tramp spins and vaults is being repaired and is actually totally absent. Tramp moves with grace, mastery, and virtuosity on the edge of a precipice.

The Place in the Scene

What follows is memorable: struggling to take her first unsteady steps on her roller skates, Gamine realizes with horror what is happening; she calls Tramp to her side and guides his hand. Becoming aware of the nearby abyss, Tramp instantly loses control and balance, straightaway abandoned by the spirits of the dance and of grace as he staggers away from the precipice.

This scene is a good representation of the particular way we can be stunned during an action when the risks involved in it are suddenly revealed. In Tramp's case, this interrupts the mastery of the body which moves freely between symbolic, imaginary, and real. Stunned, Tramp loses his grace and his balance, but manages to avoid falling into the precipice, and quickly recovers his enthusiasm.

For there to be un-stunning it is necessary to second the instant between the *not any longer* and the *not yet* that characterizes the encounter with the unexpected, the moment of subjective evanescence that unfolds. It is necessary to be able to simultaneously acknowledge the horror of the action that was just revealed and the opening onto the unknown that this revelation involves. It is a passage that foregrounds a particular relation to knowledge. We cannot help but notice that Tramp's sublime high-wire act on the edge of the abyss manifests a know-how; but this *savoir-faire* is a paradoxical knowledge, possible only when the subject is "unconscious of himself, that is to say, unconscious of knowing anything."[165] Stunning introduces a suspension of this knowledge and calls forth another knowledge: it coincides with the sudden revelation of the scene on the world stage, which reveals an unexpected configuration. During the space of a slip (*l'esp d'un laps*), we are helpless.

Awareness—a word that captures the subject's realization, his or her awakening to a difference—stops and catapults into the domain of reasoning, of the "I think" of secondary elaboration; but it can also be a springboard toward an affirmation of the experience that just happened. This can build up a new dimension of knowledge, the expertise of a transit between different registers. Tramp's ease and its sudden interruption evokes the know-how of children, their extraordinary capacity to adopt the rhythm that inhabits them—to dance, frolic, sing, draw, paint, and so forth—before their encounter with the horror of

---

[165] *Ibid.*, 326.

The Place in the Scene

Charlie Chaplin, Modern Times

The Place in the Scene

the action, with castration anxiety, installs inhibition, which becomes sedimented in the latency period.

Carried by the rhythmic scansion, Tramp had put on his roller skates; and it is thanks to enthusiasm that, un-stunned, he starts to skate again, discovering with Gamine the creative opportunities offered by the department store. This desire peculiar to enthusiasm, might it be the desire to act in the direction of life, the desire of the living?

At the beginning of the movie, Tramp works on an assembly line where he carries out one task: he tightens bolts by the millions, which alienates him to the point of provoking "boltitus"; he sees bolts everywhere, confuses buttons with bolts that need to be tightened, sees them on a young woman's behind, on a lady's breast, mistakes noses for bolts and so forth, and ends up being committed to a psychiatric hospital. His alienation causes a mania, a kind of mad enthusiasm for the job. Another rhythm already takes precedence over the harmful rhythm of the repeated alienating task. The hospital returns him to reality: when he leaves he finds himself dealing with the lugubrious atmosphere of the Great Depression, with famine, unemployment, strikes, the struggle for survival and the desultory efficiency of modern industrialization. An extraordinary series of incidents and misunderstandings have him entering and leaving prison several times. But each time he encounters an obstacle, Tramp finds new resources to help him reverse the situation.

Tramp is the subject of the "find." In order to survive in an alienated and alienating world, he keeps coming up with an invention, an action that overturns every premise and every expectation. The scene on the roller skates at the edge of the precipice is the prelude to another sensational stunning that happens later in the film, to which Tramp finds an answer thanks to a particular invention. This is the famous restaurant scene, where he has to sing to keep his job (he, who knows no songs and thinks he doesn't know how to sing). Gamine writes on his cuffs the lyrics of a song the tune of which Tramp knows. But once on stage, he inadvertently waves his arms: the cuffs fly off and he finds himself, in front of everyone, stunned, without words or voice. The time it takes to understand precipitates the time it takes to conclude: Tramp improvises a song with words invented on the fly, a mixture of words from several languages that imitates a signifying structure. Tramp *lets himself be sung*. His performance is a success, although it fails to stop the series of vicissitudes that occur as the film concludes, suggesting an uncertain future in which anything can still happen.

It is interesting to remember that *Modern Times* (1936) is the first film in which we hear Chaplin's voice, precisely when he is singing gibberish—"The Nonsense Song"—to the tune of the comic ditty "*Je cherche après Titine*" by Léo Daniderff. The first time in the history of cinema that Chaplin's voice is heard is in order to give voice to nonsense and rhythm. Up to that point, his films were completely silent, even though the motion picture industry had long ago adopted sound.[166]

Modern Times is Chaplin's first overtly political film, a reflection on the then current Great Depression and on the alienation deriving from industrial profits and new technologies, a theme particularly close to his heart and which he discussed with Mahatma Gandhi during a meeting in London. The film is a call to awareness of the alienation and the segregation peculiar to the contemporary world, of which we are both the victims and the accomplices. But it also proposes a strategy for fighting back and breaking the cycle. Thanks to comedy and paradox, the encounter with an unbearable reality is reinterpreted and metaphorized. Un-stunning and invention express their entire ethical and political potential; they are ways of mounting a symbolic appropriation of a crushing real, which introduces in the totalitarianism of the dominant system a quotidian place of singular response strategies and unanticipated and unpredictable actions, capable of undermining from the inside the blueprints of the established order.[167]

Perspective and Gaze

The particularity of the gaze in the visual field finds its expression in the history of representation. The problem of how to render the illusion of the depth of space on a two-dimensional surface

---

[166] In 1934 Chaplin had considered the possibility of making a talkie, but quickly abandoned this idea fearing that the voice might transform the Tramp character and alienate his non-English-speaking admirers. It's worth noting that "The Nonsense Song" is the prelude to the comic use of semi-intelligible words in the Dictator's speeches in *The Great Dictator*, released in 1940.

[167] See M. de Certeau, *L'invention du quotidien I: Arts de faire* (Paris: Éditions Gallimard, 1990).

spanned several centuries. It is well known that the discovery of linear perspective during the Renaissance revolutionized its parameters by introducing mathematical and geometric principles into the representation of the image "as it is seen" in reality. While there has been much debate about the scope and the implications of this invention, its impact on the art of the Renaissance and on the history of modern thought has certainly been enormous.

During the Middle Ages, the Latin term *perspectiva* meant the whole of the science of optics. It was based on an essential precedent: the theory formulated by Euclid during the third century BCE in his treatise on optics, in use for a millennium, according to which the gaze proceeds in a straight line, and the lines that leave the eye and encounter an object constitute a visual cone (a theory that was later supplanted by the idea that it was rather the light that went in a straight line and that it was reflected by the objects onto the eye).

During his early years, Filippo Brunelleschi, the inventor of perspective with a single vanishing point (or concentric linear perspective), had been in contact with optic studies and *perspectiva*, considered at the time a way of calculating distances and lengths; he had probably consolidated his knowledge in this area by frequenting the mathematician and astronomer Paolo dal Pozzo Toscanelli. As Leon Battista Alberti has shown us, Brunelleschi's famous experiments on panels—one representing a view of the Florence Baptistery from the central door of Santa Maria del Fiore, the other representing Piazza della Signoria seen from the Via dei Calzaiuoli—allowed him to establish a proportional constant between the painted image and the reflected image, as well as a vanishing point toward which objects shrank. The success of this discovery was such that not only was it integrated into the century's representative canon, it also became an integral part of the Renaissance worldview and of the conquest of the natural world by mathematical abstraction; it was absorbed by the era's science and mathematics and later served as the basis for new remarkable mathematical developments. Treatises on perspective proliferated in the sixteenth, seventeenth, and eighteenth centuries, from *Due regole della prospettiva pratica* by Vignola (1583) to *L'Exemple de l'une des manières universelles* by Gérard Desargues (1636), *Principle of Linear Perspective* by Brook Taylor (1719), and *A Complete Treatise on Perspective in Theory and Practice on the Two Principles of Brook Taylor* (1779) by Thomas Malton.

Perspective gives itself an impossible task: that of representing three-dimensional objects on a two-dimensional surface. Panofsky defines it as a systematic abstraction of the "structure" of "psychophysiological" space, as its transformation into mathematical space: a transformation that denies the difference between front and back, left and right, body and empty space; that forgets that we do not see by means of a fixed point, but indeed thanks to two eyes that are in constant motion, the principle of a spherical field of vision; that does not take into account the difference between a "visual image" and a "retinal image" that is imprinted on the eye.[168] And so on and so forth. Yet, it wants to represent on a two-dimensional surface the image as it is grasped by direct sight, which involves, among other things, restrictive conditions of observation (for example, the necessity that the viewer share the same vantage point as the painter).

The use of linear geometric perspective immediately raises a number of questions, such as the classic one of the putting into perspective a tile floor made up of square tiles, which poses the problem of the shrinking of the depth scale: "This problem has several solutions. What all those that were proposed in the classic treatises have in common is to introduce a 'third point' (third, relative to the two other points: the eye and the main vanishing point)."[169] It was Desargues who introduced two decisive elements to the problem: the first is the fact that the problem can be solved by using any point on the horizon (besides the main vanishing point), which strips the third point of the picture of its privilege; the second is that if it appears that the parallel straight lines are always convergent, it is because "they happen to converge to infinity. The plane of the picture is therefore to be completed by the infinite straight line."[170]

In Desargues' hands, perspective becomes projective geometry. What happens, as Panofsky points out, when replacing the Euclidian visual cone with the geometric beam of multilateral rays is that per-

---

[168] E. Panofsky, *Perspective as Symbolic Form* (Cambridge, MA: Zone books, 1991), 30-31.

[169] J. Brini, "Du tableau au plan projectif," *Le regard: Cahiers de L'association freudienne internationale* (Grenoble: Journées d'étude, 1999), 41.

[170] *Ibid.*, 42. "This second idea took two centuries to reach completion with the works of Chasles and Poncelet, in the nineteenth century, which rigorously laid the foundations of projective geometry."

spective sets aside the gaze's direction and opens space in every direction in an identical fashion. This is a conquest of an infinite, homogenous, and "isotropic" space, which, where art is concerned, still owes much, as Panofsky points out, to the homogeneity of the Medieval style, without which "not only infinity but also the directional indifference of space would not have been conceivable."[171]

According to Panofsky, Descartes' philosophy and Desargues' theory of perspective belong to a historical and cultural moment when the concept of space tries to purge itself of any subjective content. With the passage from geometric linear perspective to projective geometry, the eye in space, which is what the subject came down to, "is delocalized. It is everywhere and nowhere, since nothing but directions are involved."[172] The space in question, consequently, loses its sensory and intuitive character and is reduced to a series of mathematical laws, to a series of transformation practices. Space *is* this very transformation.

The projective plane is an abstraction of the perspective arrangement: contrary to the ordinary plane, its parallel straight lines merge at infinity, which reflects the multidimensionality of real space and shows that the global drawing of the projective plane on a two-dimensional surface is inherently impossible. The topological characteristic of the projective plane's straight line is at the same time to have a point at infinity and to be a closed straight line, which makes it homeomorphic to a circle. Among the properties of the projective plane, there is the fact that it is a non-orientable surface that is divisible into two parts, one as a Möbius strip (which keeps the property of non-orientability) and the other as a disc. The immersion of the projective plane in Euclidian space produces a sphere equipped with a cross-cap.

Lacan considers the invention of perspective an essential pre-Cartesian moment in the history of Western thought, which witnesses a structural correlation between the emergence of the subject of science and the problematic of the subject of vision. He uses the construction of linear perspective, as well as its transformation in the projective plane, in order to examine the relationship between vision and gaze, as well as the particularity of the structure of fantasm. In

---

[171] E. Panofsky, *Perspective as Symbolic Form*, op. cit., 71.
[172] J. Brini, op. cit., 43.

fantasm the gaze as object has its own specificity, which in no way detracts from the importance of other objects *a*. The scopic fantasm, "inasmuch as it is the representative of any possible representation of the subject," exercises a particular function, showing the subject's position in relation to the world scene:[173]

> Here, I am taking the structure at the subject's level, but it reflects something that is already to be found in the natural relation that the eye inscribes with regard to light. I am not simply this punctiform being located at the geometrical point from which perspective is grasped. No doubt, the picture is painted in the back of my eye. Certainly, the picture is in my eye. But *I* am in the picture.[174]

The Screen

A screen comes between the subject and the world: it coincides with the scopic fantasm and veils the real. Lacan notes that it is on the level of opening one's eyes to the world that the world necessarily appears as picture. He considers the "the plane of the fantasm" to be the plane that is parallel to the picture where the painter is situated. And it is precisely in the interval between the fantasm plane and the picture plane that the gaze lands, inherently ungraspable, invisible, and unrepresentable, a pure real that supports the image. The fantasm coincides with the window through which, once his or her eyes are open, the subject sees the world, *is* in the world: "The existence of this window is thus absolutely fundamental, but it is always elided in the relation of the gaze to the world seen, like the slit of the eyelids or the opening of the pupil."

---

[173] J. Lacan, *Le Séminaire livre XIII: L'objet de la psychanalyse*, 1 juin 1966.

[174] "Je prends ici la structure au niveau du sujet, mais elle reflète quelque chose qui se trouve déjà dans le rapport naturel que l'œil inscrit à l'endroit de la lumière. Je ne suis pas simplement cet être punctiforme qui se repère au point géométral d'où est saisie la perspective. Sans doute, au fond de mon œil, se peint le tableau. Le tableau, certes, est dans mon œil. Mais moi, je suis dans le tableau." J. Lacan, *Le Séminaire livre XI: Les quatre concepts fondamentaux de la psychanalyse*, op. cit., 89. Alan Sheridan's translation *The Four Fundamental Concepts of Psycho-analysis* (New York: Norton & Company, 1977) concludes by stating the opposite of what Lacan says: "But *I'm not* in the picture," a mistake that renders the content of Lacan's discourse incomprehensible.

The Place in the Scene

Lacan finds in the projective plane the topological structure of fantasm. The projective plane allows thinking the continuity between inside and outside, the cut between the divided subject of the unconscious and the object *a*, and the properties of that object. The property of unilaterality of the projective plane shows that the internal order of the body is in perfect continuity with its environment: "The body is closed and yet the milieu that surrounds it is inside it. Or, inversely, the milieu surrounds a closed body of which it is yet the most intimate core."[175] This is the property that allows the non-reductive presentation of clinical evidence in psychoanalysis. It restores the particularity of subjective space.

While the development of projective geometry delocalizes the subject, Lacan, in his famous reading of Velázquez's *Las Meninas*, shows that the subject's place is situated at the heart of the picture. There is nothing beyond representation, since representation is the very shape of the world as scene. This is what is illustrated by the famous challenge between Parrhasios and Zeuxis about the representative excellence of painting, recounted by Pliny the Elder: Zeuxis painted grapes that looked so natural birds pecked at them. With this he seemed to have won the competition. But Parrhasios painted a curtain so realistically that Zeuxis asked him to draw the curtain that covered his painting. What is involved in representation, concludes Lacan, is indeed the fooling of the eye. And it is to the extent that it is deceptive that the gaze has a privileged position in fantasm: "Beyond appearance there is nothing in itself, there is the gaze."[176]

The Edge: Angst and the House of Man

The eye that opens is a window onto the world landscape. Within that landscape, there can emerge what Lacan calls an "edge phenomenon" (*un phénomène de bord*), a phenomenon that shakes our illusory feeling of recognizing the world. Suddenly, the relation to the world is revealed as scene.

---

[175] J.D. Nasio, *Introduction à la topologie de Lacan* (Paris: Petite Bibliothèque Payot, 2010), 77.

[176] J. Lacan, *Le Séminaire livre XI: Les quatre concepts fondamentaux de la psychanalyse*, op. cit., 95.

The Place in the Scene

The appearance of an edge—from the unexpected revelation, for instance, that the landscape out the window is no more than a painting leaning on the window, as Magritte masterly illustrates—implies a break, a suspension. It's the unexpected. Suddenly, the place reveals the presence of a fault in the signifying network that organizes it, something that cannot be put immediately into words. The real that inhabits the place appears surreptitiously.

Lacan has pointed out that the edge phenomenon is consubstantial to the feeling of angst. "Angst is framed," as he puts it.[177] Angst emerges on the limit where fantasm reveals its nature as frame, as screen facing the real; enigmatic, it marks the edge that strips from the world scene its fantasmatic reality. It summons the imminent, the unknown.

According to Lacan, angst is an affect that does not lie. If the signifier produces the world, the essential characteristic of this world is that within it, it is possible to mislead and be misled; and if, as Freud says, the characteristic of affects is to move away from what produced them through displacement, they tend to lie about their cause. Which is not the case with angst, the veritable substance of which is *"that which does not mislead*, the beyond any doubt."[178] The certainty that accompanies it is rooted in a persistent yet veiled real.

According to Freud, angst is a signal in the ego; and since for Freud the ego is surface, or the projection of a surface, this signal is in the sphere of the imaginary an edge phenomenon. The process of identification that attributes an image to the body results in the writing of a lack: the libidinal investment that sustains such a process doesn't exhaust itself on the specular image, since part of it remains auto-erotically invested in the body—at the level of primary narcissism, of the cause of desire—and does not have a reflected image. This lack of reflection, which inscribes a lack (designated as *–phi* by Lacan) beyond and within the virtual image, indicates a structural function necessary

---

[177] J. Lacan, *Le Séminaire livre X: L'angoisse*, op. cit., 89. The Wolfman's dream is an example of it. In this dream, the fantasm is revealed through its structure, in a pure, schematic way, and the gaze plays an essential role: "Now, what do we see in this dream? The sudden gaping—the two terms are noted—of a window. The fantasm is seen beyond a windowpane, and by a window that opens. The fantasm is framed." *Ibid.*, 92. We translate the French *angoisse* with *angst*. Freud's notion of *Angst* was incorrectly translated into English as "anxiety."

[178] *Ibid.*, 92.

to the constitution of the ego; it is the support and the refuge of the ego, an empty place that preserves the subject's desire and gives a consistency to the identifying operations that unfold between the subject and the other. The structuring quality of secondary narcissism is based on this support.

This place, the place of the lack –*phi*, is what Lacan calls *Heim*: the house of Man, a house situated in the Other, which represents "the very absence where we are."[179] It orients and polarizes desire. However, as Freud pointed out, *Heim* is intrinsically connected with *Unheim*: the house of man shelters what is most radically strange in the familiar. The feeling of the *Unheimliche* suddenly surfaces in the register of identification where something appears in the empty place of the lack, a feeling akin to the emergence of angst as lack of lack.

> In this *Heim* point, not only does what you have always known manifest itself, namely that desire is revealed as desire of the Other, desire *in* the Other here, but also that my desire, I would say, enters into the lair where it has been expected for all eternity in the shape of the object that I am, inasmuch as it exiles me from my subjectivity, by resolving by itself all the signifiers to which it [my subjectivity] is attached.[180]

The formulation rings both poetic and a-ontological, in line with the particularity of the *parlêtre*, who by definition prevents any return to ideas of being or substance: by nature, the subject is a *sujet troué*, "subject with a hole," who summons the object *a* as cause, irreducible remainder of the operation of advent of the subject in the Other's place. In the context of this operation, angst relates to the register of separation, expressing a threat *to the very possibility of separating* from the Other. If it strikes the ego, it is so that the subject is alerted to a desire "that does not concern anything other than my very being, which calls me into question. Let's say, it annuls me. In principle, it is not addressed to me as present, it is addressed to me, if you wish, as being expected, and even more so, as lost. It solicits my loss for the

---

[179] *Ibid.*, 60. "Man finds his/her house in a point situated in the Other beyond of the image we are made of."
[180] *Ibid.*, 61.

Other to find its place there. That's what angst is."[181] In the empty place where our own house stood, we find that we are expected. It is an occupation that aims at loss, at annihilation.

The indeterminacy of the Other's *jouissance* breaks into the body's imaginary. Colette Soler proposed declining the Lacanian thesis according to the *jouissances* inscribed by the Borromean knot of the real, symbolic, and imaginary registers: 1) *joui-sense*,[182] relative to the body's imaginary; 2) phallic *jouissance*, outside the body; and 3) the Other's *jouissance*, outside the symbolic. As she observes, on the level of *joui-sense*, angst directly connects to meaning, to breaks in meaning; on the level of phallic *jouissance*, angst is linked to having (impotence, loss, failure, success, etc.); on the level of the *jouissance* of the Other, the height of angst is angst of the real (traumatic quality of existence, angst of non-phallic *jouissance*, etc.). "In the three cases, the subject is prey to the feeling of being 'reduced to his or her body,' destitute as being outside of meaning."[183]

This is an observation that corresponds to clinical experience, to the different occurrences of angst that threaten narcissistic integrity. In the flattening of the Borromean knot, angst is confirmed as an edge phenomenon, a phenomenon that surfaces on the edges of the different forms of *jouissance* involved in the encounter with the real, symbolic, and imaginary registers. It signals that something is threatened at the heart of the encounter, in *Heim*, at the empty place of object *a*, in the house of man.

Labyrinth-Space

When, in the process of identification, "the absence where we are" is shown to be what it is, "it seizes the image that supports it, and the specular image becomes the image of the double, with everything

---

[181] "…qui ne concerne rien d'autre que mon être même, c'est-à-dire qui me met en question. Disons qu'il m'annule. En principe, il ne s'adresse pas à moi, comme présent, il s'adresse à moi, si vous voulez, comme attendu, et bien plus encore comme perdu. Il sollicite ma perte, pour que l'Autre s'y retrouve. C'est cela l'angoisse". J. Lacan, *Le Séminaire livre X: L'angoisse*, op. cit., 179. Angst signals a threat to the structuring distinction between -*phi* and *a*.
[182] *Joui-sense*: *joui* (enjoy) and *sense* (meaning).
[183] C. Soler, *Les affects lacaniens*, op. cit., 27.

The Place in the Scene

this involves in the way of radical strangeness."[184] The subject's lack of autonomy is suddenly revealed. Exiled from his or her subjectivity, the subject only accedes to his or her desire by substituting himself/herself to one of his or her own doubles.

Edgar Allan Poe's tale "William Wilson" is a famous expression of this phenomenon. What is striking, upon re-reading it, is the impression of finding within it, one after the other, the different aspects of the ego's vicissitudes in the identification process.

The tale begins with the narrator's declaration about his name: "Let me call myself, for the present, William Wilson."[185] He does not want to "sully" "the fair page now lying before [him]" with "[his] real appellation": it is a name tainted with infamy. From the very outset we sense we are entering the realm of classical tragedy, of myth. Might he ever, he wonders, become a fit object of sympathy or pity? Might he ever manage to shed some of the burden of his destiny, as "the slave of circumstances beyond human control"? The story is told by someone who is dying. The myth he embodies is that of the fellow, the fraternal rival. But as a modern hero, William Wilson doubts; he doubts that the law to which he is submitted can be situated anywhere but in his own subjectivity. Thus he questions himself as a divided subject.

The narrative of his past history opens with the description of his later school years. He describes in detail the scene of his encounter with the double.

> I shall be pardoned for seeking relief, however slight and temporary, in the weakness of a few rambling details. These, moreover,... assume to my fancy, adventitious importance, as connected with a period and a locality when and where I recognize the first ambiguous motions of the destiny which afterwards so fully overshadowed me.[186]

These details pertain to the precise space of his school, of which he traces a sort of map. This domain has its limits set, in the garden, by prison-like ramparts that establish a strict boundary line. Yet, within this circumscribed line, something makes it very hard to find one's bearings:

---

[184] J. Lacan, *Le Séminaire livre X: L'angoisse*, op. cit., 60.
[185] E.A. Poe, *Poetry and Prose* (New York: The Library of America, 1984), 337.
[186] *Ibid.*, 338.

But the house!—how quaint an old building was this!—to me how veritably a palace of enchantment! There was really no end to its windings—to its incomprehensible subdivisions. It was difficult, at any given time, to say with certainty upon which of its two stories one happened to be. From each room to every other there were sure to be found three or four steps either in ascent or descent. Then the lateral branches were innumerable—inconceivable—and so returning in upon themselves, that our most exact ideas in regard to the whole mansion were not very far different from those with which we pondered upon infinity. During the five years of my residence here, I was never able to ascertain with precision in what remote locality lay the little sleeping apartment assigned to myself and some eighteen or twenty other scholars.[187]

An inconceivable space, a topography that defies mapping. The space that cannot be mastered, the labyrinthine space, is one of the typical topoi of the emergence of angst, very often used in fiction as a trigger for horror. In the place, angst emerges when the familiar, the habitual, the intimate, is suddenly haunted by an unknown element that decomposes it. What does it mean to know a space if not to grasp its structure, the order of things that inhabit it, its topography? You know a space if you can draw it, even superficially. What distinguishes our house, the space that we are closest to, is that we can master it, even with our eyes closed. What would happen if, in the dark of night, while moving through our familiar space, we suddenly perceived, through touch or hearing, a foreign, unrecognizable element? This is what happens in the phenomenon of the *Unheimliche*, in the revelation of strangeness in what is most intimate: a drawing comes apart, shaking every frame of reference. The real gains the upper hand in the knotting of the three *dit-mensions*.

William Wilson's way of describing the complexity of the structure that houses his school enhances the feeling of an inconceivable unity. Passing through it gives one the impression of crossing detached parts of a body, an organism in pieces. In his seminar of 1952–53 on the "Wolf-Man," Lacan observes that the primal scene, represented to the subject through the dream of the wolves, reemerges when the patient tries to mediate his desire by creating a symbolic relation with his father: "In his unconscious, it is a matter of a passive homosexu-

---

[187] *Ibid.*, 340.

al relation," he notes, following Freud's conclusions. But narcissism demands that this be repressed. What is narcissism?, asks Lacan, who ventures the hypothesis of a possible conflict between what he calls a feminizing impression and an experience of the complete, specular body. If identification with the mother in the primal scene is "rejected," it is because it evokes the image of the fragmented body. The phallic quality of the unified image is erected against the threat of a bodily disarticulation; it indicates the restorative function of narcissism, which comes to the rescue of the subject's integrity before the real of the drives. In the case of the Wolf-Man, the hypothetical circulation of *jouissance* between father and son poses a risk for narcissistic identification. Narcissistic identification, Lacan stresses, is frail and always threatened; it is akin to the transitivism of the mirror stage, to the fact that whenever the subject is apprehended as a form and as an ego, his or her desire is being projected outward. But if it is true that it is "in a see-sawing motion, a motion of exchange with the other, that man is apprehended as a body, as an empty bodily form," the frailty of the narcissistic identification underscores the vacillation that can be produced between this empty form and its dissolution in the body's real.[188]

If, on the one hand, the inconceivable space of William Wilson's school suggests the image's structural instability, on the other hand, it invokes the emergence of a completed image. In its place the double appears.

See-Saw: Of Transitivism

What characterizes the double's appearance is that he has the same name as the narrator. William Wilson had gained a certain influence over all his comrades with the exception of one pupil who had the same first and last names as he. This peculiar circumstance, as well the newcomer's "most inappropriate, and assuredly most unwelcome *affectionateness* of manner" and the fact that he arrived at the school

---

[188] J. Lacan, *Le Séminaire livre I: Les écrits techniques de Freud* (Paris: Éditions du Seuil, 1975), 193.

the same day as his namesake, had created the idea that they were brothers:[189]

> But assuredly if we *had* been brothers we must have been twins; for ... I casually learned that my namesake was born on the nineteenth of January, 1813—and this is a somewhat remarkable coincidence; for the day is precisely that of my own nativity.[190]

The same name, the idea of being brothers, the same date of birth. Suddenly, the symbolic seems to collapse into the imaginary, to get swallowed up in it. One can imagine the paradox of a mother who leads her child to a peer in order to say, "You see this child? It's you."[191]

The fantasy of a failed recognition seems to underlie the tale. The appearance of the double does not shore up the fragmentation of a space that cannot be mastered; it elicits a symbolic mark, capable of breaking a deadly spell.

Let us note that the elaborately described school, in all its points, resembles the one at which Edgar Allan Poe studied in his childhood, during his stay in England. The headmaster mentioned by William Wilson, the Reverend Bransby, is named after Poe's teacher in real life. Furthermore, William was the first name of Poe's brother, two years older than he (having been born in 1807). The date of birth Poe attributes to William Wilson is one sometimes attributed to the author himself, though he was in fact born on January 19, 1809. In his biography of Poe, Kenneth Silverman underlines that Poe attributes to himself three different years of birth: 1809, 1811, and 1813, corresponding to the interval between his age and his brother's.[192] Poe's brother, William Henry Leonard, was also a writer and poet; for a time,

---

[189] E.A. Poe, *Poetry and Prose*, op. cit., 342.

[190] *Ibid*.

[191] Which reminds me of a good joke: a man visiting a foreign city runs into an old friend he hadn't seen in years. Happy to see him, the friend invites him home. Showing him around his property, he says: Do you see this villa? It's mine. Do you see this beautiful swimming pool? It's mine. Do you see this Rembrandt? It's mine. And so on, until, during the tour of the house, he stops in front of the door to a room and opens it cautiously: in the bedroom a beautiful woman is making love with a man. Do you see this woman? She's my wife. And the man? That's me.

[192] K. Silverman, *Edgar A. Poe: Mournful and Never-ending Remembrance* (New York: Harper Collins, 1992).

the two brothers wrote together. There are some poems whose authorship it is impossible to establish with certainty. It should be added that William also wrote a story, "The Pirate," whose hero is named Edgar-Leonard. Edgar Allan Poe, moreover, never ceased to embellish his own life with episodes actually from the life of his brother, such as the famous arrest by the police on a trip to Russia, a country in which Edgar never set foot. It was William who, during his years in the navy, had the opportunity, like William Wilson, to travel throughout Europe, whereas it was Edgar who, inclined toward gambling like William Wilson, lost nearly two thousand dollars in just one year at the University of Virginia, a huge sum for the time. William Henry Leonard had drunk himself to death by the age of 28. Edgar Allan Poe would later suffer a similar fate, enigmatic and equally tragic.

The fantasy of a failed recognition congeals, in the figure of the double, an aspect of the heightened transitivism that seems to have marked Poe's life. The qualities of the double in "William Wilson" reproduce the different aspects of the articulation of the ego. Seized at first with curiosity, then with rage and feelings of rivalry, and finally with an alienating dispossession of his own individuality, William Wilson soon finds himself having to recognize the superiority of his adversary, a superiority which others apparently don't notice. The captivating quality of the image of the other crystallizes into an ideal. This *Ideal-Ich*—encountered, rediscovered, repeated—is soon enough transfigured into a moral model. Yet, for the entire first part of the tale, this transfiguration is unstable. Only later, after William Wilson has left school, will the double reappear in the guise of an *Ich-Ideal*, a persecutor, spokesman for the moral law. But about his school years, William Wilson remarks:

> It may seem strange that in spite of the continual anxiety occasioned me by the rivalry of Wilson, and his intolerable spirit of contradiction, I could not bring myself to hate him altogether.... It is difficult, indeed, to define, or even to describe, my real feelings towards him. They formed a motley and heterogeneous admixture;—some petulant animosity, which was not yet hatred, some esteem, more respect, much fear, with a world of uneasy curiosity. To the moralist it will be unnecessary to say, in addition, that Wilson and myself were the most inseparable of companions.[193]

---

[193] E.A. Poe, *Poetry and Prose*, op. cit., 343.

An animosity that is not yet hate, admiration, fear, curiosity: there is a sort of fluctuation between fascination and alienation. It is in this very back-and-forth movement, in this see-saw (constituted, precisely, by the alternation between "seeing" and "having seen"), that the transitivism inherent in the mirror stage is defined. "See-sawing," we are told, comes from sawing. Webster's gives the following etymology for "see-saw": "a doubled form of the word 'saw' that comes from the action of 'sawing.'" One might suggest, then, that the back-and-forth movement invoked here operates a cut. Thanks to it, a shape, a silhouette, is constituted.

If it can be said that the ego, once articulated, becomes an especially rigid structure always about to defend itself against the other (through the famous mechanisms on which Anna Freud put such great emphasis) and we recognize in it the ego's paranoiac tendency, we can also observe that this rigidity constitutes a response to that teeter-tottering motion that can always threaten it.[194] Confronted with this vacillation, the ego reacts with a paranoiac turgescence. This is precisely what allows it to reestablish a well-defined line of demarcation, re-drawing itself as a closed form.

One and the same phenomenon establishes both the domain of love and that of the struggle to the death. If transitivism presents alienated desire in the area of the fellow, its single outcome will be "desire for the disappearance of the other as support of the subject's desire."[195] Here we may well wonder what the other, the fellow, reveals of the subject's desire whenever ferocity flares up in history. This ferocity lays bare a moment of frailty in the ego, following a destabilizing see-sawing moment. It is said that if we back off, faced with the harm we wish to inflict on another, it is because we identify with him or her. This identification may also be a necessity "of the skin": the need of the subject to preserve himself/herself as a separate entity through the recognition of the fellow, a need to keep a distance with regard to the image and to respect the coordinates of a drawing. Such is the enigma of William Wilson: at the moment at which he finally kills his double, he realizes he has only destroyed himself.

---

[194] A. Freud, *Ego and the Mechanisms of Defense* (London: International Universities Press, 1979).

[195] J. Lacan, *Le Séminaire livre I: Les écrits techniques de Freud*, op. cit., 193.

The Place in the Scene

As is noted, the aggressivity that characterizes the relation to the fellow is displaced to within the superego only in order to be turned against the subject himself/herself, preventing him or her from crossing a certain barrier toward the destruction of the other. Indeed, the identification of the mirror stage is strengthened if one receives from the Other—the third term in the scene—a sign, a symbolic mark that returns to the subject his or her desire, hitherto experienced in the realm of the fellow. If, therefore, it is the symbolic that "contains" the imaginary, if it is the Other that sustains the operation of identification, we can ask ourselves what the position of this third term is in the case in which the struggle for pure prestige is transformed into sheer destruction of the other, of the fellow. In the struggle for pure prestige, indeed, the pact is everywhere prior to the violence before perpetrating it, and the symbolic "dominates the imaginary."[196]

This implicates the position of the Other as much as the question of his/her desire. Lacan stresses the difference between the Hegelian Other—who is Other as consciousness, Other who sees me—and the Other that psychoanalysis deals with, who is there as unconscious, as place of the signifier: "The Other interests my desire to the extent of what it is missing and what it does not know."[197] Its truth is expressed in angst:

> The desire of the Other does not recognize me. Hegel believes it does ... that would be too easy, I could always make it through struggle and violence. It calls me into question, it questions me at the very root of my desire as *a*, as cause of that desire....[198]

Blindness in the Frame

The key moment of "William Wilson" is an enigmatic scene whose secret Poe does not divulge to us. One night, around his fifth year at this school, after a fight with his double, William Wilson suddenly decides to visit the latter in his tiny apartment. Once again, the

---

[196] J. Lacan, "The Subversion of the Subject and the Dialectic of Desire in the Freudian Unconscious," *Ecrits: The First Complete Edition in English*, trans. B. Fink, op. cit., 686.

[197] J. Lacan, *Le Séminaire livre X: L'angoisse*, op. cit., 33.

[198] *Ibid.*, 180.

narrator lingers over the details of the building's endless subdivision, with its series of dim, interlinked nooks and crannies, closets and cupboards turned into little rooms. Thus he reaches this cramped, dark area; he pauses to listen to the easy sound of his rival sleeping. Slowly he parts the curtains surrounding the bed, so that the lamp he is holding suddenly illuminates the scene. There, something unnamable takes place:

> I looked;—and a numbness, an iciness of feeling instantly pervaded my frame. My breast heaved, my knees tottered, my whole spirit became possessed with an objectless yet intolerable horror. Gasping for breath, I lowered the lamp in still nearer proximity to the face. Were these—*these* the lineaments of William Wilson? I saw, indeed, that they were his, but I shook as if with a fit of the ague in fancying they were not. What *was* there about them to confound me in this manner? I gazed;—while my brain reeled with a multitude of incoherent thoughts. Not thus he appeared—assuredly not *thus*—in the vivacity of his waking hours. The same name! the same contour of person! The same day of arrival at the academy! And then his dogged and meaningless imitation of my gait, my voice, my habits, and my manner! Was it, in truth, within the bounds of human possibility, that *what I now saw* was the result, merely, of the habitual practice of this sarcastic imitation? Awe-stricken, and with a creeping shudder, I extinguished the lamp, passed silently from the chamber, and left, at once, the halls of that old academy, never to enter them again.[199]

An unbearable horror accompanies the sudden revelation. *What I now saw*, insists William Wilson, how is it that *what I now saw* should be nothing other than the result of a sarcastic imitation? Taking William Wilson literally, we might imagine that this seeing instantly reveals the truth of the double: there is no distinction left, there is no longer an ego that is not other. It is the radical uncanny. The absence where we are is thus revealed for what it is: the master of the game, it seizes the image that supports it. "To use terms that derive their meaning from their opposition to the Hegelian terms, it makes us appear as object, by revealing to us the subject's lack of autonomy."[200]

---

[199] E.A. Poe, *Poetry and Prose*, op. cit., 347.
[200] J. Lacan, *Le Séminaire livre X: L'angoisse*, op. cit., 60.

This scene is the prelude to the last scene of the tale, in the course of which William Wilson, after having mortally wounded his double, sees *himself* bleeding in a mirror.[201] Entering the abode of his rival, William Wilson has to cross a sort of boundary, a limit: he has ventured into the field of the other, in his place. But what he encounters is a stunning frame that repels him, that restores a threshold. It is the same threshold that is finally defined by the mirror: the mirror stops, it is only a surface, a reflecting plane. Distancing is necessary "to give the subject the distance from himself that the specular dimension is made to offer him."[202] What then is this horror that makes one back up?

The horror is a response to the crossing of an imaginary threshold, where something of looking is seen. A gaze materializes in the frame, but the frame also materializes in the gaze. In "William Wilson," it is as if the body and the features of the double took on the consistency of an unsustainable look, a gaze detached from one's own seeing. Children know quite well how impossible it is to sustain looking at one's own gaze. In this phenomenon something demonstrates, I would say, the *blind spot* that *sustains* the imaginary. What is intrinsic to this gaze is that it shows how it is detached from the subject's very seeing.

Lacan points out that the closer the subject gets to the object of desire, the more the subject is redirected toward its specular image; the angst provoked by the double signals how its apparition comes to fill, to stifle with its presence, the empty space of the object. Moreover, a trope that is often found in the stories of the double is that the double comes to disturb or undermine the subject's relationship to the object of his or her desire.

---

[201] Let us note that, in this last scene, William Wilson can see himself in the mirror because a third figure manifests his presence and breaks the spell of the doubling: "[I] plunged my sword, with brute ferocity, repeatedly through and through his bosom. At that instant some person tried the latch of the door. I hastened to prevent an intrusion, and then immediately returned to my dying antagonist." E.A. Poe, *Poetry and Prose*, op. cit., 356.

[202] J. Lacan, *Le Séminaire livre X: L'angoisse*, op. cit., 141.

Of the Uncanny and the Malevolent Gaze

If this particular night William Wilson has ventured into the place of his rival, it is because something altogether peculiar has been taking place. In the course of an extremely violent altercation with him:

> I discovered, or fancied I discovered, in his accent, his air, and general appearance, a something which first startled, and then deeply interested me, by bringing to mind dim visions of my earliest infancy—wild, confused, and thronging memories of a time when memory herself was yet unborn. I cannot better describe the sensation which oppressed me than by saying that I could with difficulty shake off the belief of my having been acquainted with the being who stood before me, at some epoch very long ago—some point of the past even infinitely remote.[203]

According to Freud, *das Unheimliche* is a feeling that one suddenly has when "repressed infantile complexes are evoked by an impression, or when primitive convictions that have been overcome seem to receive fresh confirmation."[204] The *Unheimliche* is triggered to signal what is most radically intimate in what presents itself as foreign, remote.

Freud enumerates the factors that produce it: animism, magic, enchantment, the omnipotence of thought, the relationship with death, involuntary repetition, the castration complex. The other factors are seen as no more than corollaries. Basically, all these factors involve elements relating to secondary narcissism. This is also the case with what Freud understands by "the relationship with death," which, following Otto Rank's remarks, he associates in this context with a moment in the life of the psyche characterized by animism.[205] As far as the castration complex is concerned, it goes without saying that in the Freudian conception it involves a threat to narcissistic integrity.

In the Freudian universe the phenomenon of *Unheimliche* is mainly related to the domain of the imaginary. Freud stresses how

---

[203] E.A. Poe, *Poetry and Prose*, op. cit., 346.
[204] S. Freud, Das Unheimliche (1919), *Gesammelte Werke XII* (Frankfurt am Main: S. Fischer Verlag, 2006), 263.
[205] O. Rank, *The Double: A Psychoanalytic Study*, trans. and ed. Harry Tucker (Chapel Hill: University of North Carolina Press, 1971).

the phenomenon of the uncanny can occur each time the frontier between fantasy and reality is weakened. The first example Freud gives in his essay on the *Unheimliche* concerns the passage between the animate and the inanimate, a question of borders. He cites, as an example, Hoffmann's tale "The Sandman" to show that the *Unheimliche* involved here is the angst connected to the infantile castration complex.

In the first traumatic scene of his childhood, Nathaniel, surprised while spying on his father and Coppelius, who are talking in his father's office, is grabbed by the former who, not content with trying to gouge out his eyes in order to throw them in the fireplace, unscrews his arms and legs the way a mechanic would those of a doll. What happens is a kind of disassembly of the corporeal apparatus; not only is a piece of the body detached, but also a unity is coming apart. It isn't for nothing that the one Nathaniel falls in love with is a doll, Olympia, the automaton created by the mechanic Spalanzani. What is an automaton, after all, if not an assemblage of spare parts infused with movement? It is the articulation of movement, its mastery, that transforms the inanimate into a kind of mirage of living unity. We are dealing with a trope related to horror. One might wonder to what extent the fantasy of the passage between the inanimate and the animate, rather than referring to death, as it is traditionally believed, refers to the knotting of the imaginary with the real and the symbolic that structures the subject.

Olympia represents Nathaniel's *Urbild*: she shares no less than her eyes with him, those detached organs that circulate between the two of them to the rhythm of a movement of identification, of that "mad love," as Freud calls it, that is the narcissistic one. But the eyes, in the tale, don't just circulate between the protagonist and his double; from the start they acquire a special status: eyes to steal, eyes to cast in the fire, eyes to gouge out, eyes to buy, etc. Something here calls into question the position of the eyes, one fundamental in identification. However, each time the *Unheimliche* emerges during the course of the tale, these eyes appear as subjects of a gaze, be it that of Coppola, Coppelius, or the Sandman. One might even claim that these three characters are one and the same, are but a hole of pure gaze, a gaze that suspends the sight of the mirror and freezes the subject in place. This is when angst appears, to interpose itself and summon a barrier to an annihilating *jouissance*.

Here we can grasp the malevolent function of the Other's gaze, the other side of the coin of its function of support and confirmation in the process of identification. The deadly force of the Other's gaze, once internalized, hardens into the nefarious and violent nature of the *jouissance* with which the superego turns on the subject's ego, chipping away at its image, enumerating one by one the ideals that bolster him or her in order to hold them in contempt and reduce them to ashes, something clinical experience frequently shows where self-image is concerned, be it the image of the body or the mind.

Repetition and Enchantment

In "The Sandman," Nathaniel's madness develops to the rhythm of the repetition of the *Unheimliche*. It is not by chance that the closer the object of Nathaniel's desire is—be it pointed in the direction of the body of the father, of Olympia, or of Clara—the more the uncanny is triggered. One can see how angst presents as an intermediate term between *jouissance* and desire.

Freud noted the relationship between the *Unheimliche* and repetition, which is flagrant in the case of the double. For example, he mentions it when he recalls a personal experience regarding place. In a small Italian town where he has gotten lost, he walks down the same street three times, without realizing it, until he is surprised by an uncanny sensation, prompted by the same seductive looks coming from the same young women at the same windows. In the uncanny, the repetitive quality of the event—the same milieu, the same shape, the same image—is struck by something on the order of the 'all at once,' of the sudden revelation, which constitutes an interruption of the signifying structure that supports the subject's scene of the world. Yet, Freud's definition of the *Unheimliche*—the return of the repressed or new confirmations of primitive, overcome convictions—seems to leave this element aside. The triggering of the uncanny, the fact of finding yourself suddenly disconcerted, short on mastered words and gestures, is less indicative of the return of something symbolized than of the encounter with a limit to the symbolic.

We can wonder about the nature of this encounter. The phenomenon of the *Unheimliche* evokes that of the *déjà-vu*: something here tends toward the extra-temporal character of remembrance. Lacan explains: "One might say that the feeling of *déjà-vu* ... is the imaginary echo that arises as a response to a point of reality that belongs to the limit where it has been excised from the symbolic."[206] Uncanny and *déjà-vu* share this quality of imaginary echo of a point at the limit of the symbolic.[207] This echo would be the answer to the immemorial forms that come from a boundary point where the subject's standing vacillates, where the landscape of the world reveals the facticity that belongs to it. The lack of words, the loss of a mastered space, signals this fugitive suspension outside of space/time, where the symbolic's hold on the imaginary is loosened and where the real has the upper hand.

Buñuel's *El ángel exterminador* (1962) is an enigmatic representation of the space/time relationship between repetition and *Unheimliche*. It stages the arrest of the temporal flow and simultaneously dilates a portion of it, delineating a space separate from time. A series of troubling repetitions—the very scene of the guests' arrival, the firing, one after the other, during dinner, of the servants who are preparing it—enigmatically foreshadow the advent of an uncanny the nature of which is unclear. It is at the end of the post-dinner society chatter and exchange of bourgeois pleasantries, at the moment of leave-taking, that there is a change of venue: the guests have no intention of leaving and, "naturally," get comfortable on the drawing room sofas and rugs in order to spend the rest of the night. The following morning, the scene reveals its entire uncanniness: in short, the guests, the host and hostess, and the only servant left all find themselves prisoners in the drawing room, now separated from the adjacent anteroom by an invisible border, a border that is mysteriously impossible to cross. No one can leave the drawing room even though the exit is totally accessible.

A frontier crosses the body of the house and separates the here from the there: extrinsically, from the spectator's point of view—or

---

[206] J. Lacan, "Response to Jean Hyppolite's Commentary on Freud's 'Verneinung,'" *Ecrits: The First Complete Edition in English*, trans. B. Fink, op. cit., 326. The way Freud explains *déjà vu* it is not so different, at least in part, from what he has to say about the *Unheimlich*: it involves the emergence into consciousness of an older unconscious perception, thanks to the influence of a current perception, similar to the older one.

[207] Freud observes that the forms that provoke the *Unheimliche* can be classified in the same way: "It is a question here harkening back to certain phases in the evolutionary history of the feeling of the ego, of a regression to a time when the border between the ego and the outside world, between the self and others, was not yet neatly drawn." S. Freud, Das Unheimliche, op. cit., 248.

The Place in the Scene

Luis Buñuel, El ángel exterminador

that of the sheep and the little bear who wander surrealistically around the stairs, the anteroom, and the kitchen, or that of the neighbors, or that of the rest of the village—time passes as usual; inside, beyond the invisible frontier, time passes but is spellbound by an "outside of time" that has transformed a mysterious, ineffable moment into a veritable prison. In this scene within a scene, joviality and surprise turn into impatience, hunger, and malaise; they turn into aggression, insults, sickness, hallucinations, and death, as though the dilated subtraction of a moment in time allowed observation through a magnifying glass of angst and human dejection. One detail: only the sheep, who do not know the signifying dimensions of time, are able to cross the invisible border. Angst is expressed by the representation of an interminable occupation of a finite space, with a border that cannot ever be crossed. The empty space of the *Heim* is invaded.

Curiously and imperceptibly, after an indeterminate span of time, the curse is lifted thanks to a guest who, it seems, discovers its secret: repetition. The entire series of gestures and words needs to be repeated, preceding the imperceptible moment that removed a segment of space from time, the scene from the scene. Once executed with precision, the repetition restarts the signifying flow, allowing everyday banality to start back up. At the end of the movie, the sheep's entrance into the village church presages a new spell, a new repeated pause of the scene on the scene of the world.

Buñuel catches the *Unheimliche*, its suddenness, and tries to dilate it, to draw out as much as possible the consequences of its stagnation in the very midst of everyday life. Of course, it is a fiction, but it has the virtue of examining the relationship of the subject to time, of highlighting the hem of the real which forms a trim to repetition, shaking the network of desires which weaves the quotidian landscape. Much could be said about the fact that the protagonists are a group of respectable bourgeois, as is often the case in Buñuel's films, reflecting a critical and sarcastic take on his own era and culture.

Phobic Strategy and the Limit of Place

According to pediatricians and pedagogues, there exist classic infantile fears: the fear of the dark between six months and two years, the fear of large animals around three years of age, the fear of small animals around four, the fear of flying things, and so on. They speak of "natural" fears, as if the experience of fear were a condition of each child's "development." It took Freud to understand that, in effect, infantile fears mark the crossing of a territory shared by speaking beings in their relation to sexuation. By staging the emergence of the castration fantasy, infantile fears trace the domain in which the subjective sexual configuration is going to be articulated.

Freud discovers that for both sexes the access to sexuation involves confronting a loss, which he represents as follows: on the one hand, we think we have the phallus and we are anxious about the idea of losing it, and, on the other, we are convinced we lost it and we wish to recover it. The assumption of human sexuality is confronted by a lack. According to Freud, the castration fantasy is structurally tied to the Oedipal prohibition, which establishes a conflict between the urgency of the drive and the law. Lacan re-elaborates and specifies the Oedipal configuration: in the distress of his or her entry into the world, what the newborn desires is the mother's desire, in the position of the primordial Other, upon which his or her survival depends. Since she desires, she is subject to a lack, as we can only desire what we do not have. Castration is thus first encountered in the mother, in *trou-matisme,* in the encounter with what the Other is missing; the signifier of this lack is called "phallus," the signifier of the mother's desire.[208] The law is encountered in what Lacan calls the 'paternal metaphor'—metaphor indeed—the law of the third, in the position of the signifier of maternal desire, which acts as an obstacle to the mother's whims. Not only has the child had to recognize not being the signifier of the mother's desire, but s/he also has had to reckon with the fact that there is someone else who seems to possess it (be it a male or female partner, a friend, an uncle, work, and so forth), which engenders a sense of structural inadequacy. This involves the recognition of a difference which is also a difference in desire.

Castration angst is triggered by this unavoidable inadequacy; uncertainty about the Other's desire turns into an imaginary absence, into a threat to the body. Infantile fears signal the proximity of angst, the obligation of having to deal with the Other's desire; but they also prevent it, keep it under control thanks to fear, thus giving a form, or

---

[208] The French *trou* means "hole."

a name, to the indeterminate and the unnamable. They mark the territory wherein the choice between neurosis and perversion is decided, on which the subject progressively traces the outlines of his or her place as it relates to the domain of the Other, making the relationship between drive, law, and desire the coordinates of his or her sexuation.

Phobia, which takes root in this infantile territory of passage, expresses a particular relation to the place. If the Other's desire addresses me as awaited or expected, this establishes a temporal relationship of antecedence that I'm forced to enter into. In this temporal dimension that is angst, the subject remains suspended in the immanence of something close by and yet without name and indefinite. The phobic solution, however, restores the routine of the temporal flux introducing fear. While the characteristic of the phobic object is to be an object from the world treated like a signifier, its function is to substitute an object of fear for angst. The subject thereby frees up his or her field of action; this comes at a price, though: that of his or her territory's reduction, since, from that point on, a piece of reality becomes forbidden to him or her. As someone puts it with satisfaction, he is very strong, he is almost invincible; and indeed, in his daily life, he is involved in very dangerous situations without being bothered. There is only one problem: he is afraid of squirrels, and jogging in the park or hiking in nature, where squirrels proliferate, are his favorite pastimes.

By raising an object to the status of untouchable taboo object, the phobic strategy allows targeting the object as what never stops lacking, escaping. The world thus becomes organized according to a prohibition that seems arbitrary in appearance but is shaped by a singular truth, and the subjective landscape is delimited by a theory of fear: don't go near squirrels, don't travel by plane, don't cross open spaces, and so on, all of which often requires elaborate detours in one's everyday itinerary. It shows how theory, the signifying construction of the world, tries to dispatch the encounter with the unthinkable. By delimiting the scene, it founds an ethic thanks to fear.

The phobic object upholds a law; this is obvious in infantile phobia, which invokes the Oedipal prohibition—a parental other who knows how to say no—as is the case with Little Hans, described by Freud. Faced with an Other's desire that questions the subject at the root of his or her own desire, faced with encountering an unavoidable difference, a barrier is erected to separate the subject from the object of desire and turn the phobic object into the signifier that makes up for "the Other's lack."[209] Thus, the phobic strategy gives an answer that acts as a border. By establishing and reestablishing the limits of the subjective field of action, it re-designs the world landscape in order to conceal its most intimate nature, the real that inhabits it.

Inside-Outside, Love-Hate

According to Freud, at the beginning of psychic life, the ego-subject is able to auto-erotically satisfy its drives. While love is the relationship between the ego and its sources of pleasure, as Freud defines it, at this stage the outside world coincides with the indifferent, or, as a source of excitation, with the unpleasant. It is only with the appearance of the object that an antithetical relationship develops between love and hate. Hate then becomes a possible destination for the circuit of the drive, the only occurrence of the transformation of a drive into its opposite. The object relation traces a spatial relation: a motor tendency that tends to approach the object and incorporate it (we talk about the "attraction" an object that gives us pleasure exerts on us and we say we "love" this object) and also a tendency to move away from it (we then feel the "repulsion" exerted by this object and we "hate" it).[210] This hatred can then be accentuated to the point of becoming an aggressive inclination toward the object, with the intention of annihilating it.

Freud lingers on the fact that saying the drive "loves the object" is something acceptable, whereas to say the drive "hates the object" produces a strange, discordant effect. Whereas "to love" is limited to the sphere of the pure pleasure relation the ego entertains with objects, "to hate" does not have such an intimate connection to sexual pleasure; it only involves displeasure: "The true prototypes of the hatred relation do not come from sexual life but from the ego's struggle for self-preservation and affirmation."[211] Yet, since *Beyond the Plea-*

---

[209] J. Lacan, "The Direction of the Treatment and the Principle of its Power," *Ecrits: The First Complete Edition in English*, trans. B. Fink, op. cit., 510.

[210] "Wir empfinden die 'Abstossung' des Objekts und hassen es," S. Freud, "Triebe und Triebschicksale," op. cit., 229.

[211] *Ibid.*, 230.

sure Principle, the self-preservation drives disappear, reabsorbed in the dialectical tension between life drives and death drives. On the one hand, and specifically as concerns the relation to the outside world represented by hatred, they move in the direction of the death drive; on the other, where the vital bond is concerned, they move in the direction of the libido, now representing the life drive. The simultaneous presence of life and death drives in the object relation reflects their fusion, as does the fact of incorporating or devouring during the oral stage, where love is compatible with the abolition of the object's separate existence, or the impulse to appropriate the object during the anal-sadistic stage, not caring about hurting or destroying it. Affective ambivalence informs this movement.

It should be noted that for Freud, however, hatred as the outcome of the transformation of the drive into its opposite is rooted in, and simultaneously differs from, something far more primitive in the very nature of hatred. Hatred remains more archaic, more ancient, than love. Not only does Freud associate it with the hostile side of the absolute Other, of *das Ding* as *Nebenmensch*, and with the advent of the psychic scene derived from primary drive movements (where the original pleasure-ego wants to introject all the good and reject all the bad), he also associates it with the very advent of the living and its relation to being and, intimately, with the inertia belonging to the death drive. Life itself, moreover, is considered a transformation of the death drive. Hatred would seem to be a kind *of resistance against life in the living being*.

It is possible to question the relationship of this notion of hatred with what Freud calls *die Mordlust*, the lust for killing, and the *jouissance* associated with it. Clinical experience shows the force of the destructive drive that can be triggered by the defenseless; this is the case, for example, with the fantasies and feelings prompted sometimes by the newborn: the temptation to let them fall, to attack them, to abuse them. Fantasm and drive, here, respond to the very vulnerability of the living, so well represented by the impotence that causes the newborn's life to be completely dependent on the caregiver. This is also the case with feminine vulnerability and with body frailty in general. It is the case, furthermore, with pets who, deprived of speech and any form of defense, are exposed to all kinds of violence.

The vulnerable exerts a particular and enigmatic fascination, which harbors, among other things, the desire to extinguish a *jouis-*

sance perceived as radically Other. Faced with the vulnerable, we find ourselves in a position of omnipotence over the living.

The Space of Hatred

In Mali, in each village in Dogon country, there is a singular shaded house: the Toguna (the debate or discussion hut). The Toguna is more or less three feet high and rests on a base made of pillars in the shape of a Y, decorated with sculpted wood, some of them magnificent. The roof is made of woven millet stems.

In the Toguna, the village chief, the Hogon, confers with the ancients; they talk about village business, discuss news of the world, and consult, sometimes rendering justice. The debate hut is the place where men meet to discuss and settle their differences. What is remarkable is the fact that the roof is so low: if someone aggressively stands up to leave, he will hit his head and have to sit down again.

Here is a form of architecture that envisages anger, that foresees that the differences within the social bond can turn into a break. It is an architecture of gathering that applies a restriction on acts of rejection or refusal. That it is specifically the house of conversation and discussion that requires such a restriction is remarkable. The speech of exchange and communication harbors discord.

As Lacan notes, "I speak without knowing. I speak with my body and this without knowing. I always say more than I know."[212] This surplus of the saying over the knowing, a surplus that I am constantly missing (*"inter-dit entre les mots"*) accompanies the difference between enunciation and statement, the miscommunication and misapprehension peculiar to the act of speaking, the gap that keeps me at a distance from my own declarations.[213] And to speak with the body, with a body shaped in a signifying way, summons the affects, those effects of *lalangue* that are beyond language.

"What speaks without knowing it does make me *I*, verb subject. It is not sufficient to make me be." "There is some relationship to

---

[212] J. Lacan, *Le Séminaire livre XX: Encore*, op. cit., 108.
[213] *Ibid*. Lacan is playing with the French word *"interdit"* (forbidden), which he cuts in two. This can be approximated by the English "inter-diction," which evokes the forbidden and at the same time what is written in between the lines.

being that cannot be known."[214] And, Lacan adds: the passion of hatred "is indeed what comes closest to being, [this being] that I call the 'to *ex-sist.*' Nothing comes closer to hatred than that speech wherein *ex-sistence* resides."[215]

According to Lacan, speech locates hatred where the subjective split happens as expressed in the act of speech, in the *ex-sistence* peculiar to the *parlêtre*, in its lack of being. Hatred is located in the structural discordance between knowing and being, on the side of speech that is closest to the subject's eternal exile. Separate from a knowledge that s/he is ignorant of—called unconscious—but the consequences of which s/he experiences daily, divided by a rational thought process which, as Freud notes, constantly avoids truth in favor of whatever logic will do, the subject of language finds himself or herself perpetually cast aside by the lack of coincidence between knowledge and truth. Yet, his or her subjective truth does not cease returning to him or her when s/he least expects it, from an unforeseen and unpredictable place in the speaking body. It returns in the shape of a surprise.

Surprise can be welcomed. But faced with surprise, it is possible to stiffen and seek a return to the signifying routine that was interrupted by the emergence of the unexpected, in the hope of plugging the breach that was suddenly opened; one can abhor it and try to annihilate it. Is there a relationship between this type of horror and the emergence of hatred?

The horror of surprise brings to the mind the irreducible aspect of the encounter with difference in the real, its traumatic quality. The confrontation with the limits of the symbolizable—as is the case when the infantile sexual theories are in crises—calls into question the very tenor of thought and of the symbolic register in which it functions. Taking on the horror of castration, the horror engendered by the encounter with the maternal incompleteness (*trou-matisme*), represents as absence an impossibility of knowing, an impossibility concerning both the Other's *jouissance* and the encounter with an unassimilable real.

It is not by chance that Freud insists on the rejection of femininity (*Ablehnung der Weiblichkeit*) as an essential factor in the sub-

---

[214] *Ibid.*

[215] "[La passion de la haine] est bien ce qui s'approche le plus de l'être, [cet être] que j'appelle l'ex-sister. Rien ne s'approche plus de la haine que ce dire où se situe l'ex-sistence." J. Lacan, *Le Séminaire livre XX: Encore*, op. cit., 110.

ject's resistance to the truth belonging to him or her, whatever his or her sex; measuring its extent is, for Freud, an indispensible aim of the psychoanalytic treatment. Since, in the encounter with the maternal *trou-matisme*, the privileged object of desire turns out to be the subject of lack, Piera Aulagnier-Spairani proposes calling femininity "the name given, by the subject of desire, to the object where it cannot be named because it is missing."[216] The relentlessness against the feminine—the desire to dominate it, to annihilate it, which is so often the soul and foundation of hatred—manifests the intolerable confrontation with a difference that is, in fact, an encounter with the lack of being that is peculiar to the very subject who abhors it. The love of totality, the faith in an imaginary, turgescent phallic plenitude, reveals its fundamentalist tendency, its possible terrorist drift, following the denial of subjective *ex-sistence*.

If hatred is closer to *ex-sistence*, is it a response to the emergence of a hole in the symbolic? Is it an attempt to circumvent the inefficiency of the symbolic faced with the real, to foreclose the revelation of a tear in its net? This is what evokes an aspect of the perverse solution, which is recognition of the real and its simultaneous negation, as is the case with *Verleugnung*, a solution that rests on the idea that the symbolic law has an intrinsic malleability, that it sets a limit and, at the same time, its possible transgression. It expresses the credo in a symbolic that could circumvent the real, make it yield, as in the idea of the final solution, of the achievement of death after death, of the subjugation of the laws of nature.

Between the Two

The discussion hut, the social space that foresees that the act of speech may engender hatred, reminds us of the relationship between subject and collective.

The collective has its own specificity. Once a specific number of people have been inserted into a synchronic relationship within the social bond, their relationship changes: subjectivity is then introduced

---

[216] P. Aulagnier-Spairani, "La féminité," in *Le désir et la perversion* (Points: Éditions du Seuil, 1967), 69.

"between individuals," determined by the way each sees himself/herself and conceives of himself/herself in relation to the other.[217] As we indicated earlier, Lacan shows that the subject of the assertion, of an assertion of the "I am white" kind (but also: black, or red, or good, or tired, or angry, and so forth; an assertion supporting the right to exist and the logic of existence, the logic of desire, of life, of the anticipation of death) is a result of a process of identification that involves the passage through an indefinite subject and a reciprocal subject, logical instances within the collective. The emergence of the subject of the assertion involves a new way of counting, which reflects the fact that "the collective is nothing but the subject of the individual."[218] Each of the subjects is, relative to the two others, at stake in their thought, in the position of object *a* under the gaze of the others.[219] This new way of counting shows that factors such as drive, desire, and identification influence the way the speaking being expresses his or her own existence, showing the complementarity between the subject's emergence and the object cause of desire.

"Between two, whomever they are, there is always the One and the Other, the One and the little *a*," which shows the plural nature of the social bond.[220] But in the relation of the one to the other, it is impossible not to take into account that *Y' a de l'Un*, to use Lacan's formulation (a formulation that, among other things, brings the unconscious to the fore).[221] The One in question equivocates between signifier and number, according to its "bifidity," as Lacan calls it: of the

---

[217] E. Porge, *Des fondements de la clinique psychanalytique*, op. cit., 50.

[218] J. Lacan, "Logical Time and the Assertion of Anticipated Certainty," *Ecrits: The First Complete Edition in English*, trans. B. Fink, op. cit., 175.

[219] If they are three, they are in reality "two plus *a*"; and, from *a*'s point of view, this two plus *a* is equivalent to "One plus *a*." *Séminaire livre XX: Encore*, op. cit., 47. This new way of counting derives from the spatio-temporal knotting that accompanies the emergence of the subject of the assertion and the inadequacy of the rapport between the one and the Other in the reciprocal relation. This is mathematically illustrated in the Golden ratio.

[220] J. Lacan, *Le Séminaire livre XX: Encore*, op. cit., 48.

[221] *Y' a de l'Un*: the formulation could be translated as "There's some One," but this translation does not reflect its complexity. *Un* in French designates both the indefinite article "a" and the number one. In addition, Lacan accentuates the double nature of the signifier with a pun: "*de*" (which sometimes Lacan writes *d'*) can be heard as both the partitive article 'some' and the number two (*deux*). Finally, *un* in French evokes Lacan's use of the German term *Unbewusste*—unconscious—since it underlines the *Un* of Un*bewusste*.

unary, symbolic slope on the one side, marked by repetition and difference, and of the *unien* slope on the other, according to the numeric nature of the One. Lacan invents the term *unien* to name the genesis of the One as emerging from the empty set: set theory demonstrates that the One begins on the level where *there is one that is missing*.[222] This is correlative to the fact that *there aren't two* that make One, which is also the case in the sexual domain. The structurally divided nature of the One, in between unary and *unien*, is radically opposed to the imaginary notion of the One as "union," as "whole," including in the sexual relation.

"There's some One. But that means there's some feeling anyway. This feeling that I have called, according to the *unarinesses (un-arités*), that I have called the support, the support of what I do have to recognize, hatred."[223] Hatred once again has a structural connotation, both in relation to the discordance between being and knowing and in relation to the divided nature of the One. We might ask ourselves to what extent the very nature of the subject-effect of the collective—another form of its structural *ex-sistence*—can lead to the radical fierceness against the other's unarity, the other's singularity, to what extent it can lead to a rebellion against what determines him or her as speaking being.

Associated with the structural exile of being, hatred targets the irreducible nature of the One in difference. The One suffers from solitude: "it doesn't truly bond to anything that seems to belong to the sexual Other."[224] The Other is not added to the One, it is never complementary; on the contrary, it differentiates itself from the One, accentuating the discordance that is peculiar to it and undermining the

---

[222] "L'Un commence au niveau où il y en a *un qui manque*. L'ensemble vide est donc proprement légitimé de ceci qu'il est la porte dont le franchissement constitue la naissance de l'Un." J. Lacan, *Le Séminaire livre XIX: ...ou pire* (Paris: Éditions du Seuil, 2011), 143. "One begins on the level where there is one that is missing. The empty set is therefore properly legitimized in that it is the doorway leading to the birth of the One." In introducing the notion of the *unien* with set theory, Lacan adds a facet to Frege's definition of the One as "signifier of inexistence," with which he agrees but which he finds insufficient.

[223] J. Lacan, *Le Séminaire XXIV: L'insu qui sait de l'une-bévue, s'aile à mourre*, 10 mai 1977.

[224] J. Lacan, *Le Séminaire livre XX: Encore*, op. cit., 116.

dream of an ideal and satisfactory complementarity that could make One of the two.

The partner in the sexual couple remains Other, unattainable.

Trespassing

On the world scene, hatred is often a border passion; it calls for a separation in space, a here and a there. It suffices to think of the hatred triggered by territorial situations, as has been the case with the many wars we have experienced and continue to experience. There have been quarrels regarding property and implantations, confrontations over rights.

There is an interesting word that refers to the relationship between space and transgression: *trespass*. It derives from the old French *trepas*—from *trepasser*, "passing beyond" (from *tres*, "beyond"; from the Latin *trans* and *passer*, originally "to transgress," "to offend")—which points to a threshold, specifically the threshold we cross at the time of death. In English, *to trespass* signifies, above all, crossing, going beyond accepted limits: transgressing, intruding, which is the equivalent of committing an infraction. In legal language, *a trespass* is an illegal act against another person, a right, or a property. It is worth noting that the word ties together space, properties, and rights, with death in the background.

In the yards of California villas in Los Angeles, in the middle of town, there are signs saying *"No trespassing, armed response."* These are meant, of course, to dissuade; however, the sign shows that the transgression of the boundary can bring about a legitimate loss of life. The warning is more serious than it may seem, seeing as it is based on the right to protect private property and on the right to bear arms, both established by the United States constitution.

Whether it is real or metaphorical, the territorial question involves the relationship the subject has with his or her place; at the same time, it concerns the relationship with the fellow and the frame that defines it. Hate, which Lacan situates originally at the intersection of the imaginary and the real, is often unleashed as a consequence of the paranoid turgescence with which the ego reacts to its alienation in the other, to its proximity to the other. In this sense it is also a boundary phenomenon, which is all the stronger as the symbolic recognition stemming from the third party, from the Other, is weak. This is where the drive's reversal of love into hate takes place. By expressing the alienation peculiar to the operation of identification, it is the expression of one of the forms of the subject's *ex-sistence*.

The reference to death raised by the notion of *trespass* harkens back to Freud's remarks about the origin of the moral and civil order. Our own death cannot be inherently represented or conceived of, Freud observes. The subject knows nothing of his or her own death, s/he remains inherently convinced of his/her own immortality; the death of one of his or her fellows leaves him/her indifferent; s/he even harbors all kinds of destructive feelings about this fellow, and is easily ready to get rid of him or her. The enemy's death is pure satisfaction of the lust of killing (*die Mordlust*). The questions surrounding death arise solely as a consequence of an emotional conflict faced with a satisfied desire. This conflict is manifested on the occasion of the loss of a loved one: it is the affective ambivalence toward the "loved yet alien and hated" person, which makes death the central element of social order:[225]

> In the presence of the loved one's corpse, not only did the doctrine of the soul come into existence, but also the belief in immortality and the origin of man's sense of guilt, as well as the earliest moral commandments. The first and most important commandment of awakening moral conscience was: "Thou shall not kill." It arose as a reaction against the satisfaction of the hatred felt in the presence of the loved one's corpse, concealed by grief, and was gradually extended to strangers, and finally even to enemies.[226]

There would be no morality, no 'natural' knowledge would exist concerning what is allowed or 'right' to do or not do, without emotional ambivalence, without the affective plurality put into motion by desire. According to Freud, the reaction to the satisfaction of hate is at the root of moral commandments, of the sedimentation of an *unwritten law* that antecedes their formulation, but which is no less impera-

---

[225] S. Freud, Thoughts for the Time of War and Death (1915), *Standard Edition XIV*, op. cit., 293.

[226] S. Freud, "Zeitgemässes über Krieg und Tod" (1915), *Gesammelte Werle X* (Frankfurt am Main: S. Fisher Verlag, 1959), 348–349.

tive for being so, being the witness and expression of the relationship between subject and desire. It becomes internalized in the superego, a superego that is the reliquary of the first object choices *and* the reaction formation against these choices, conveyor of inherently contradictory injunctions.[227]

Hate and violence are thus constitutive elements of the social order. At the beginning, power is based on the law of the strongest; it is pure violence. The law that emerges to oppose it represents the force of the community, a force that, according to Freud, nevertheless continues to be violence, ready to be unleashed against anyone who opposes it. While the law establishes a separation, a threshold that should not be crossed, it is always *someone's* law, as Simone Weil notes, which implicitly establishes an idea of claim.[228]

A boundary passion, hatred seems to fulfill a structuring function in the regulation of the social bond. It exposes at the same time the intrinsic tension between the notion of subject and that of the individual; while by its nature the subject is divided and exiled, it enters the social as 'individual,' as undivided, which establishes his or her rights and his or her duties, his or her place in the symbolic universe.

Freud finds a particular form of social bond in the "crowd": the fact of putting the same object of veneration in place of the ego ideal sediments the libidinal identification and attachment among its members, which feeds the group's strength and allows its adherents to express affects which would otherwise be inhibited or repressed (among these, the passion of hatred and the fact of conceding its exercise, with all the resulting effects). Racism is one example: upholding the group's paranoid and turgescent identity, it institutionalizes hatred within the social body. An isolated racist, Gérard Haddad notes, "would be no more than a psychiatric curiosity."[229]

The notion of crowd allows Freud to "entify" the idea of the "all," echo of an Eros that would be the principle of union.[230] The *Mas-*

---

[227] Freud expresses the contradictory nature intrinsic to the nature of the superego in the phrase "You *ought to be* like this (like your father)," and, at the same time "You *may not* be like this [like your father]." *The Ego and the Id, Standard Edition XIX*, op. cit., 34.

[228] S. Weil, *La personne et le sacré: Ecrits de Londres*, in OEuvres de Simone Weil (Paris: Éditions Gallimard, 1957).

[229] G. Haddad, *Les folies millénaristes* (Paris: Grasset, Biblio-Essais, 1990).

[230] J. Lacan, *Le Séminaire livre XIX: ...ou pire*, op. cit., 167.

senpsychologie thus misses, according to Lacan, "the nature of the *not all* that founds it."[231] By placing the object *a* in the crowd framework outlined by Freud, Lacan subverts the relationship between the individual and the crowd: the subject divided by *a* is not commensurable to the unit. There is no common measure between the object *a* cause of desire and the One of the ego ideal's unary trait. The unary trait, which is the mark of the primary identification of the ideal, is the trait of difference; it founds repetition, and repetition never makes an "all." So, while the crowd is created thanks to putting the same ideal in the object's place, it cannot make up an "all." At the same time, Freud stresses the fact that the crowd inherits its nature from the horde: the horde is founded on the father's exception. If the Freudian myth of the *Urvater*—of the One who possesses "all" the women and is a dead father by definition, the basis of the social bond—is a necessity, it is a logical one: the One here is rooted in the logical function of the exception, in the "at least One" that is an exception to castration.[232] It is from the One—from the One that is lacking—that a structural asymmetry between sexual partners appears, an impossible that targets the real of the incompleteness of the *jouissances*.

"Like Janus, the crowd is two-faced."[233] One of its faces has the features of a logic of the all, the other derives from a logic of the not-all, a duplicity that blazes new trails to oppose every social discourse that proclaims the totalitarianism of the 'All,' and that allows us to appreciate the subversion, introduced by the subjective division, in the relation between the individual and the crowd.

One might wonder to what extent the crowd aspires, by its very nature, to produce an imaginary totality that conceals the real lack intrinsic to the relation of the One to the Other. *Hainemoration* would be consubstantial to it, the way it is consubstantial to the idea of the 'All.'[234]

---

[231] *Ibid*.

[232] See Lacan's writing of the sexuation formulas, *Le Séminaire livre XX: Encore*, op. cit., 73–82.

[233] E. Porge, *Truth and Knowledge in the Clinic: Working with Freud and Lacan* (New York: Agincourt Press, 2016), 152.

[234] *Hainemoration* is a punning neologism created by Lacan; it contains *haine*—hate—and *énamoration*—enamoration.

Should we distinguish several forms of opposition to the other? We observe that there exists a passion for the other's annihilation; but there exists also a reaction to this passion—a revolt against the transgression of the natural law that supports coexistence in difference and that signals the subject of desire's right to belong to the symbolic universe that characterizes him or her—a law that always exceeds the written law regulating social exchanges.

To Die of Shoes

In *If This Is a Man*, Primo Levi tells that after interminable days of deportation—piled into boxcars, left in the cold, without a drop of water to quench their thirst and without any sign of reason to calm incredulity, stupor, and terror—one of the first of many operations of degradation upon arrival at the concentration camp was the order to get completely undressed—wool garments to one side, everything else to the other—and to place in an ordered way their own shoes in a specific corner of the room. Once this was done, the shoes were then swept up by a trustee in front of everyone and piled up outside, in a jumbled mass. This was an enigmatic and absurd operation that confirmed the feeling of disorientation experienced by those who, stupefied, realized—as violence followed violence—that they had crossed the threshold of the unimaginable.

If in the camp the idea was to exploit human labor at the lowest cost, why this footwear ceremony? Why make people remove them and break up the pairs only to impose other ones with a wooden sole, ones that don't fit, that lacerate and make you drag your feet? In the camp, it's true, "*ist kein warum*," as Levi is brutally told by a large man.[235] The fact that there is no why, that it is impossible to understand any of what is happening, is overwhelming; it may also be salutary, Levi points out, seeing as how we still share a conception of the world in which this degradation of the human continues to be unthinkable.

---

[235] P. Levi, *If This Is a Man*, *The Complete Works of Primo Levi I*, ed. A. Goldstein (New York: Norton & Company, 2015), 25.

And do not think that the shoes constitute a factor of secondary importance in the life of the lager. Death begins with shoes; for most of us, they prove to be instruments of torture, which, after a few hours of marching, cause painful sores that become fatally infected. Anyone who has them is forced to walk as if he were dragging a ball and chain (this explains the strange gait of the army of phantoms that returns, on parade, every evening); he arrives last everywhere, and everywhere receives blows. He cannot escape if he is pursued; his feet swell, and the more they swell the more unbearable the friction with the wood and cloth of the shoes becomes. Then only the hospital is left: but to enter the hospital with a diagnosis of *dicke Füsse* (swollen feet) is extremely dangerous, because it is well known to all, much less the SS, and especially the SS, that there is no cure here for that complaint.[236]

The shoe torture was one of many meticulously applied in the camp according to a very precise plan. It was—like all torture—emblematic in that it accentuated the sensation of radical disorientation caused by the arrest and deportation and it directly targeted an intimate aspect of the human: ambulation, the possibility of moving, of measuring a place. This was a way of immediately bringing the prisoners to their knees, of taking away the upright position that makes them human. It was the crowning blow of the spoliation operation undertaken upon arrival at the camp: denuding, shaving, tattooing, elimination of one's name, of one's language, all this accompanied by thirst, hunger, beatings, insults, and humiliations. It was a radical spoliation of one's own singularity that resulted in the systematic destruction of one's own libidinal and narcissistic standing, in an attack on the human right to protect oneself behind a fashioned image, where modesty sustains dignity.

Modesty is an organizing element of the subjective relation to the world. It traces limits, creates fabrics and envelops, builds thresholds, hangs doors, installs windows, curtains, orients the way man inhabits space; it seconds the architectonic nature of language, the tying together of the real, symbolic, and imaginary dimensions that allow man to find the measure of the place, to draw discontinuous spaces, to separate, for example, a bedroom from a bathroom, a coat closet from a dining room, to lower blinds or to turn out a light. Lacan calls

---

[236] *Ibid.*, 30.

modesty "the only virtue," an affect necessary to the *parlêtre* to protect what is most intimate in its relation to the libidinal body.[237] It isn't by chance that this affect is unknown in the animal world. To attack it is to unravel one of the threads thanks to which the subject weaves his or her place on the world scene; it is to mock the sexed nature of the human being, to humiliate him or her.

Via the disintegration of the subjective place, the project dictated by Nazi hatred and executed in the camps aimed at a person's disintegration. From capture to detention, the elements that characterized the particularities of the place were undermined, the attributes that contribute to creating the libidinal landscape were eliminated. This intentional uprooting and spoliation had as its initial goal the breaking of the new arrivals' capacity for resistance; its implicit goal was the total exploitation of human resources followed by extermination, an extermination that represented the pinnacle of the hatred and contempt promoted by Nazi propaganda:

> Here was not only death but a host of maniacal and symbolic details, all intended to demonstrate that Jews, Gypsies, and Slavs are beasts, fodder, garbage. Recall the tattoo of Auschwitz, which branded men with the mark that is used for oxen; the journey in cattle cars that were never opened, forcing the deportees to lie for days in their own filth; the number used in place of the name; the failure to distribute spoons (and yet the storehouses of Auschwitz, at liberation, contained quintals of them), so that the prisoners would have to lick their own soup like dogs; the pitiless exploitation of the corpses, treated as some anonymous matter, the gold extracted from their teeth, the hair serving as material for textile, the ashes for agricultural fertilizers; the men and women debased to guinea pigs, used in medical experimentations and then killed.
>
> The very method that was chosen (after careful experimentation) for extermination was openly symbolic. The same poison gas employed for disinfecting ships' holds and rooms infested by bedbugs or lice was to be used, and was used.[238]

---

[237] J. Lacan, *Le Séminaire livre XXI: Les non-dupes errent*, 12 mars 1974.
[238] P. Levi, *If This Is A Man*, *The Complete Works of Primo Levi I*, ed. A. Goldstein, op. cit., 188.

Over the centuries more cruel deaths were invented, but none that was as laden with hatred and contempt.[239]

This is an exasperated use of symbolism typical of racism and hatred, and of its political expressions of yesterday and today. By loading the world with symbols and significations, by filling it up with meanings, it bears witness to an extreme effort to get around the real, the irreducible real of singularity and difference. Levi enumerates the standard explanations of Nazi hatred—intolerance, anti-Semitism, nationalism, militarism, the need to find a scapegoat, the madness of a maniacal dictator, and so forth—and notes that any explanation and the sum of all these explanations remain in any case insufficient, reductive, disproportionate relative to the acts committed that await explanation. They are not proportionate to the impact and the extent of Nazi fury against the other's singularity: "Maybe what happened cannot be comprehended, or rather, *shouldn't be* comprehended, because to comprehend is almost to justify." "But we can and must understand [Nazi hatred's] roots, and be on our guard."[240]

Significantly, Levi highlights the amazing faculty man possesses to "dig a niche for himself, to secrete a shell," even in desperate circumstances.[241] It's what some were able to do in the camps, at least temporarily: to plant a nail above their bunk to hang their shoes from at night, to make non-aggression pacts with the neighbors and accept the laws of the Kommando, to anticipate these laws. In other words, to reconstitute a place, the *semblant* of a place, in a place thought out and organized for its very destruction. The absence of mirrors in the camp completed the wound inflicted on the narcissistic frame necessary for survival. It is not by chance that the will to not give up and to keep minimal and ritual hygienic practices, however paradoxical given the context, turned out to be essential to avoid being immediately crushed.

---

[239] P. Levi, *Se questo è un uomo* (Torino: Giulio Einaudi Editore, 1976), 254.
[240] P. Levi, *If This Is A Man, The Complete Works of Primo Levi I*, ed. A. Goldstein, op. cit., 190.
[241] *Ibid.*, 53.

The Place in the Scene

Producing a Place

In *Schachnovelle*, Stefan Zweig illustrates the vital need to "carve out" a place, pushed to the extreme. The story occurs during a cruise in South America. A group of passengers, informed of the presence on board of the world chess champion, decides to challenge him. During a rematch, on the heels of the first and immediate defeat, a stranger steps forward and intervenes on the side of the challengers, saving them from what would have been a disastrous move, and, to everyone's amazement, equalizing the play.

He tells the narrator his story. As a lawyer in Austria, in possession of crucial information concerning the properties of monarchs and the clergy, Dr. B. was arrested by the Nazis and imprisoned. His prison was one of the rooms of a hotel used as the headquarters of the Gestapo, where he was held in the strictest isolation. No physical torture, but the sparsely furnished room turned into an asphyxiating instrument of torture. It quickly assumed the shape of a bell jar placed on a dark ocean of silence, in a void lacking space or time. This state of complete isolation compromised his mental faculties and his ability to conceal critical information during interrogations.

> ...After every interrogation by the Gestapo my own thoughts relentlessly continued the torment of questioning and examining and harassing—even more cruelly, perhaps, for the former came to an end after an hour but the latter never did, thanks to the insidious torture of this solitude. And all the time nothing around me but the table, the bureau, the bed, the wallpaper, the window, no distraction, no book, no newspaper, no new face, no pencil to write anything down with, no matches to play with, nothing, nothing, nothing. Now I saw how diabolically practical, how psychologically deadly in its conception, this hotel room system was.[242]

It was under these circumstances that one day, before an interrogation, while he was waiting in a vestibule, Dr. B. was able to furtively grab a book. It turned out to be a collection of one-hundred-fifty chess matches played by the greatest players in the world. Studying their

---

[242] S. Zweig, *Chess Story*, trans. J. Rotenberg (New York: New York Review Books, 2006), 45.

The Place in the Scene

language and their finesse, he memorized them, transforming their symbolic and imaginary combinations into a virgin and plural territory, capable of piercing the bell jar of his isolation. The ability to travel via mental spaces opened up for him a place in the place, a horizon within the coercion. But, once the appeal of practicing the games he learned had passed, Dr. B. wanted to play new ones; to do so, he would force himself to play himself, taking on in turn the role of each of the adversaries in a succession of matches in which the imaginary confrontation elated him and divided him at the same time, unleashing competition, aggression, and hatred in a single internal space. The acceleration of possible configurations—he confides to the narrator—was reflected in a temporal precipitation, in an insatiable avidity that led him to a state of delirium and, following a hospitalization, to an unexpected liberation.

After the mastery of all these imaginary games, and the disorientation this apprenticeship had produced, it was on the cruise ship that Dr. B. came across a real chessboard with real pieces for the first time. At first struck dumb, later on he couldn't help intervening and thus block the disastrous move of the world champion's challengers.

Surprised by this story, the narrator invites him to play the grandmaster again the following day. He accepts. At the agreed upon time, surrounded by spectators, two diametrically opposed characters and styles of play face one another: one is purely abstract, quick, practiced in an exclusively mental space; the other concrete, slow, tied to the chessboard and its matter. About the champion, known to be a boor completely lacking in education, the narrator notes a particular and unusual characteristic: his inability to play blind, as chess players say, without the chessboard's material support.

Dr. B. beats the champion. But in the intervals between moves, he becomes impatient, pacing back and forth over a short distance that is always the same, as though his steps propelled him against an invisible barrier that forced him to turn back. In the heat of competition, he reproduces the dimensions of his former cell, the physical support he needs to allow him to move within the mental space of the game. During the next game, the champion takes advantage of his opponent's flagrant weakness and slows down his moves to the maximum limit. Caught up in his impatience and in the acceleration of dozens of imagined moves from several mental games played simultaneously, Dr. B. makes a bad move: he makes, in the here and now of

The Place in the Scene

the real, present chessboard, a move meant for another game that he is playing on an imaginary board.

It is a story of deep alienation in which, for both of the adversaries, opposites by virtue of their style and their social origin—two sides of the same historical coin—the space of the chessboard and the infinite combination of moves become the place of possible resistance, a bridge toward an elsewhere. It is not by chance that this is Zweig's last short story, the only one in which he directly portrays Nazi persecution and the intimate effects of a lacerating subjective contradiction in the wake of a changing world from which he is constantly in exile, from Salzburg to London to New York to South America, with many travels in between.[243] It is not by chance that *Chess Story* is his last work, finished, it is said, with his biography *Yesterday's World*, on the eve of his suicide, February 22, 1942. The possible combinations of wandering, of the production of other places, do not seem to be able to soften the coercion exercised by the world of time, the distance from the world of yesterday that nothing seems able to bridge.

Language and Place

In exile in England (having entered the war against Germany), Zweig complains that he is being deprived of his language: not only can he no longer publish in Germany, but, as a refugee, as an "enemy alien," he is warned against speaking German. As he puts it in his journal, he finds himself imprisoned in a language he cannot use, on a kind of useless chessboard.

Primo Levi associates the most heartrending aspect of the dehumanization in the camp to the subtraction of language, to the impossibility of communicating, of understanding and making oneself understood, an incapacity that, in fact, led directly to death. Speech, this "necessary and sufficient mechanism by which man is defined," was forbidden, crushed, eliminated.[244] To speech suppressed in the mouths of the victims corresponded the ferocious screaming of in-

---

[243] He ends up fleeing to Brazil in 1941, a politically contradictory place that he nevertheless described as the "land of the future."

[244] P. Levi, *The Drowned and The Saved, The Complete Works of Primo Levi III*, ed. A. Goldstein, op. cit., 2474.

comprehensible, incoherent shouted orders, where the sound of the voice was reduced to an imperative that could not be decoded.

"All the human races have speech; no non-human species does": that is what defines the *universal* to which man belongs, a universal that was attacked and taunted in the camps, with the intention of showing its paltry character, of circumventing the law of the symbolic.[245]

The amplitude of this operation, the use of industrial technologies to bring it about, the number of people exterminated, make the Nazi camps a dividing line that traces a radical before and after. And it is precisely because we are concerned with this after that we cannot not reflect on the fact that language, that universal to which man belongs, continues to be called into question in an underhanded way by contemporary life.

After the immediate, post-war silence surrounding *If This Is a Man* and the cool reception of its publication in 1955, it was precisely the psychiatrist Franco Basaglia—founder of the anti-psychiatry movement in Italy—who pointed out the crucial importance of Primo Levi's observations, giving his discourse its first and profound social resonance. Basaglia immediately recognizes in Levi's analysis of subjection and exclusion implications similar to those he experienced, specifically in psychiatric commitment.

> The fact that the outcast of the Nazi camps might have the same aspect as a mental patient does not mean that—through deprivation, hardship, and tortures—the prisoner has gone mad. Rather that, interned in a place where mortifications, humiliations, and arbitrary events are the norm, a person—whatever his mental state—gradually becomes objectified within the rules of internment and identifies with them. His constructions of a crust of apathy, lack of interest, insensitivity is probably then just his extreme act of defense against a world that first excludes him and then annihilates him: the last personal resource that the patient, as internee, sets up in opposition in order to protect himself against the unbearable experience of living consciously as an outcast.[246]

---

[245] *Ibid.*, 2473. "Tutte le razze umane parlano; nessuna specie non umana sa parlare." *I sommersi e i salvati, Opere I* (Torino: Giulio Einaudi Editore, 1987), 721.

[246] F. Basaglia, "Un problema di psichiatria istituzionale: L'esclusione come categoria socio-psichiatrica," *Rivista Sperimentale di Freniatria* 6 (1966), in M. Bucciantini, *Esperimento Auschwitz/Auschwitz Experiment* (Torino: Giulio Einaudi Editore, 2011), 136–138.

Levi reacted with reticence to the exporting of his thoughts concerning the experience of the Nazi camps to other alienating social contexts, because in the camps the primary and ultimate goal of subjugation was death rather than confinement. Nevertheless, he was the one to establish continuity between the logic of the desubjectification he experienced and the logic of alienation in the contemporary world, as it is expressed in different current segregative practices aiming at control and normativization.[247]

"Imagine now a man who has been deprived of everyone he loves, and at the same time of his house, his habits, his clothes, of literally everything: he will be a hollow man, reduced to suffering and needs, heedless of dignity and restraint, for he who loses everything can easily lose himself."[248] Basaglia pursues this line of thinking in order to condemn the dehumanizing premises of psychiatric commitment: once it has occurred, it quickly becomes difficult to tell whether the mental problem comes from the disease or the confinement itself, from the effects of a space that chips away at the subjective place. Fifty years after the condemnations coming out of anti-psychiatry and the dismantling of various psychiatric institutions, the problem remains. The search for alternatives to hospitalization, therapeutic community housing, the critique of the binary logic of inside/outside the institution, keeps encountering new forms of coercion. While certain forms of internment are more flexible, segregation, special treatments, and pharmacology continue to be the means used to destroy the subjective place and attack the subject's modesty and dignity.

The stakes are eminently political, seeing how "madness" calls the social bond into question and at the same time is its effect. The way of contending with it is based as much on a variety of conceptualizations of suffering as it is on a variety of political intentions. They reflect radically different conceptions of the human: the first, positivist in origin, disavows the particularity of the subject of language and reduces the human being to material causality, reduces behaviors and

---

[247] Regarding this, refer to Levi's science fiction, where he comments with bitterness and irony on segregation in the modern world and on the legacy of the camps in the present. P. Mieli, *A Silver Martian: Normality and Segregation in Primo Levi's Sleeping Beauty in the Fridge* (New York: CPL Editions, 2014).

[248] P. Levi, *If This Is A Man, The Complete Works of Primo Levi I*, ed. A. Goldstein, op. cit., 23.

emotions to neurophysiological and chemical reactions; the second, psychoanalytical in origin, while respecting neurological and physiological components, reckons also with the particularity of the subject and of the social bond s/he is part of.[249]

Primo Levi shed light on the role played by science and the new technologies—with the collaboration of the medico-university system—in the extermination carried out in the camps as well as in the alienating practices of the democratic system. As a scientist, he expresses himself forcefully in the debate on the responsibility of scientists in the modern world:

> Whether or not you are a believer, whether or not you are a "patriot," if you are able to choose, don't let yourself be seduced by material or intellectual interest, but choose in the zone that can render least painful or least dangerous the path of your contemporaries and of those who will come after you. Do not hide behind the hypocrisy of neutral science: you are savvy enough to be able to evaluate whether a dove, a cobra, an idle dream, or maybe nothing at all will emerge from the egg you are incubating.[250]

One cannot help observing that the division between *res cogitans* and *res extensa* as platform of the conceptualization between observer and world—and the faith in "objectivity" that accompanies it—predisposes science to the production of paradigms that separate the researchers from what is sought, freeing them, at the same time, from *responsibility for their actions*, for the results produced by their research and for its eventual implications. This de-responsibilization goes hand in hand with the bracketing of the subjective particularity,

---

[249] An example of the latter comes to us thanks to the conceptualization of the space of the cure proposed by Guy Dana and his team in the services sector associated with Longjumeau Hospital in Paris. It is based on the idea that space, "when it is structured by an institutional array, gives birth to a language." Distributed over the territory and considered a place of reception (not hospitalization), the sector presents as "a container with several areas." Eschewing the binary logic of inside/outside, the plurality of places reflects in physical space a mobility in the structure, establishing a fluidity between city and sector, that introduces discontinuities in the space of the cure and supports "a knowledge of the interval," essential for the treatment of psychoses and diverse forms of psychotization. The grammar of real space introduces divisions within mental space. G. Dana, *Quelle politique pour la folie?: Le suspense de Freud* (Paris: Stock, 2010).

[250] P. Levi, "Covare il cobra," *La Stampa*, 1986.

of both the researcher and of the many subjects to whom the results of these paradigms are applied.

The ignorance of the subject of language, of his or her exclusively singular nature, pervades a large part of the scientific discourse that is widespread in the contemporary world, a discourse that—casually adopted by many intellectuals, scientists, the media, consumers, and so on—does not seem to ponder its genealogy, nor the effects of its application in the recent past. The alienating consequences of the reduction of the human being to pure organic materiality and of the emotions to chemical and neurophysiological reactions are not measured or are deliberately ignored. In large part supported by the medical and pharmacological industries, this discourse is rooted in the mercantile exploitation of the *res extensa*. With its battery of neurological, behavioral, and cognitive tests and myriad correlative treatments, it generates good profits, but also, and to a great extent, segregation.[251] Denying the way in which language permeates living substance, it forecloses the subject of language, what is most human in the relationship between the speaking being and his or her world. The fact that "science" and norms are called upon to silence the human being—instead of dealing with the psychic and social reasons that are behind his or her malaise—shows the continuity between past and current solutions, the persistence of a biopolitical logic that combines alienation, control, and profit.

It is strange that a society dedicated to the exploitation of the cult of the personal image, such as the current neoliberal society, does not consider the evocative and indecent nature of certain pseudo-scientific measures it puts in place that manipulate the relation of the subject to the place. This is the case with certain procedures performed on the body for medical reasons; it is also the case with the homogenization to which workers and students are subjected through

---

[251] Let us cite, by way of example, the IQ tests to which preschool and school-age children are subjected, tests that decide, among other things, the successive steps of their educational itinerary, blocking access to schools or tracks, causing homologation on the one hand and discrimination on the other. In this context, one needs to point out the central role played by psychology, the discipline that is perhaps currently most responsible for the work of normativization accomplished by biopolitical power. It isn't by chance that the protocols of torture at Guantanamo Bay were decided and applied by members of the American Psychological Association. Such a participation was finally denounced and opposed by other members of the association.

the imposition of uniforms, whether material or ideological, real or symbolic.[252] Too often, everyday medical and bureaucratic practices do not take into account the fact that human beings' sense of their own dignity is essential in order to face life, sickness, and trauma; too often these practices forget the respect for human speech and image, the ideal envelope that supports the body's real. They disregard the symbolic order that humanizes the organic, producing a body of veils, modesties, desire, *jouissance*.

Imponderabilia

Imponderabilia is the title of a famous Marina Abramovich performance, staged in 1977 at the Galleria Comunale d'Arte Moderna of Bologna: Marina and Ulay, completely naked, stood facing each other just inside the entrance, forcing the public that wanted to gain access to the galleries to pass sideways between their bodies, one at a time, so tight was the space. At the time, the arrival of the police and the artists' arrest put an end to the performance, which gave the notion of performance as well as that of imponderability all of their weight.

I had the opportunity to see *re-performances* of this piece—as Abramovich calls them—at New York's Museum of Modern Art in 2010, on the occasion of the retrospective and the performance-recreation *The Artist Is Present* (March 14–May 31, 2010). Here, *Imponderabilia* was installed between two rooms: a naked man and woman, in the same position as the original performance, narrowed the passage from one room of the exhibition to the other, while Marina Abramovich performed full time (736.5 hours, the length of the entire show), sitting motionless in the museum lobby in the company of different visitors, who were free to sit facing her and to gaze into her eyes for as long as they wished.

---

[252] Take for instance a common practice in many hospitals: as soon as you set foot in one, you have to exchange your own clothing for paper uniforms or humiliating half open gowns (in which you navigate the hospital hallways, on the way to consults, exams, and so on), in the name, of course, of convenience and hygiene. From the outset, the support provided by the singularity of the subjective image and the feeling of decency is eliminated, underlining the vulnerability of the sick person, the intimidation inherent in being admitted to the hospital, and the libidinal spoliation required by medical practices.

The Place in the Scene

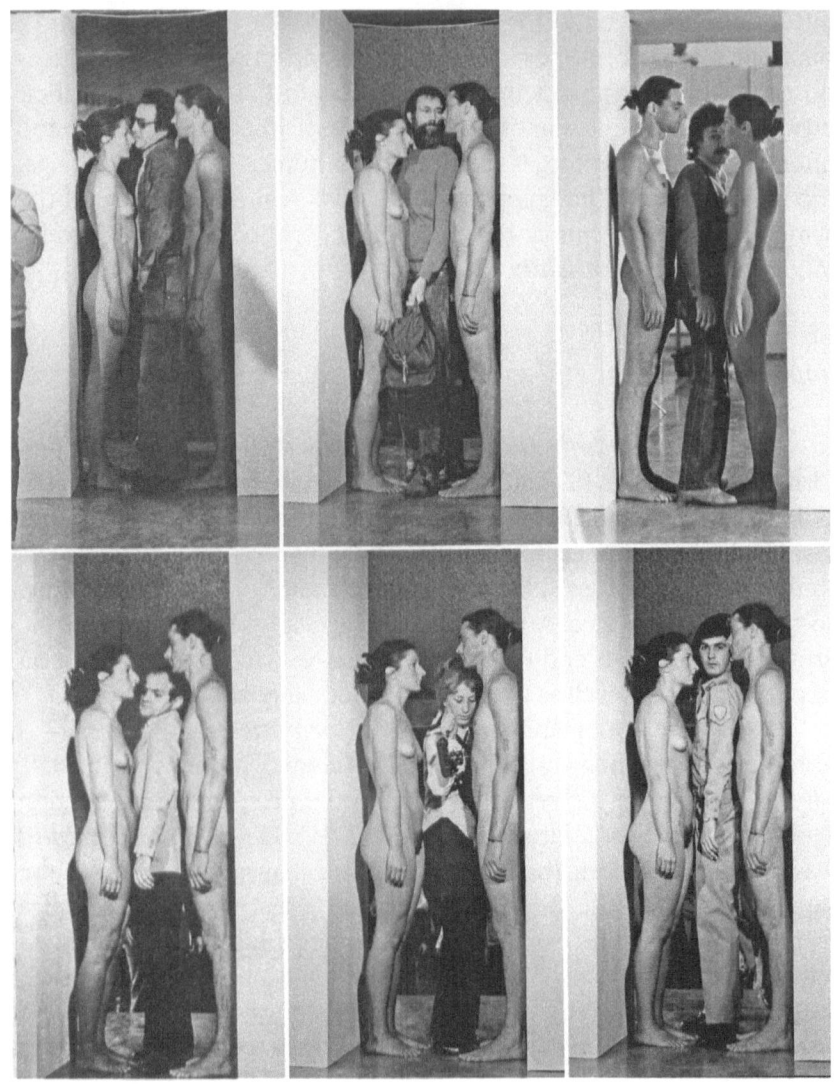

Marina and Ulay, Imponderabilia

The notion of performance, and the ephemeral character that is specific to it, involves in its uniqueness all the variants relative to the action that defines it and to the public that participates in it, always associated with a here and now, with a discrete space/time. This sheds light on a truth relating to the role of the visitor in general, which remains hidden in a classical exhibit: to whit, their structurally active role, even when they think they are just passing through an exhibit space that does not concern them directly. The presentation of a work is never only a presentation: the moment we encounter it, when our eyes land on it, *we become part of its accomplishment*, each time unique and renewed, which highlights the fact that the relation to art, like the relation to place, is always singular.

The space of an exhibit is the implicit promise of an encounter that traces novel coordinates of place. If, as Freud stresses, the artist gives birth to a new species of true things, each of these things adds a new dimension to the subjective landscape, engages differently the gaze, the voice, movement. Performance art has the virtue of highlighting the dialectical nature of the place; it breaks with the tradition of contemplative art, overturning its premises by putting into play the artist's body and action, not as an actor or interpreter of a pre-established role, but indeed as pure presence in action, in the unpredictability of the circumstances to which it is exposed. This challenges the classical notion of representation and accentuates the transferential relationship between performer and spectator, turning the work into the result of their encounter.

Imponderabilia is a radical action on the threshold, that particular space which never ceases appearing in the place in the encounter between the dimensions of the symbolic, the imaginary, and the real. The presence of a naked man and woman, who shrink and obstruct the passage, forces the visitor to choose whom to turn toward in order to pass through. Some say the performance is dated, that more than thirty years of the Body Art Movement have diluted its novelty. And yet its performance at MOMA demonstrated more of a timeless quality, at once original, repetitive, and structural. I crossed *Imponderabilia*'s threshold and observed the visitors who crossed it. I observed them moving their bodies sideways and brushing up against the naked bodies, each person making a different choice, with his or her own style and his or her own expression, each participating in the performance itself.

Imponderabilia forces one to confront sexual difference in an immediate way; the irreducible aspect of this difference appears from the outset in all its real, symbolic, and imaginary value. You are in a gallery you want to visit and you want to move to the next room, and to do so you suddenly realize you have to go through this passageway. This exposes the logic of the act: the instant of the glace and the time of comprehending are quickly followed by the moment of concluding; people are waiting. Not only is the unexpected presence of two naked bodies involved, but also the relationship that you have with these bodies, witnessed by everyone else; you have to decide whether to face the woman or the man, all the while knowing that you won't be able to avoid touching both of their bodies. Embarrassment, modesty, unease, irony, curiosity, irritation: observing the visitors, it clearly seems that each person, in his or her own way, above all, crosses an internal threshold to be able to pass through this body door.

The scene stages the tension between public and private and the way in which the context transforms the experience of place; the voyeurism intrinsic to the act of looking is fueled by the performance, and yet slowed by the other's gaze, a gaze through which the subject is presentified. *Imponderabilia* is provocation and interdiction in a single act.

One cannot help noting the tripartite nature of the choice in question: the visitor, a masculine nude, and a feminine nude, slipped into the real, at once enigmatic and flagrant, of anatomical difference. It is what implicitly evokes the ternary nature of the oedipal configuration—its mythic inevitability—and, as a consequence, the nature of human sexuation. Every speaking being is allowed, as Lacan puts it—whether or not s/he is endowed with the specific attributes ("attributes that remain to be determined")—to position himself or herself in the masculine or feminine sphere.[253] This position involves different places in regard to sexuation, to the sexual relationship, and to the object cause of desire. On the one hand, in the masculine sphere, there is phallic *jouissance*, the possibility of reaching the sexual partner only through the intermediary of the object cause of desire;[254] and, on the other hand, in the sphere of those who take on the status

---

[253] J. Lacan, *Le Séminaire livre XX: Encore*, op. cit., 74.
[254] Which relies on the phallus as a signifier lacking a signified, symbolizing the failure of meaning.

of woman, there is the access to the signifier of the Other and at the same time the possibility of a relation to the phallus.[255] This is what determines not only an asymmetry between the positions of the sexes (as Freud had noted based on the structural lack to which the subject is confronted in sexuation), but also a failed encounter by nature, the impossibility of making one out of the two: that is, the impossibility of writing the sexual relation, which never ceases not being written, as Lacan puts it. This foregrounds the solitary nature of the act, the impossibility of being One in the sexual relationship, in "this game of which the stakes consist of being One in the same *jouissance*."[256]

By forcing the visitor to take a position, *Imponderabilia* summons the solitary nature of the subjective choice within the space of the exhibit; it imperceptibly reminds us of the irreducible nature of the real that underlies the sexed nature of the place. That there were manifestations of aggressivity during its re-performance at MOMA is significant: expressions of hatred surfaced in the attitude of some visitors surprised by this obligatory passage, surprised by the forced encounter with the discordance between waiting and acting, between knowing about sexual difference and being compelled to confront it.

One day when I returned to see *The Artist Is Present*, the couple on the threshold of *Imponderabilia* had been temporarily changed (because of a lack of available performers, it seems): instead of a man and a woman, two naked men faced each other inside the passageway. Needless to say, the imponderability of the work was nullified and, in fact, the performance was now little more than an out-of-context echo of 1970s body art. This demonstrates the—albeit imponderable—weight of difference in the real.

---

[255] Of the woman barred, as Lacan stresses, since she "expresses herself from a *not-all*." Ibid., 75.

[256] P. Audi, *Le théorème du Surmâle: Lacan selon Jarry* (Lagrasse: Verdier, 2011), 155.

PLACES ON THE SCENE:
THREE CASES

Inhabiting the Place: History, Truth

There is no space that is not affected by place. Each of us inhabits the world scene from the perspective of our own relationship with place, of which we are the producer and the product. This sheds light on the way the subject acts on the landscape that is his or her own and allows considering the uniqueness of the impact on the social, political, and cultural contexts that belong to him/her.

The space/time of the landscape is replete with history. If we are the children of our landscape, we need to deal with the symbolic debt that comes from the generations who preceded us; whether we like it or not, inhabiting the place is a way of acquiring what we inherited, an acquisition that is transmission between old and new.

In this regard, a Freudian clarification concerning the notion of history is in order. Freud's contribution overturns the understanding of the notion of individual time, as well as the understanding of the finitude of historical time. Besides the relationship between synchrony and diachrony specific to historical materiality, to the succession and the interlocking of real events of which human beings are participants and protagonists, Freud examines the particular temporality through which this history affects the individual and the collective, transcending the generations. He studies diverse aspects of time: chronological time, made up of the synchronic and diachronic network of real and imaginary events (which involves antecedence, progression, contemporaneity, succession); historical time, which accounts for the series of real events that reflect material reality and the context in which it happens; the time peculiar to psychic causality, which Freud defines with the term *Nachträglichkeit* and which has a logical and structural character, not on the order of evolution; and the time of the absence of time that characterizes the drive. The diverse aspects of time interact, producing the experience of subjectivity as well as the subjective experience of history. In particular, the logical character of *Nachträglichkeit* allows for a radically new conceptualization of the shaping of history. Woven into the fabric of signifiers that traverse the generations, this temporality invests a past inscription and reactivates it in the individual and collective psychic formations of the present.

While by material truth Freud means the reality external to the subject, verifiable on the basis of concrete evidence—specifically called proofs of reality—by historical truth Freud means a form of return of the repressed (*Wiederkehr des Verdrängten*), the return and the persistence in the present of a fragment of truth (*ein Stückchen Wahrheit*). The latter returns in a warped and warping envelope, as is the case, for example, of the kernel of historical truth that appears in delirium or in certain symptomatic manifestations. Not only does madness have a method, but it also contains a share of historical truth. If we consider humanity as a whole, Freud observes, and put it in place of the individual, we observe that it has also developed delirious formations—religions, traditions, myths, legends—which, although they contradict reality, exert an extraordinary influence: "They owe their power to the element of historical truth derived from the repression of the forgotten and archaic past."[257]

But what quotient of reality does this past truth possess? The fragment of historical truth restores the traces of an external, material reality and of its impression on the psychic scene; it signals the persistence of its inscription and its efficacy in the present. Such and such a collective manifestation, such and such an individual manifestation, embody a version of a process of deciphering an impression inscribed at an inaugural moment, the trace of which has been solidified by a period of latency.

The logical structure of temporality, identified by Freud on the basis of the study of trauma, makes it so that the unassimilable aspect of the encounter with the real is transmitted between generations. This is a fundamental discovery of the psychoanalytic clinic: to whit, the fact that the symptom can express in the present effects of meaning that relate not only to the experience of the person manifesting them, but to the generations preceding him or her and within which

---

[257] S. Freud, "Konstruktionen in der Analyse," *Gesammelte Werke XVI* (Frankfurt am Main: S. Fischer Verlag, 1981), 56.

his/her personal history is inscribed. That the subject ends up having to deal in the present with a symbolic debt coming from a past that precedes him or her is a consequence of the processes of identification of which s/he is the effect, of the transferential nature of his or her relationship with the social environment. In addition to genetic and environmental transmission, symbolic transmission between the generations—as well as the imaginary and real transmissions to which it is linked—bequeaths to the newborn the culture, traditions, traumas, and inclinations that permeate the history of the group to which s/he belongs, as well as the expectations that accompany his or her birth and that will mark his or her itinerary.

In opposition to the "bounce between truth and lie" of a certain deconstructionist drift, which implies that *any* reading of a text is good if the text allows it, it is worthwhile to rehabilitate the terms 'history' and 'truth.'[258] As far as history is concerned, it is worth remembering, for example, that it rests on the separation between events and mythic elements, on the analysis of the sources and of their eventual distortion. And while the analysis of the distortion is already a form of construction, as Carlo Ginzburg rightly points out, it is not incompatible with the proof, nor with the disclaimers inflicted by the reality principle. This is something with which Freud would be in agreement: "Knowledge (even historical knowledge) is possible."[259]

As for the notion of truth—concealed as it is by the predicative definition that characterizes it in Western philosophy—it should not be forgotten that it is not possible to say whether something is true or not true outside the boundaries of language. This is what Lacan stresses when he states, " I, the truth, am speaking," shaking up a tradition in which the fact of saying something and the form in which one says it are inseparable.[260] The linguistic form is above all "the condition for the accomplishment of thought," as Benveniste notes with finesse, showing, among other things, how much the Aristotelian attributes of being coincide with the predicative forms of the Greek language and predispose being to its philosophical vocation.[261]

---

[258] C. Ginzburg, *Rapporti di forza* (Milan: Feltrinelli, 2000), 38.
[259] *Ibid.*, 49.
[260] For exemple in "La science et la vérité," *Ecrits*, op. cit., 866.
[261] E. Benveniste, "Catégories de pensée et catégories de langue," in *Problèmes de linguistique générale I* (Paris: Éditions Gallimard, 1966), 64.

Truth does not reside in the predicate, in a verb to be that adapts being to the object, but rather in the relationship between said and saying. However, as Lacan adds, the fact that truth speaks does not mean it speaks the truth: "It's the truth, it speaks. As for what it says, it's up to you to work with what you have."[262]

Outside of the act of speech, truth offers no guarantees; only another word is able to attest to its validity. This means that its value derives as much from its subjective quality as from its effects in the collective, since the subject of the subjective in question here, the subject in language, is the effect of the act of speech, of the division that results from the relationship between the one and the other, peculiar to the nature of the collective within the social bond. But the fact that truth speaks without being *adaequatio rei et intellectus* does not diminish in any way its nature as effraction; on the contrary, it does not diminish its impact on the one who voices it and the one who listens to it, an impact that is always specific, singular, unique, irreplaceable, not interchangeable with another truth. If one considers the truth effects of a given letter, their possible readings will be limited to those allowed by their contextualization.

There is history and there is knowledge of history; there is a memory of history and there is a subjective truth. To treat the subjective relation to place—a relation steeped in individual uniqueness and in the history in which it develops—I have chosen three kinds of figure. Despite their diversity and their distance, each of them illustrates a crucial moment of revolt and transformation. Each sheds light on a singular 'treatment' of the relation to the real and bears witness to the progressive subversion of the world scene during the periods in question. This transformation involves the logic of the act: an act is what divides the now and institutes a before and an after.

The first example is inspired by Melville's tale *Benito Cereno*. It is a tale based on events related in 1817 by Captain Amasa Delano about the singular rescue of a Spanish ship. The narrative unfolds from the perspective of two logical moments: that of the facts that occurred in material reality and that of their reading by Melville, a reading that stages the violence of the historical reality they transmit, that shatters the certainties of the period.

---

[262] J. Lacan, *Le Séminaire livre XVI: D'un Autre à l'autre*, 12 février 1969.

The second is inspired by the study of a controversial historical document: the painter Pontormo's journal, written in the sixteenth century while he was working on a grandiose decoration of the choir stall of the San Lorenzo Basilica in Florence. Pontormo's journal is a precious testimonial not only to the period's intellectual vision, steeped in the foundations of modern science and the spirit of the Reformation, but also to the artist's subjective position in relation to his act. The journal itself is a key element in tracing the coordinates of the place; it leads us into the twists and turns of the relationships between bodies—earthly and heavenly—and nature, showing to what extent the place contains the reciprocal reflection of body and world, and to what extent the body is a threshold between nature and culture.

The third is the case of a unique place: Vienna at the turn of the century, where the architectonic and urbanistic applications of the second half of the nineteenth century open onto a new configuration of the city scene, onto a redefinition of place that reflects the passage from one period to another, the opening of a new vision of the subject and of history.

1.
OF THE SCENE WITHIN THE SCENE

If the signifier produces the world, then the fact that mistakes can be made there is one of its characteristics. This is the case, for instance, with communication, the intentions of which often collide with the evidence of miscommunication, with misunderstandings (a word that highlights both comprehension and meaning). While the symbolic register is specifically that of double meaning, where sense and nonsense hold hands, the imaginary register is the empire of meaning, where everything seeks and finds an explanation, even a fictitious one. The love of meaning is the weaving of the *semblant* that unfolds in the fantasm's opening onto the world.

Delano's Place

Herman Melville's novella *Benito Cereno* is emblematic of the relationship between the symbolic and the imaginary and their connection to a persistent and unassimilable real.[263] Melville bases many of his stories on actual events to allow his writing free rein, combining material truth with historical truth, as is the case for *Moby Dick*, for *Omoo*, and for "Bartleby." *Benito Cereno* is based on a singular occurrence, harkening back to 1805, reported by its protagonist Captain Amasa Delano in the account of his voyages, *A Narrative of Voyages and Travels, in the Northern and Southern Hemispheres: Comprising Three Voyages Round the World, Together with a Voyage of Survey*

---

[263] *Benito Cereno* belongs to the collection *The Piazza Tales*, published in 1856. A first version was published in 1855 in issues 34, 35, and 36 of *Putnam's Monthly Magazine*, New York. I'm referring here to H. Melville, *Benito Cereno*, in *The Piazza Tales and Other Prose Pieces, 1839-1860*, ed. H. Hayford, A.A. MacDougall, G. Thomas Tanselle, and others (Chicago: Northwestern UP, 1987).

and Discovery in the Pacific Ocean and Oriental Islands, published in 1817.[264] Melville rewrites the facts and subtly transforms them, an appropriation that becomes a literary, stylistic, and rhythmic invention conferring historico-political complexity and resonance to the events. He takes up Captain Delano's account but lightens the tone of the description; in certain places he changes the narrative slightly, in others he resorts to complete invention. The change he makes in the date of the actual events is crucial and significant: he moves them back to 1799, which is an allusion to the Haitian Revolution (1791–1804) and to the constitution of the Republic of Haiti, the first state "where after the abolition of slavery, the government passed to and *remained* in the hands of the descendants of the African populations imported to work as slaves on the immensely profitable sugar cane plantations."[265] This reference is confirmed by the name change of the ship on which the events take place: *Tryal*, according to the facts related in Delano's account, transformed into *San Dominick* by Melville, the phonetic relative of *Santo Domingo*, destination of the first mass importation of African slaves to the Americas and colonial geographical name of Haiti before the Haitian Revolution. This was a change of context that made *Benito Cereno* an essential and complex punctuation mark in the debate over slavery, which pitted abolitionists against slavers at the time of its publication.

In Melville's tale, Amasa Delano—the American captain of a merchant ship hunting seals, anchored in the harbor of Santa Maria island near the southern end of Chile—is one of the story's three main characters. Having noticed a ship in distress, Delano decides to board the ship to offer his aid. Once on the bridge, and after having taken note of the ship's extreme state of degradation, he spends all day waiting for a breeze that will take him to shore. From the ship's captain Benito Cereno—who is in a pitiful state of health—and from the many blacks and the few whites he encounters on board, he learns about the misadventures of a voyage described as both disastrous and interminable,

---

[264] Captain Amasa Delano, *A Narrative of Voyages and Travels, in the Northern and Southern Hemispheres: Comprising Three Voyages Round the World, Together with a Voyage of Survey and Discovery in the Pacific Ocean and Oriental Islands* (Boston: E.G. House, 1817), 313–354.

[265] L. Ballerini, "Ombre di un presente che adombra l'avvento di ombre più cupe," in Herman Melville, *Benito Cereno*, trans. L. Ballerini (Venezia: Marsilio Editori, 2012), 31.

1. Of the Scene within the Scene

which decimated, or rather exterminated, the officers and the passengers, of whom only the captain and a few sailors remain, along with a large number of Senegalese slaves, the ship's main cargo, their owner having perished during the voyage. A faithful and zealous black servant named Babo is Benito Cereno's inseparable companion.

So much for the tale's introduction. From the start, as soon as the unknown sailing vessel appears, a series of clues signal the strangeness of the situation—no flag, hesitant maneuvers, an obvious lack of knowledge about the area—all preambles to the sequence of oddities that succeed one another during the course of the day. Captain Delano reacts immediately through a confident interpretation, because he is a man "of a singularly undistrustful good nature, not liable, except on extraordinary and repeated incentives, and hardly then, to indulge in personal alarms, any way involving the imputation of malign evil in man."[266] Moreover, the sea is the Captain's place, as is the anchorage of Santa Maria island where he has been several times; his way of inhabiting it is to turn the unknown into the known, to transform signs into interpretations that produce meaning, and the interpretations into veritable certainties, which makes his worldview the very emblem of the fantasmatic relation to the world.

It is impossible not to notice the characteristics of the place itself, on which Melville lingers with minute mastery, painting a landscape at once calm and disturbing, as is the case, indeed, when the strange pokes through the familiar and the calm seems to anticipate the storm. There is the sea, of course—"Everything was mute and calm; everything grey"—but also the gradual encounter with the mysterious ship, gliding through the mist, its bleached aspect, its derelict state, its fallen grandeur, its figurehead wrapped in white canvas like a shroud, and the strange inscription beneath: "*Seguid vuestro jefe* [Follow your leader]." Finally, the boarding of the foreign ship:

> Always upon first boarding a large and populous ship at sea, especially a foreign one, with a non-descript crew such as Lascars or Manilla men, the impression varies in a peculiar way from that produced by first entering a strange house with strange inmates in a strange land. Both house and ship, the one by its walls and blinds, the other by its high bulwarks

---

[266] H. Melville, *Benito Cereno*, in *The Piazza Tales and Other Prose Pieces, 1839-1860*, op. cit., 47.

like ramparts, hoard from view their interiors till the last moment; but in the case of the ship there is this addition; that the living spectacle it contains, upon its sudden and complete disclosure, has, in contrast with the blank ocean which zones it, something of the effect of enchantment. The ship seems unreal; these strange costumes, gestures, and faces, but a shadowy tableau just emerged from the deep, which directly must receive back what it gave.

Perhaps it was such influence as above is attempted to be described, which, in Captain Delano's mind, heightened whatever, upon a staid scrutiny, might have seemed unusual.[267]

Delano is not shaken by this living spectacle in the middle of the ocean's emptiness. As representative of the respectable New England mentality of the early nineteenth century, he is a reasonable, optimistic man, sure of his worldview, from the beginning to the end of the story.

Benito Cereno

The character who bears this name, the story's protagonist, is far from being a hero. He moves with detachment through a place ruled by a total lack of discipline. He rarely speaks and, during the first part of the story, unwillingly. Wearing extravagantly luxurious clothes under the circumstances (we later learn that he was forced to wear this outfit), the young nobleman Don Benito, 29 years old, at first gives ceremonious and formal replies to Delano's questions and later minimal explanations, colored by the somber mood of those who are not in good health, who are beset by nebulous listlessness. In the eyes of the American Captain, the Captain of the Spanish ship is the victim of a chronic depression caused by the terrible vicissitudes he experienced, and of a physical and mental impairment that prevents him from exercising the authority he needs to command his ship. It isn't by chance that his faithful black servant Babo never leaves him for a moment—eager, diligent, and preoccupied, an irreproachable substitute, a true right-hand man—to the extent that Delano says about him: "Don Benito, I envy you such a friend; slave I cannot call him."[268]

---

[267] *Ibid.*, 49–50.
[268] *Ibid.*, 57.

1. Of the Scene within the Scene

Waiting for the breeze that will allow the *San Dominick* to get to the anchorage, Delano orders his sailors to restock the vessel with water and food; he promises a future in which yesterday's and today's tragedy will melt away like snow in the sun. Meanwhile the day goes by, marked by a series of misunderstandings in which each thing has a logical explanation, though quite removed from the facts. Only an action on the part of Benito Cereno will reveal their true nature: after the ship's mooring, just as the two Captains are saying farewell, Don Benito suddenly has a surge of energy and unexpectedly bounds into the boat transporting his benefactor, followed by Babo in his wake, brandishing a knife. All of a sudden, things appear under a different light. But Delano continues to be mistaken: when Babo precipitously follows Cereno into the boat—to kill him, actually—Delano thinks the slave is acting to protect his master, and suspects the Spanish Captain of being an ingrate, capable of God knows what plot against the very person who went out of his way to save him. It is a comedy of errors in the midst of tragedy.

In reality, what is happening on the *San Dominick* is a fabrication conceived by the clever Babo. A mutiny took place on board: hundreds of slaves massacred their masters and most of the crew, sparing the Captain and a few sailors (the few sailors needed, in the minds of the rebels, to pilot the ship and bring them back to Senegal, their native land). The head of the mutineers is Babo, the sole author of a theatrical artifice meant to avoid a dangerous confrontation with the American ship, to mislead Amasa Delano and extort the aid needed to be able to proceed to another destination. After having transformed the bridge of the *San Dominick* into a formidable theatrical performance, Babo hatches plots, directs like a Pirandellian impresario a troupe the majority of whom (the mutineers) voluntarily play their roles, and the minority of whom (Cereno and the surviving sailors) do so because they are forced to.

The casual management of the conflict between consenting actors and compelled ones would be enough for Babo to earn our admiration. He is simultaneously busy on two fronts: on the Delano front, where he has to convincingly play the role of the slave tending to his master's well-being; on the Benito Cereno front, where he must tacitly but unhesitatingly reinforce the message that he is now the master of the ship and of the lives of those who are on it. By playing the slave, he is taking on a role that is very familiar to him; the split between role and being, which is so radical in conditions of subjugation and segregation, is now doubled up and reversed.

Babo and Cereno display plural identifications that reflect one another. The identification with the lost object (loss of freedom, power, place of origin) here involves the slave's camp as much as the master's; it appears on the horizon where slavery and abolitionism, as well as hatred and the ethics of desire, are directly confronted. The story's catalyst, Babo, allows Melville to avoid a stereotypical representation of racial conflicts and to highlight the complexity of the forces in play in a historical tragedy that is, above all else, a singular human tragedy.

Benito Cereno does not act like a hero. He is clumsy in his role of victim and continues to be; he remains burdened after his liberation and his own redemption, indelibly marked by events that do not seem to heal. The end of the adventure includes the storming of the mutinous ship by Delano's sailors, the chaining of the rebellious slaves, and the side-by-side navigation of the two ships to Conception and then to Lima, a navigation during which the two Captains have an opportunity to reflect on the events. But before concluding, the tale is interrupted by the partial transcription of the testimony offered during the trial of the mutineers (who are, as far as the men are concerned, all sentenced to death). Thus we are able to read passages from Benito Cereno's deposition made under oath. The documents from the trial used by Melville are authentic as far as the facts are concerned (being excerpts from the account of the voyages by the real, historical Delano), but skillfully edited and reassembled compared to the originals. In the novel the same events are thus recounted twice: once from Delano's point of view, another time from that of Benito Cereno's testimony at the trial. This is what allows a confrontation between two radically different reports about the same place, highlighting the production of irremediably discordant, singular places on the same scene.

With the passage from narrative to testimony, and then the return to narrative, Melville breaks with stylistic congruence, which dictates that each genre should be composed in the form that defines it; he mixes prosodies, rhetorical devices, and lexicons, convinced as he is that the friction between the mythic core and the narrative vehicle brings about a salutary disintegration of expectations. In this way, he decomposes the landscape that he had been progressively painting for the reader by inserting multiple registers that shed light on unexpected areas. In the back and forth between semblant and material reali-

1. Of the Scene within the Scene

ty—moving to the cadences of different styles, where each successive detail paints over the landscape that preceded it—the traumatic real insinuates itself and the echo of an irreducible historical truth resonates.

Of the Imaginary and the Real

With genius and mastery, Melville recounts eminently tragic events through the eyes of someone who is unaware of their tragic nature. This allows him, among other things, to decline, through commentaries, consoling maxims, reassuring words, and predictions, the long procession of terrible storms, lengthy lulls, devastating fevers, and innumerable deaths. On several occasions this contrast spills over into the comic, without diminishing the nefarious nature of the events: rather, it emphasizes their crudeness, it emphasizes the tragic nature of the facts and of a fantasmatic relation to the world (that of Amasa Delano, who does not cease being unaware of it). Delano never questions himself as a divided subject.

The American Captain is armed with the best intentions; he is generous, altruistic, and optimistic. It is for him alone that Babo has orchestrated a play in which the real power dynamics, triggered by the slave rebellion, are masked by the dynamics of usual power. And it is the usual that always wins in Delano's eyes, which allows him to be unaware of the extreme danger he runs by boarding the *San Dominick*; to realize it would mean signing his own death warrant. Ineptitude is his safe-conduct. This is one of Melville's messages. It isn't the banality of evil yet, but the complicity intrinsic to the norm, bearing the greatest responsibility for the *status quo*. Amasa Delano is certain that he is living respectful of justice and of the most laudable social practices, including helping those in need, whether it is a ship in distress or the right of a slave to not be killed but to be used as a slave. In the end, he learns the reality that runs counter to all his theories; but he does not recant. The nature of facts, their bitter contradictions, the human reasons for the conflict, these seem not to touch him. Like a good psychotherapist, Delano encourages the trauma's neutralization and the patient's pacified integration into the routine of the daily norm.

At the other end of the spectrum, there is Benito Cereno's silence, his stammering and reticence; unequivocal signs of a crisis that

Places on the Scene: Three Cases

will not heal despite the operation's successful outcome. After escaping danger, there is no happy ending for Don Benito. Tormented, agitated, "broken in mind and spirit," he refuses to go home to Chile and retires to the Monastery of Mount Agonia outside the walls of the city of Lima.[269] The violence of the encounter with the real has irremediably upended his destiny, his position in the world; this is what Melville emphasizes, thereby giving a political and psychological depth to the human incompatibilities highlighted by the events.

During the long navigation toward Lima, after the ship's rescue, a conversation between the two Captains sheds light on Don Benito's deep malaise:

> "So far may even the best man err, in judging the conduct of one with the recesses of whose condition he is not acquainted. But you were forced to it; and you were in time undeceived. Would that, in both respects, it was so ever, and with all men."
>
> "You generalize, Don Benito; and mournfully enough. But the past is passed; why moralize upon it? Forget it. See, yon bright sun forgotten it all, and the blue sea, and the blue sky; these have turned over new leaves."
>
> "Because they have no memory," he dejectedly replied; "because they are not human."
>
> "But these mild trades that now fan your cheek, do they not come with a human-like healing to you? Warm friends, steadfast friends are the trades."
>
> "With their steadfastness they but waft me to my tomb, Señor," was the foreboding response.
>
> "You are saved," cried Captain Delano, more and more astonished and pained; "you are saved; what has cast such a shadow upon you?"
>
> "The negro."
>
> There was silence, while the moody man sat, slowly and unconsciously gathering his mantle about him, as if it were a pall.[270]

It is impossible to fail to register all the power of Cereno's answer about the source of his anguish: "The Negro," a concise and sin-

---

[269] The Benito Cereno to whom the actual Captain Delano refers in *A Narrative of Voyages and Travels* is a completely different man: once freed, he turned out to be a vindictive and corrupt ingrate. Far from being broken, he found a way to turn the events to his own advantage.

[270] *Ibid.*, 116.

1. Of the Scene within the Scene

cere answer, where the word *negro* summons a multitude of implications. In his tale, Melville uses both of the terms *black* and *negro*. As Luigi Ballerini has rightly pointed out, this is a most important clue in the analysis of the text. The narrator, as well as the Amasa Delano character, use the term *black* most of the time, but not when the climate of revolt appears. Don Benito, especially in the Melvillian excerpts of his deposition, uses the term *negro* like a drumbeat. It is a Spanish-based term that originated in Latin American idioms during the end of the eighteenth century and the beginning of the nineteenth century, a term by definition permeated with colonialism and slavery. On Cereno's lips the word *negro* condenses the "shadows present, foreshadowing deeper shadow to come."

To Delano's adage—"But the past is passed; why moralize upon it? Forget it. See, yon bright sun has forgotten it all, and the blue sea, and the blue sky; these have turned over new leaves"—Cereno answers by invoking the human dimension: if they forget, it is because they have no memory, it's that they are not human, which is as much a reflection of the difference in subjective position between the two interlocutors as a reflection of Cereno's concern. He is confronted, following the rebellion, with the question of knowing what is a human being and what is human. Delano replies in a calming tone; he evokes the steadfast and warm friends that are the trade winds, the winds that blow East to West, that accompanied the exploration of the New World, helping enable the conquest as well as the massacre of human beings *in situ*, the importation of slaves and their exploitation. As Glenn C. Altschuler puts it, "if Delano does not mean the slave trade, Melville wants the reader to remember it."[271] And Delano, the righteous, who comes from Duxbury, Massachusetts, the land of the abolitionists, does not hesitate to hope for new winds and new commercial opportunities.

"With their steadfastness they but waft me to my tomb, Señor," Cereno replies, revealing the extent of a personal break that is a break

---

[271] G.C. Altschuler, "Whose Foot and Whose Throat?: A Re-Examination of Melville's *Benito Cereno*," in *Melville's Short Novels*, ed. D. McCall (New York: Norton & Company, 2002), 302. "It has been said that Americans recognize no past, that the present exists only as a means of propelling them into the future. Melville recognized the burden of the past and chose a real incident from it to comment on its value and our rejection of it." *Ibid.*, 303.

Places on the Scene: Three Cases

in history, of its repetitive course and of the *status quo*, the expression of present conflicts and conflicts to come. The painful and fatal silence in which Cereno cloaks himself is echoed by the haughty silence of Babo, who, once captured, does not utter a single word: "His aspect seemed to say, since I cannot do deeds, I will not speak words."[272]

A special fate awaited Babo, leader and brain of the rebellion: he would be hanged and then burned. Separated from his body, his head was attached atop a pole and exhibited on the Plaza de Lima, where it redefines the place with its fixed and implacable stare. This is how the story ends:

> Some months after, dragged to the gibbet at the tail of a mule, the black met his voiceless end. The body was burned to ashes; but for many days, the head, that hive of subtlety, fixed on a pole in the Plaza, met, unabashed, the gaze of the whites; and across the Plaza looked toward St. Bartholomew's church, in whose vaults slept then, as now, the recovered bones of Aranda; and across the Rimac bridge looked toward the monastery, on Mount Agonia without; where, three months after being dismissed by the court, Benito Cereno, borne on the bier, did, indeed, follow his leader.[273]

The severed head proudly meets the whites' gaze and links the church of Saint Bartholomew to the convent of Mount Agonia, tracing in the landscape a triangle of fatal bonds that summon all the violence of exploitation, slavery, and rebellion. In Saint Bartholomew's church are the bones of Don Alexandro Aranda, the master of the mutinous slaves on the *San Dominick*. We learn of his terrible end through Cereno's deposition at the trial: Babo had informed Don Benito of his decision to kill Don Aranda, Cereno's childhood friend, as a warning if one of them stood in their way. Hacked to death with a hatchet, Don Aranda's corpse had disappeared for three days in order to reappear as a skeleton at the prow of the ship, replacing the original figurehead of Christopher Columbus—discoverer of the New World, good luck charm, and promise of tranquility and opulence. Under the fig-

---

[272] H. Melville, *Benito Cereno*, in *The Piazza Tales and Other Prose Pieces, 1839-1860*, op. cit., 116.
[273] *Ibid.*, 116–117.

urehead, thus transformed, the following phrase was written: "*Seguid vuestro jefe.*"

Follow your leader. An eloquent phrase that unpacks multiple meanings. First, the imperative command directed at the slave, an imperative that defines his or her position as slave. There is also the idea that the master must be followed because he knows how to steer. Or, as Altschuler suggests, the idea that the blacks—who all seem to faithfully follow their leader—can, in fact, want to overthrow him; or the idea that the whites who follow their leaders and support slavery can follow them to certain death.

And Don Benito, in a coffin, *did indeed follow his leader*. The story ends thus, opening the door to a series of possibilities. Is Aranda his leader? Is Babo? Is the cause for which he dies? Or the end of a cause? By declaring that the sickness that torments him and that will lead to his death is "the Negro," Cereno highlights the radicalness of an ineluctable encounter. Once freed, he refuses to have any contact with Babo and is unable to tolerate, even for an instant, his sight or his presence.

Whether it is a matter of being unable to stand the fact of being fooled and crushed, or a matter of being confronted with an order of things that have revealed their explosive nature or with the paradigms of a world that no longer exists, the encounter with *the Negro* is above all the encounter with Babo, with a very refined human intelligence, and in this case an inalienable one. It is the encounter with the irreducibility of difference—not so much and not only of class and position but of intentions and desire—and, within it, with the uniqueness and singularity of the other, with the human nature that is his own. This unleashes hatred and the revolt against the exile that dwells in the subjective divide. Isn't hatred a form of recognition of the other as fellow?

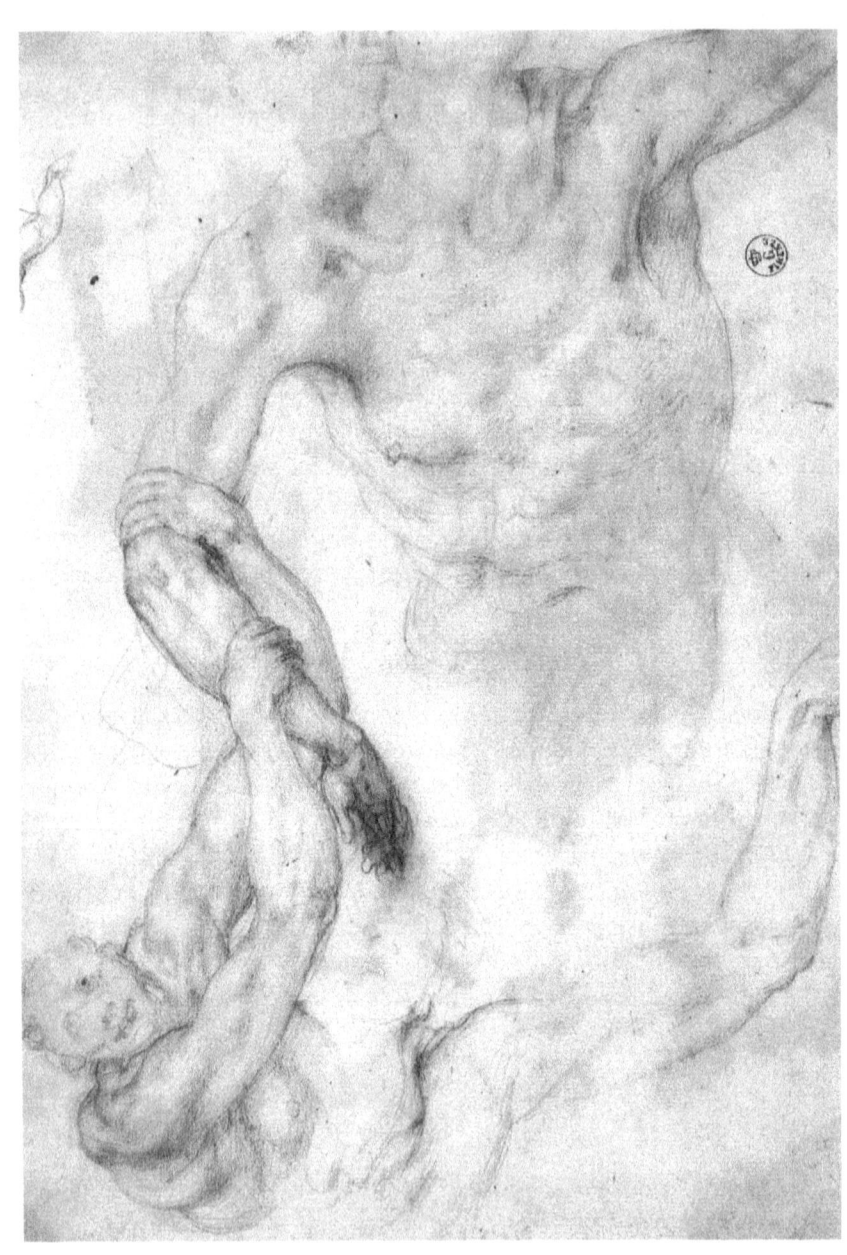

Pontormo, Ascent of Souls, Study

2.
OF THE HEAVENS ON STAGE

While the first windows on the world scene are the eye that opens and the ear that listens—but also the skin that feels, the mouth that savors—the scene revealed there is an extension of the landscape. The body is its condition. Within it, there is the nearby and the distant, the visible and the invisible, thanks to the physicality that inhabits it and is a part of it.

As distant or invisible as they are, the distant and the invisible have their place in the landscape. Such are the firmament, the stars, the sun, the moon, the planets (existing and non-existing). Their presence in the gaze and the mind of man invites interpretation, the search for a logical explanation of the relationship between things. Inhabiting the territory has always involved the inclusion of the nearby and the distant, as is the case, as we have seen, in the architecture of many prehistoric sites and that of ancient temples that reflect a complex cosmology. These constructions are, in and of themselves, readings and, simultaneously, new systems of writing.

The Open Book

Naturally, the world's interpretative grids vary according to the century, the culture, and the symbolic system that produced them. In Western culture, the Renaissance was a period in which novel and surprising readings proliferated. They were so innovative that they became the basis of modern science and the modern world. They are especially focused on the past, reclaiming ancient classicism to transform the present and shape the future. This re-appropriation is an investigation, an experimentation, an invention that—by seeking a transparent and rational relationship among things, and between reason and religion—restores the human to its place and redefines its relationship with the universe. If there exists an order of things, albeit one determined by God, it is up to man to read it, to study it, and to divulge it. If the subject situates himself or herself in the picture—as is the case with the discovery of perspective—s/he has the power to redraw its parts, and also to appropriate the laws of representation in order to show the invisible in the visible. Moreover, man *is* the body that shelters the mind, a body that also belongs to the order of things, a body close by and yet distant, that needs to be understood, studied, and sustained.

Man's place, the universe, is a very big book open to our eyes, Galileo concluded. But while this vision leads to the mathematical model of reading the world, which rules modern science, it happens in stages, through passages and encounters among the philosophical, medical, astrological, literary, and artistic conceptions that spanned two centuries of ferment, of a revolt of reason.

Florence was certainly the epicenter of this effervescence, a masterful example of which is provided at the end of the Renaissance by the works of the Mannerist painter Jacopo da Pontormo, in whom the revolt of reason takes the shape of a revolt of form, according to an ethic that unites near and far, reading and experience, aiming at a novel artistic project that constitutes a militant action regarding place. As is well known, Pontormo left a journal full of annotations, which has long been a source of misunderstandings and elucubrations, but nonetheless a precious resource with which to tackle his period, his worldview, and his intent to operate on place.

Pontormo's Journal

At the beginning of the sequence of papers that make up Pontormo's *Journal* or *My Book*—a sequence confused by its seventeenth-century folding—we find an undated annotation of a medical nature,[274] immediately noticeable at a first glance at the Magliabech

---

[274] S. Nigro observes that the name "diary" is given to Pontormo's notes improperly: in the sixteenth century, "diary" meant the recording of public events. Referring to a specification by Lorenzo Lotto in a March 1532 letter to the brotherhood of Bergamo ("de man in mano ho tenuto notato al mio libro"), Nigro proposes the name *Il mio libro* (*My book*) for Pontormo's journal. S. Nigro, *L'orologio di Pontormo* (Milan: Rizzoli, 1998), 46.

autographic manuscript because of its broad, regular, and precise writing.[275] It occupies an inaugural spot with respect to Pontormo's almost daily annotations. In all probability, it pre-dates the journal and motivated its drafting.[276] Its contents illustrate why it might have been written before or during the first months of the journal's composition:

> If it finds you disorderly in the way of clothing, coitus, or an excess of eating, in a few days it can do you in or harm you. Thus, one must use prudence in June, July, August, and half of September and sweat moderately and particularly in the breeze when you have exercised and take care in eating and drinking when you are hot. Then be on alert from the middle of September to autumn, because the days are becoming shorter and the weather begins to be wet and [because of] the moisture from the over-drinking that you did during the summer, you need to fast and drink little and stay awake long and exercise to prepare yourself so that the cold of winter does not harm you as they do not find you ill-disposed. And do not eat too much meat, and particularly pork, and from the middle of January onward do not eat any because it causes fever and is bad, and live moderately in all things, because the humors and phlegm thaw from February, March, and April, because in the winter the cold had frozen them. And be careful because sometimes, depending on what is happening with the moon, there is cold, and then immediately [afterward] everything frozen melts, and from this there arises much ruinous phlegm or strokes or other dangerous illnesses. Because everything proceeds from over-eating and drinking when it is cold, because the cold acts on you and takes hold, but as soon as the weather is good and moist, it warms and grows and swells again. And thus, as I said above, in the beginning, when you are full in this way, be careful of the cooling process for it kills either right

---

[275] Pages 74r and 75r of the Magliabech autographic manuscript.

[276] Like Lebensztejn and Nigro, I favor the hypothesis that it pre-dates *My Book*. J.-C. Lebenstejn, "Dossier Pontormo," *Macula* 5/6 (1980) and, subsequently, *Le Journal de Jacopo da Pontormo* (Paris: Aldine, 1992). See also S. Nigro, *L'orologio di Pontormo*, op. cit. Conversely, in his *Introduzione* to *Jacopo da Pontormo, Diario: Codice magliabechiano VIII 1490 della Biblioteca Nazionale Centrale di Firenze, Commentario* (Rome: Salerno, 1996)—with a note by Stefano Zamponi and a comment on the sketches by Elena Testaferrata—Roberto Fedi treats Pontormo's medical annotations and the notes appearing on pages 74r, 75r, and 75v as "composite material" external to the diary; he isolates these pages and gives them a separate title, *Prescrizioni e ricordi*, an editorial intervention that intentionally separates from the diary a part that is intrinsic to it. Here, we have followed the original pagination of the manuscript and added punctuation marks.

away or in a few days. And so, if you have an excess of humors acquired in the winter, keep to the instructions that I have said, and in particular, be mindful in March.[277]

There are two three-part additions to this opening prescription, in the form of notes compiled during the drafting of the journal. One refers to an episode of November 5, 1554, and the other (divided into two parts) is from April 22, 1555. They seem to clarify the prescription's meaning or exemplify its instructions. The note referring to November 5—which fell into one of the two periods when Pontormo suspends his annotations (October 23 to December 17, 1554)—mentions an episode of illness, one among the many listed in the diary. It seems that Pontormo meant to emphasize it, perhaps to indicate the consequences of a transgression of the initial prescription. He adds in the margin, "because I know that not doing so, I will regret it."[278] The additions of April 22, 1555 signal a special day that, as the diary confirms, celebrates the end of a month of fear and uneasiness ("I was frightened") marked by the fateful March moon, that from which it is most important to take precautions.[279]

The journal unfolds over the arc of two years, 1554 to 1556, a time when Pontormo, through the assignment of Duke Cosimo I, was painting the choir of the basilica of San Lorenzo, presumably commissioned around 1545 and begun in 1546.[280] The oldest event that we find mentioned in it occurs on January 7, 1554 ("I fell and struck my shoulder and arm and was ill"), which appears on the reverse side of the second folio of the opening prescription, in all probability re-

---

[277] Translated passages herein from Pontormo's diary and other writings have been developed directly for the present book.

[278] J. Pontormo, *My Book*, 75r.

[279] J. Pontormo, *My Book*, 75r and 75v.

[280] The task, "the most important commission of the decade"—G. Vasari, *Vite* (Rome: Newton Compton), 1024—"was assigned to Pontormo around 1545, when, for some time after the death of Andrea del Sarto in 1530 and the final distancing from Michelangelo, he was the most established painter active in Florence, with over thirty years of service to the Medici," M. Firpo, *Gli affreschi di Pontormo a San Lorenzo* (Torino: Einaudi, 1997), 13. For the reasons that set the beginning of the work in 1546, see J. Cox-Rearick, *The Drawing of Pontormo* (Cambridge, MA: Harvard UP, 1964), 318. During the period of the diary's drafting, Florence (along with Emperor Charles V) found itself involved in a war against Siena and its ally, France. The break in the war is noted in the journal on March 28, 1556.

Pontormo, Journal, p. 74r

Pontormo, Journal, p. 75r

Pontormo, Journal, p. 75v

Places on the Scene: Three Cases

corded at the same time, or subsequent to, the true beginning of the near-daily annotations on March 11, 1554.[281]

Starting from March 11, the diary proceeds with varying regularity, with annotations that are not necessarily daily and that at some points skip entire months. Pontormo records the day of the week, the festivities, foods eaten, the weather, his physical states, and the progress of the work at San Lorenzo, sketching the figures frescoed in the margins and sometimes specifying with a line the part of the body composed that day.[282] The daily events are mentioned in the same style, tone, and rhythm as the foods eaten and the bodies drawn.

The names of friends and acquaintances highlight the regularity of Pontormo's meetings and the repetitiveness of an organized daily life completely centered around the execution of his work at San Lorenzo, but peppered with deep and cordial human relationships. His closest friends (his student Bronzino, his attendant Daniello di Bartolomeo and his wife Alessandra Allori, Piero, the farmer Matteo Naldini, the young Batista Naldini, who came to the workshop at age twelve, and his disciple Dandrino Allori) ensure the emotional atmosphere and the carrying out of the daily drudgery. At the same time, the noted meetings illuminate the character of Pontormo's learned and literate encounters and the artistic environment that characterized them, valuable clues to Pontormo's personal style and the era in which he lived: this is the case for the ever-present Bronzino as well as for Luca Martini, Benedetto Varchi, Giovan Battista Gelli, Giovan Battista Strozzi, Vincenzo Borghini, and others.[283]

---

[281] J. Pontormo, *My Book*, 75v. According to Nigro, the annotation dated March 11, 1554, was added by Pontormo to the pages of his journal in April 1555, three months after an event recorded on January 27, 1555, regarding a bet with Bronzino concerning a quote by Petrarch. Negri observes that the reference to some expressions in Petrarch's *Triumphus Mortis* II (vv. 43–45), which had influenced the way of mentioning the bodily ailments of many authors "having a literary mind frame"—Michelangelo, Aretino Tasso—also influenced Pontormo in his note of November 5, 1554 (S. Nigro, *L'orologio di Pontormo*, op. cit., 42–43).

[282] There are forty sketches "that render with great clarity the idea of the figure, or groups of figures, in the process of execution." E. Testaferrata, "Gli schizzi del diario e gli affreschi del coro di S. Lorenzo," in R. Fedi, op. cit., 128. Testaferrata's proposed numbering differs from that of Cox-Rearick, who counts forty-three sketches (*ibid.*, 130).

[283] For Pontormo's culture and environment, see R. Fedi, "La cultura del Pontormo," *Pontormo e Rosso: Atti del convegno de Empoli e Volterra*, ed. R.P. Ciardi and A. Natali

2. Of the Heavens on Stage

The Body and the Sky

The journal has the appearance of a *promemoria* more than anything else. In his private recording, Pontormo reports on climatic and physical conditions, foods eaten, and work done. This responds to a specific design of which the opening prescription is an indication. It is a matter of staying alert, achieving and respecting a certain physical balance, and preventing the arrival of illness or providing for it.[284]

"Yet the heavens within us do not lie before our eyes, but rather behind our eyes, so that we cannot see them. Who after all can gaze through the skin?"[285] In its derivation, man—in microcosm—hosts and reflects the laws of the macrocosm. "The heavens, in fact, are man and man is the heavens."[286] The properties of superior bodies being the form and power of inferior ones, man is the seat of the four elements and mirror of the world. But as Pico della Mirandola emphasizes in his criticism of the dominant astrological concept, the gifts and faculties of celestial bodies derive from the principles themselves and from the forms that govern them.[287] The influence that the superior spheres possess over the inferior ones is not of a supersensible order; there are no "dark" qualities. Investigation of the macrocosm illuminates knowledge of the microcosm. A single law governs the firmament and the human body.

Illnesses, then, are in the heavens that govern them. As we read in the *Picatrix*, the corporeal matter of terrestrial things and the spir-

---

Marsilio (Venice, 1996), 26-46. Pontormo knew Latin, had experience with the classics, and attended the meetings of the Florentine Academy.

[284] Such health-related notes were rather common at the time. Regarding their style, Fedi (op. cit., 31) makes reference to the fourteenth-century *Reggimento* by Francesco di Barberino, the *Memoirs* of Giovanni Di Paolo Morelli, and those of Michelangelo. According to Negri, Pontormo was inspired by the "rule" and "manner" of Michelangelo's life, following the publication of Ascanio Condivi's *Life of Michelangelo*, which appeared in Rome in 1553 (Negri, op. cit., 113).

[285] Paracelsus, *Paragranum: Astronomia* in *Paracelsus (Theophrastus Bombastus von Hohenheim, 1493–1541), Essential Theoretical Writings*, ed. A. Weeks (Leiden: Brill, 2008), 177.

[286] *Ibid.*, 163.

[287] G. Pico della Mirandola, *Disputationes adversus astrologiam divinatricem* 3.24, ed. E. Garin (Florence: Valecchi, 1946), 385–9.

itual matter of the stars are a single matter.[288] From this comes the need to pay attention to the unfolding of time, which is subject to the heavens, the need to know how its rules take effect with the variation of the seasons and their signs, and the need to study its similarity to—or effects upon—the human microcosm. If illness is in the heavens, it cannot be eliminated. However, it can be known, predicted, or softened by avoiding and impeding nature's course and making nature's wisdom one's own, since what is invisible in the isolated part is illuminated in its relationship to the whole. This is the secret of the alchemist, already distancing himself from the magic arts: knowing how to achieve fully that which carries out the "condition ordained by nature."[289] From this came medical study of phenomena dependent on the particular, individual character of the body, interest in its hygiene, and detailed study of the effects produced by assimilation of external elements (the first step in a complex process of transformations).

In this framework, food occupies a privileged place. Behind the skin that separates internal from external, the two skies of a single cosmos, it is necessary to know how to follow the destiny and design of what is ingested: "No truth will be found in you if you do not follow the figure that nature has preordained. You thus see that there is nothing in man that has not been sketched outside of him," since "nature designs him."[290] If Pontormo's *tacuinum sanitatis* reiterates the crucial points of medical-astrological knowledge of the time regarding the relationship between heavenly order and common physical order, his notes have the character of a memory-aid, a device to help implement it. This is the expression of a need that is extremely clear and determined. Food-related entries express concerns for the influences of the seasons on the body. According to the Hippocratic Corpus, illness prevails in the body "according to the season which is most comfortable with it."[291] As shown in the sixteenth century's *Treatise on Hygiene and Diet* inspired by Avicenna, medical care sets its roots in the study

---

[288] *Picatrix* 1.7. See the recent edition in English translated by J.M. Greer and C. Warnock (Iowa City: Renaissance Astrology Press, 2010).

[289] Paracelsus, *Paragranum: Philosophia*, op. cit., 163.

[290] "Nessuna verità sarà ritrovata in voi, se non seguirete la figura che la natura ha predelineato. Vedete cosi che nulla v'è nell'uomo che non sia abbozzato fuori di lui" perché "la natura lo disegna." Paracelsus, *Paragranum: Alchimia*, op. cit., 211.

[291] Hippocrates, *The Nature of Man*, in *Hippocrates IV*, trans. W.H.S. Jones (Cambridge, MA: Harvard UP, 1931), 25.

of heavenly constellations, natural seasons, body, and diet.[292] Body and heavens inhabit the same place.

Rule, Hygiene, Work

Pontormo does not seem to follow a particular regimen. There is the impression of an overall scheme in which reference to official religious regimens overlaps with prevailing medical prescriptions. He respects fasting on Fridays, Saturdays, and at least a third day during the week. This custom seems to roughly correspond with religious observance, but not with its strictness (for example, the third day of the week for abstaining from meat, beyond Friday and Saturday, should be Wednesday). The same applies to the Quattro Tempora, the three days of religious fasting corresponding to the four seasons of the year. In a note added in April 1555 to the opening prescription, Pontormo highlights their importance in relation to the illnesses that struck him:

> I remember the 5th of November [1554], and it seems necessary, although I have some impediments of the stomach or the head or pains in my sides or legs or arms or teeth that may be continuous, it is necessary that I do not do as [I did] before but [rather] immediately remedy it by eating little or by fasting, and committing myself, for the Quattro Tempora, to observing the prescribed fasts. And moreover, it sometimes happens that you then feel full from eating, worsened by sleep and by food, so that it seems that I am then bloated, and it is important to take care of oneself and avoid all excesses.[293]

Despite the tone with which he chastises himself, Pontormo does not seem to respect the Quattro Tempora faithfully. Although it is true that he fasts once in awhile (and especially at that time) he

---

[292] Anonymous ["Anonimo Tarentino"], *Trattato di igiene e dietetica* (cod. XII E 7 Biblioteca Nazionale di Napoli), probably drafted between 1502 and 1505, representative of the fifteenth-century tradition of popular medicine and the desire for democratization of scientific knowledge.

[293] J. Pontormo, *My Book*, 75r. The last sentence reads in the original: "alora è da riguardarsi perchè è sanità superflua," literally: "and it is important to take care of oneself because this is excess health." We propose to translate it: "and it is important to take care of oneself and avoid all excesses."

Places on the Scene: Three Cases

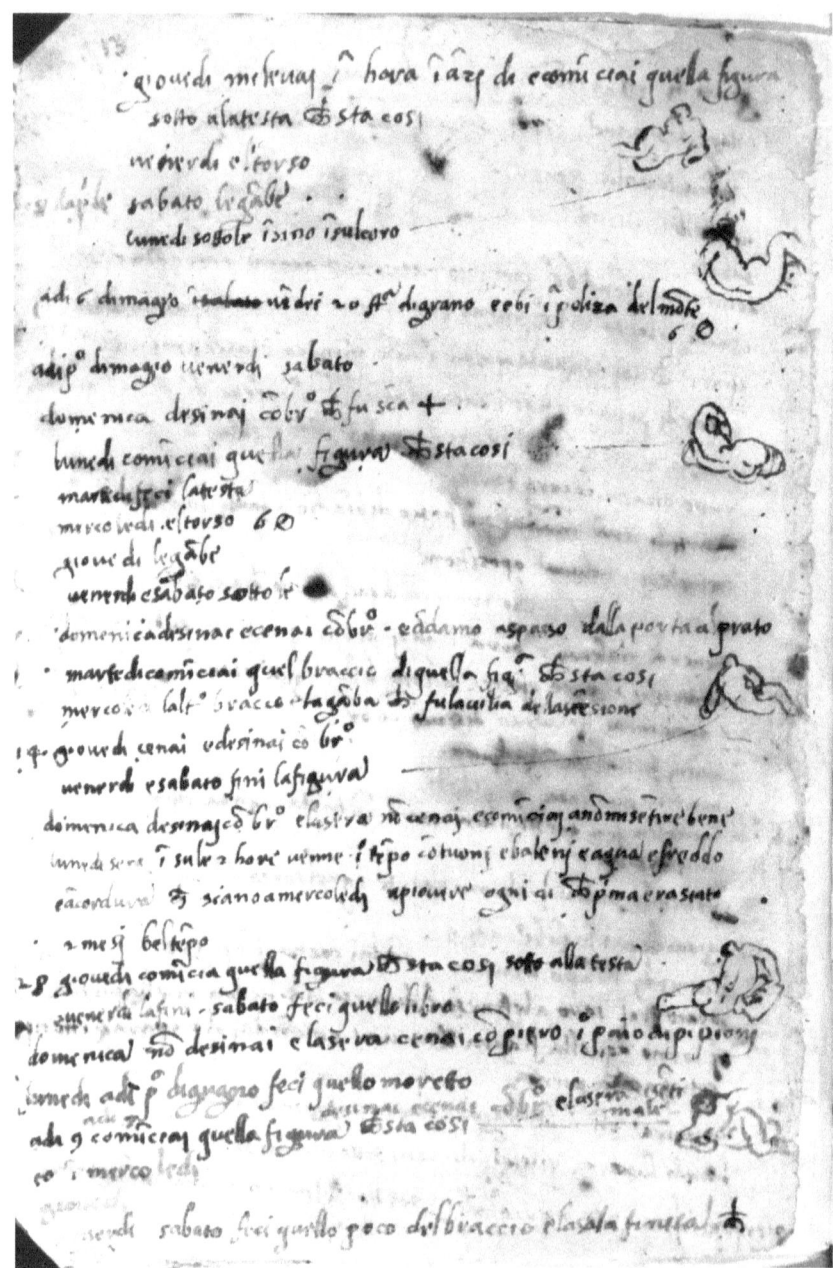

Pontormo, Journal, p. 71v

often substitutes a more prolonged abstinence from meat than *bona fide* fasting requires, and he sometimes completely neglects to note his regimen during a holiday period.[294] In the attention given to his diet, the religious question seems to pass to a secondary level, or at least it combines with other worries. Pontormo insists on the nexus that ties his physical ailments to the transgression of a rule that, more than anything else, seems like a functional rule for the body's hygiene. After all, Quattro Tempora's correspondence to the seasons originally had a hygienic character. Astrology itself was not distant from religion (as demonstrated by the numerous dedications of consolatory predictions to Popes Leo X and Clement VII) nor was it from politics: Cosimo I, supported by his court's literati, adjusted his own zodiac sign of Gemini to make himself a Capricorn and thereby share, along with their sign, the fortunes of Augustus and Charles V.[295]

> On 11 March 1554, Sunday morning, I lunched with Bronzino on chicken and veal and felt good (the truth is that when coming to my house I was in bed; it was quite late, and in getting up, I felt bloated and full; It was a very beautiful day). In the evening, I dined on a little dried roasted meat and was thirsty.[296]

> [May 10, 1555]
> Saturday evening I dined with Piero on fish from the Arno, ricotta, eggs, and artichokes, and I ate too much, particularly of the ricotta, and in the morning I lunched with Bronzino, and in the evening I did not eat dinner, and this it was my luck as I had eaten too much.
> Monday evening I ate the meat cooked on Thursday, and it did me no good. 10 ounces of bread.[297]

> [May 17, 1556]
> Sunday I lunched with Bronzino, and in the evening I did not eat dinner, and I began not to feel good. Monday evening at around 2, a storm came with thunder, lighting, and rain and cold, and on Wednesday it is still

---

[294] For example, for the Ascension in 1555 or 1556 and Easter of 1555.
[295] R. Cantagalli, *Cosimo I de' Medici: granduca di Toscana* (Milan: Mursia, 1985), 132.
[296] J. Pontormo, *My Book*, 76r.
[297] J. Pontormo, *My Book*, 66v.

Places on the Scene: Three Cases

going on, raining every day, while previously there had been two months of good weather.[298]

Doctor, patient, and observer of himself, Pontormo faithfully transcribes the events of which he is the locus. Added to, and overlaid upon, the attention he pays to his own physical state, there is the care with which he notes the progress of the work at San Lorenzo. During 1554, there are only two notes on the frescoes underway.[299] Starting from January 30, 1555, his recording of the frescoed figures becomes systematic. This is the period when "the painter was getting ready to paint the two lateral scenes of the lower area [of the choir], the Flood and the Resurrection of the dead, the largest and most surprising of the entire cycle, and the most demanding and worthy of memory."[300] It must be noted that the months when notation of food is most continuous and regular, December and January, are those when the work at San Lorenzo was suspended for the winter.[301]

It is necessary to be prepared and cautious during the winter, since the cold condenses and freezes what is stored. Then, depending on the extent to which one's own conduct had been moderated, there would occur the "pockets of humours and phlegm" that "open up in February, March, and April."[302] If, as Telesio asserts, life results from the conflicting forces of hot and cold, the matter being the same, it will differ only as to the degree of rarefaction or condensation.[303] It is a case of keeping in mind the transformations dependent upon the season, in view of the new period (*tempi nuovi*) and the upcoming work.

---

[298] J. Pontormo, *My Book*, 71v.

[299] This probably indicates that Pontormo initially intended "his diary above all as a completely private memorandum for the preservation of his health." Testaferrata, op.cit., 127.

[300] *Ibid*. I will return later to the reasons for the importance of these scenes.

[301] Pontormo indicates the dates that he restarted work: January 30, 1555, and February 6, 1556.

[302] Pontormo describes these as "le sachate degl'omori e delle scese."

[303] B. Telesio, *De rerum natura iuxta propria principia*, the first two books published in 1556 and the complete edition of nine books in 1586.

The Body between Nature and Painting

Caring for the body is caring for a center, for the chokepoint or neck of the hourglass that places the world of nature in relation to that of painting. This acts like a filter. In the body, the transformation of one reality into another occurs. With this alchemic hourglass overturned, the matter falls in changed form; what had been external becomes internal and is externalized again, producing a new reality, something that can be seen for the first time. Designed by nature, man has the power to redesign it. As Leonardo observes, man can never know nature if he does not succeed in designing it in his mind.[304] The processes that map out his center, his heaven, suggest to him the art of transformation in simulacrum: he possesses its science. In Pontormo's diary, the relationship between food and work becomes mirror-like. As he feeds his own body, Pontormo gives life to the frescoes of San Lorenzo's choir; he constructs its bodies limb by limb. It is a matter of achieving and establishing the optimal physical condition that might allow the progress of a work of exceptional importance, one comparable, in area and ambition, only to the Sistine Chapel.

"Pontormo had beautiful traits (*"bellissimi tratti"*) and was so afraid of death that he did not even want to hear it discussed, and he fled from having any contact with dead bodies."[305] In this way, Vasari first emphasized Pontormo's fear of death, which has become one of the legendary subjects critics have leaned upon to justify the diary's nature (its sordidness, as it has been said).[306] And yet, as can be seen by the tone of the notes, it is not fear of death that animates the diary, but the need to maintain a certain balance in life, to have a certain experience of life in terms of one's own work.[307]

---

[304] Leonardo da Vinci, *Treatise on Painting I*, trans. A. Philip McMahon (Princeton: Princeton UP, 1956), 48.

[305] G. Vasari, *The Lives of the Artists*, trans. J.C. Bondanella and P. Bondanella (Oxford: Oxford UP, 1991), 413. As will be seen later, this "fear of meeting death" contradicts an anecdote mentioned by Cinelli. For the possible reasons for Vasari's comments, see below.

[306] "It is difficult to imagine a document more sordid." C. Cecchi, preface to *Jacopo da Pontormo: Diario*, ed. C. Cecchi (Florence: Le Monnier, 1956), 7.

[307] As Trento puts it, "More than a book of memories, Pontormo's diary is a tool thought up by the artist within the difficulties of his daily life, to help him bring his final work to completion." D. Trento, *Pontormo: Il diario alla prova della filologia* (Bologna: L'inchiostroblu, 1984), 21.

Places on the Scene: Three Cases

The artist's goal is the creation of a new kind of true thing. "The demands of the painter's art," however, "do not suit the body, they disturb his mind rather than enrich his life," as Pontormo states in a letter responding to an academic question raised by Benedetto Varchi on "What is more noble, Painting or Sculpture?".[308] Unlike the sculptor, whose physical labors are supported by the materials' quality and durability, or by the way light radiates *chiaroscuri* on the *tutto tondo*, the painter has in his hands only the tools of highest simulation. Not only is painting "a matter of greater mental analysis, of greater skill, and more marvelous" than sculpture, not only does it imitate nature, but it also competes with it.[309] And it competes with another nature, since it may permissibly show "something nature never made."[310] The picture "is that appearance which says that it is the very thing that gives appearance."[311]

These are the things that trouble the painter's mind: "But what I called too daring is that importance placed on outdoing nature in wanting to give life to a figure, to make it seem alive and yet to place it on a flat surface, because if the painter had considered at all that when God created man he sculpted him in the round, which makes it easier to give life to a figure, then he would not have taken up a discipline so full of artifice, so miraculous and divine."[312] Having abandoned divine facilitation, the most difficult implementation of the new reality is based on the art of simulation and the power of imagination, the latter being the faculty placed by Campanella in the seventh position among those of the soul, as one of the first steps toward science.[313] Master of all things coming to man's mind, the painter has them "first in his mind and then in his hands."[314] A transfigured interiority is thus made

---

[308] J. Pontormo, "Letter to Varchi," in Mayer, op. cit., 57.
[309] Leonardo da Vinci, *Treatise on Painting*, op. cit., 34.
[310] J. Pontormo, "Letter to Varchi," in Mayer, op. cit., 57.
[311] Le tableau "est cette apparence qui dit qu'elle est ce qui donne l'apparence." J. Lacan, *Le Séminaire livre XI: Les quatre concepts fondamentaux de la psychanalyse*, op. cit., 103.
[312] J. Pontormo, "Letter to Varchi," in Mayer, op. cit., 58.
[313] T. Campanella, *Metaphysica* 5.1.3, ed. G. di Napoli (Bologna: Zanichelli, 1967).
[314] Leonardo da Vinci, *Treatise on Painting*, op. cit., 19.

visible, and a new window opens onto the world, one through which history can be viewed.³¹⁵

As in astronomy and philosophy, all of the visible must find confirmation in the invisible. Because images are subjected to the visual faculty, they will communicate universally and will not need interpretation into different languages. Therefore, infinite things to look at, "which words cannot even name, since there are no words appropriate to them"³¹⁶—names not being universal like forms are—will present themselves to the eye as "made desperate by the gaze," prominent among the senses and the bridge between the two heavens.³¹⁷

Entrance, Exit

The painter makes the entrance of nature correspond to an exit that is the composition of a piece of the universe. And it is the report of a particular "exit," among the many illnesses cited, on which Pontormo lingers, describing it most carefully:

> Thursday, on 4 July [1555], I began that figure that is like this [FIGURE]
> and in the evening I was uncomfortable waiting for the meat, because Batista was lame and it was the first time that he spent the night elsewhere, and when his father was ill, he didn't stay with him, and this is because he had a bed to sleep in at Rotella's.
> Friday, Saturday, I did up to the legs; Sunday I lunched with Bronzino.
> On the 8th, Monday, I did [wrote] I-don't-know-what letters, and my diarrhea [*l'uscita*] began.
> Tuesday, I did a thigh, my diarrhea increased with a lot of bloody and white discharge; Wednesday I was worse, maybe 10 times or more, because every hour I needed [to go], and so I stayed at home and dined on a little bad soup, and my Batista went out in the evening and he knew that I did not feel well, and he did not return and I will always keep that in mind.

---

³¹⁵ L. Battista Alberti, *On Painting II* (1435), ed. and trans. R. Sinisgalli (Cambridge: Cambridge UP, 2011).

³¹⁶ Leonardo da Vinci, *Treatise on Painting*, op. cit., 14.

³¹⁷ "Comme désespéré par le regard," J. Lacan, *Le Séminaire livre XI: Les quatre concepts fondamentaux de la psychanalyse*, op. cit., 106.

Places on the Scene: Three Cases

> Thursday, I did the other leg, and with the indispositions of my body I am a little better, because [I went] four times. I dined in San Lorenzo and drank a little *Greco*—not that I feel good really because every three hours my torment returns. On the 12th, Friday evening, I dined with Piero and I believe the diarrhea had passed, that is, those pains.[318]

This tells the story of a bodily ailment that—no less than those of the mind—is both the issue and result of work-related worries. This *issue* (exit, *uscita*) is a sign of nature's processes, the effect of particular conditions. That which liquefies sums up and reveals the influences of the season ("there was a great heat") and of the regimen, but also of the emotion that emerges with the appearance of Batista's name: "my Batista."[319] One cannot help but notice that Batista's exit corresponds to an exit of another sort: *"una colera sanguigna e bianca"* ("a bloody and white discharge").[320] After all, the hot July sun and the loosening that it causes influence the heart as much as the body, just as the moon influences the brain.

The "torment" (*"strugimento"*) impedes Pontormo in his work. One abnormal and impertinent issue seems to overlap with another, taking precedence over it and replacing it. Hence, the satisfaction that comes through in the note of the following Thursday: "Thursday morning, I shat two non-liquid turds and it came out as if they were long wicks of cotton wool—that is white fat, and I dined very well in San Lorenzo, a little very good boiled meat, and I finished the figure."[321] This time, what he carefully deposits is a sign of the body's rehabilitation, of found harmony. This new result crowns the comple-

---

[318] J. Pontormo, *My Book*, 67v.

[319] Pontormo's relationship with Batista, although made up of "breaks, annoyances, and little everyday cruelties," as Negri describes it (op. cit., 27), was one of great affection. According to Filippo Baldinucci, "such was the affectionate servitude" that Batista gave to Pontormo, "that upon his death he made a gift of all of his studies, a gift that was certainly very valuable. But because the poor young man had nothing with which to prove such a donation to [Pontormo's] heirs, he was stripped of everything, except the virtue that he had learned from his teacher." F. Baldinucci, *Notizie de' professori di disegno*, cited by Negri, op. cit., 26.

[320] The word *"colera"* cannot not bring to mind the Italian *"collera,"* "anger."

[321] J. Pontormo, *My Book*, 67v.

tion of a frescoed figure, his *result* (*ri-uscita*)[322] is accompanied by a very good dinner.

The creator "will only ever participate in the creation of a small, dirty deposit."[323] However, his art finds a basis in nature's wisdom, in the purpose it assigns to its own processes. What the painter takes from it is the secret of his transformation, his design. In this respect, his art is science: not only does he deploy the laws of nature (for example the law of light in the perfection of mathematics and geometry), but he also knows how to continue its course and celebrate its transmutations, making gold of its dross: "*Qui a natura homo tantum erat, artis fenore et uberrimo proventu reduplicatus homo vocatur et homo-homo.*"[324]

How is the Moon?

"On 30 January 1555, I began the loins of the figure that cries for the little boy. On the 31st, I did the little bit of the clothing that wraps around her; it was bad weather and my stomach and bowels hurt for those two days and the moon entered its first quarter."[325] So begins a dense series of entries that unfolds across the arc of February, March, and April 1555. In it, Pontormo records with particular care the variations of the weather in relation to his physical conditions and those of his work, a care that slowly lets tension come through, condensing suddenly in a note bridging March and April ("so I remain not knowing what will become of me")[326] and dissolving only at the end of the week:

> Easter Sunday, there was a great cold and wind and rain. I lunched with Bronzino, 6 ounces of bread, and in the evening I did not dine.

---

[322] The Italian word *riuscita*, while commonly understood as "result" or "success," can also be heard as "re-exit."

[323] J. Lacan, *Le Séminaire livre XI: Les quatre concepts fondamentaux de la psychanalyse*, op. cit.. 107.

[324] C. Bovillus, *Liber de sapiente* 24 (1510): "For this fact he who by nature was only a man, because of the very rich contribution of art can be called a double man, or man-man."

[325] J. Pontormo, *My Book*, 65v.

[326] J. Pontormo, *My Book*, 66r.

Places on the Scene: Three Cases

> Monday, colder still and wind and rain and that evening I dined at Daniello's house, 6 ounces of bread.
> Tuesday was very nice and that evening I dined, 10 ounces of bread.
> Wednesday morning it was cold and I stayed at home. I dined on 9 ounces of bread, lamb, the best that there could be.
> Thursday, I worked on the two arms and dined on 9 ounces of bread, meat, cheese, and it was rather cold. [Figure]
> Friday, I did the head with the boulder that is underneath. I dined on 9 ounces of bread, a cheese omelet [*pesce d'uovo*], and a salad, and I was quite dizzy.
> Saturday, I did the branch and the boulder and the hand and dined on 10 ounces of bread.[327]
> Sunday, I dined on 10 ounces of bread and all day remained worn out, weak, and irritable. It was a beautiful day and there was a moon.
> Monday, the 22nd of April, I was well. Every illness had gone away. I ate 8 ounces of bread, I was no longer dizzy and I was not weak, and I have much hope.[328]

Beginning with February's moon and ending with April's, these two pages contain the advent of the March moon of 1555. And it is from the second addition to the opening prescription (April 22, 1555) that we become aware of events taking place contemporaneously with the daily entries:

> In the year 1555 with the moon that began in March and lasted until the 21st of April, for all the time of that moon there began pestilent illnesses that killed many men who were moderate and good, and perhaps without ailments, and all were bled. I believe that this happened to them because there was no cold in January, and it burst forth during the March moon, when one felt a poisonous and dull cold fighting with the warmed air of the season of the longer days; it was like fire sizzling in water, such that I was very fearful. The thing to do is be prepared before the March moon begins that it may find you moderate in food and exercise and taking great care in sweating. And do not be surprised if, a few days after it has waned, an ill-disposed man who does not know how or from where it comes suddenly feels well, as happened to me today, the 22nd of April, the first day of the new moon. My feeling well, and previously having

---

[327] "Branch" translates here "*broncone*": a big branch, which was also a symbol of the Medici.
[328] J. Pontormo, *My Book*, 66r.

never felt well, all this must come from a certain coldness that had not yet cleared and had lasted to the 21st. But on this day mentioned above, I felt warm and good, because the weather has perhaps [found] its season.[329]

According to the Hippocratic Corpus, changes of season may generate illnesses and epidemics and, within each season, the sudden changes from cold to hot or vice versa: every sudden change is damaging or deadly. But the passage from winter to spring marks a crucial moment in the year.

"The dense moon/ sick dense and heavy/ how is the mo/on," Leonardo da Vinci writes in a loose-leaf notebook.[330] If the moon always governs birth and waning, the March moon presides over a special phase of generation. Placed between the end and the beginning of the natural year (we must not forget that the Florentine year began on March 25th), it both combines two seasons and separates them, encompassing the transition from cold to warm, from latency to reawakening. "Be mindful in March,"[331] urges the second addition to the prescription, "and especially in its moon, 10 days before and 10 after, that is, at the beginning of the new moon of March, and it may continue until the fiftieth day has passed, because all of the waxing moons are harmful if one is full, and it is important to take care of oneself beforehand."[332] The March moon presides over melting.

Pontormo highlights with particular attention the relationship between cooling and warming. The processes of humidification, the passage from cold to warm (that which warms, grows, and swells)

---

[329] J. Pontormo, *My Book*, 75v and 75. There are many echoes of this note, of a literary and content-related nature. Negri accurately observes that with the expression "pestilent illnesses" (*infermità pestifere*), Pontormo was referring to the introduction of the *Decameron*, "pluralizing Boccaccio's *pestifera infermità*, set off by the cruelty of heaven... between 'March and the following July.'" Negri further suggests that "men who are moderate and good and perhaps without disorders" might evoke a contrast with the disorderly bodies of Michele Savonarola's *De preservatione a peste et eius cura*, as well as those who "live without order and measure" discussed in the third chapter of Marsilio Ficino's *Consiglio contro la pestilenza*. Negri, op. cit., 114.

[330] "La lune densa/ egra densa e grave/ come sta la lu/na," Leonardo. On the hypotheses regarding the meaning of the sentence and its transcription, see note 54 in Leonardo da Vinci, *Scritti letterari*, "Pensieri" #128, ed. A. Marinoni (Milan: Rizzoli, 1980), 79.

[331] "*Sta in cervello il marzo*" literally means: "be careful in March."

[332] J. Pontormo, *My Book*, 75r.

seem especially important to him.[333] Coldness and moistness are characteristics of water. Like all animals, man is composed of two elements, "different in properties but working together in their use, namely, fire and water."[334]

According to Cornelius Agrippa, among the elements that depend on the moon are earth, water, the humors, sweat, and the superfluity of bodies.[335] If "all waxing moons are harmful when one is full," it is because swelling of the increment will be followed by liquefaction caused by the decrement. It is all the more necessary, then, to remain "moderate about food and exercise" at the advent of the March moon, since, with the first warmth, the humors subject to it can result in "terrible colds or strokes," as happened to "Cecco the baker."[336] More than once in the diary, Pontormo states that he feels "swollen" and "full." It is swelling, the retention of liquids, that particularly worries him and explains his attention to "exits," liquefaction, the firming up of the body's humors, and phlegm and discharges.

Visible signs of the invisibility of nature's processes—phlegm, sweat, urine, and feces—indicate the body's watery state. After all, Pontormo, who had turned 60 on May 24, 1554, was no longer either "young" or a "man," and according to the opinion of Hippocrates, "old men are cold and moist, because fire retreats and there is an onset of water; the dry elements have gone and the moist have established themselves."[337] If man, designed by nature, is different at different ages, it will be necessary to ensure the right balance of the elements in the body and to adopt a regimen "inclined to fire when the onset of water occurs, and one inclined to water when the onset of fire occurs."[338] Fire, giving form to water, orders the body, harmonizes its organs, and channels its humors. When swelling and fullness erupt,

---

[333] "The danger is great where heat and moisture meet." M. Ficino, *Consiglio contro la pestilenza* (1481) (Bologna: Capelli, 1983), 74.

[334] Hippocrates, *Regimen* 1.3, in *Hippocrates IV*, trans. W.H.S. Jones (Cambridge, MA: Harvard UP, 1931), 231. The water that nourishes everything draws "its own movement from fire." Cf. *Ibid.*, 233: "fire can move all things always, while water can nourish all things always."

[335] H. Cornelius Agrippa, *Three Books of Occult Philosophy or Magic* 1.24, ed. W. Whitehead (Chicago: Hahn & Whitehead, 1898), 95.

[336] J. Pontormo, *My Book*, 66r. April 10, 1555: "Wednesday two eggs and that evening Cecco the baker had a stroke."

[337] Hippocrates, *Regimen* 1.33, in *Hippocrates*, op. cit., 281.

[338] Hippocrates, *Regimen* 1.32, in *Hippocrates*, op. cit., 275.

water pervades the body. If the liquid is plentiful, it flows from its containers and thickens, making the patient pale and causing serious illnesses like "dropsical diseases."[339] And as the biographers tell us, it was dropsy that killed Pontormo, shortly before he finished the frescoes of San Lorenzo.[340]

Something is held back and swells. The last illness mentioned in the diary deals with retention. A few days before interrupting his entries—in October of 1556, two months before his death—Pontormo states, "but I have a sore throat, that is, I cannot spit up something that is stuck there that I usually have."[341]

Liquefaction, Inundation, Deluge

Between January and March of 1555, Pontormo engaged in a special relationship with water. It was during this time that he was painting the Flood, on the left side of the choir of the San Lorenzo.[342] As with all of the basilica's frescoes, nothing remains of this except a few preparatory designs and the sketches outlined in the margins of the journal. In fact, to use the words of Milanesi in his commentary on Vasari's *Lives*, "In October of 1738, these paintings were whitewashed over—certainly," he adds, "causing no great damage to the art."[343] This

---

[339] Hippocrates, *Regimen* 3.76, in *Hippocrates*, op. cit., 401.

[340] The date of Pontormo's death may be set as December 31, 1556 or possibly January 1, 1557. R. Fedi, op. cit., 25.

[341] J. Pontormo, *My Book*, 73r. October 1556.

[342] See the careful reconstruction by Elena Testaferrata of the parts of the choir frescoed by Pontormo during the drafting of the journal. On June 9, 1554, a new space to be frescoed was prepared, and shortly thereafter Pontormo started to paint the Flood, "a scene on which he worked from January 30 to March 4, 1555. Subsequently, for a little more than two weeks (March 11–27), he took up again and brought to completion the Ascension of the souls.... From March 29 to the middle of June, he returned to work on the Flood ... embarking then upon the wall in front, the scene with the Resurrection of the dead that he painted without interruption ... until November 27, 1555." Op. cit., 131. Testaferrata's opinion differs partially from that of Janet Cox-Rearick in *The Drawing of Pontormo* (Cambridge, MA: Harvard UP, 1964), 349–50, according to whom, Pontormo was probably working on the Ascension of the souls from January to March 1555, on the Flood from April to June, and on the resurrection of the dead from July to November 1555 and February to July 1556.

[343] *Giorgio Vasari: Opere VI*, ed. G. Milanesi (Florence: Sansoni, 1973), 288 note. The frescoes were destroyed during the work of strengthening the choir's walls that occurred

is a curious destiny for the magnificent work that occupied nearly eleven years of Pontormo's life. The elusive physiognomy of this work can only be traced through the approximately thirty surviving preparatory drawings, statements of old witnesses, a few partial copies, and reconstructions by scholars.

In the cycle of frescoes in the choir depicting scenes from Genesis and the Old Testament, the Flood (at the lower left) was next to the Ascension of the souls and the martyrdom of San Lorenzo, placed in the center, and across from the Resurrection of the elect. This continued the string of depictions in the upper part, already finished at the time the diary was drafted.[344] These included the Fall of man and the Expulsion from Paradise—the descent of man in the eyes of God—summarizing the punishment of guilt and the path to redemption among Noah's descendants. The water that inundates and kills is also the water of purification.

If inundation is one of God's punishments, it is so through the design of the heavens. The specter of the Flood had shaken the early sixteenth century. Starting with a 1499 prediction by Johannes Stöeffler that noted a conjunction of planets in the sign of Pisces for February 1524, a deep dispute regarding the coming of a universal flood on that date involved the most important astrologers of Italy and Germany. More than 150 pamphlets by 57 authors, with polemical, religious, and political motives, addressed the subject. In the end, the famous month of February 1524 (Pontormo was 30 at the time) turned out to be "drier than the average season."[345] But the worry had been based on a meeting of the planets under a water sign; February, it must be noted, precedes the entrance of the March moon.

Leonardo, with whom the young Pontormo had passed a brief apprenticeship before entering Andrea Del Sarto's workshop, had also been interested in the Flood. What attracted Leonardo's investigatory

---

between 1738 and 1740. See E. Ciletti, "On the Destruction of Pontormo's Frescoes at San Lorenzo and the Possibility that Parts Remain," *The Burlington Magazine* 121 (1979), 765–70. Regarding the events that led to the work's disappearance, see Firpo, op. cit., 14–21.

[344] "This can be established with certainty, because the natural order of fresco painting compels one to move from high to low and because (a reason of much greater interest) the diary itself records it." Testaferrata, op. cit., 126.

[345] P. Zambelli, "Astrologia, magia e alchimia nel Rinascimento fiorentino ed europeo," in *Firenze e la Toscana dei Medici nell'Europa del '500* (Milan: Electa, 1980), 321–322.

eye was the event's complexity and the need for a physical demonstration that corresponded to a demonstration in painting, since, in his judgment, the laws of physics must not differ from those of aesthetics. The Flood is a special case of the relationship between cosmic forces. And if the study of movement was what particularly consumed the last years of Leonardo's life, the motion of the waters in the Flood took on an exceptional complexity, since it involved all the elements and altered their relationships. From this comes Leonardo's interest in the meticulous analysis of falling, velocity, the percussion of the waters, their "angles of incidence," and their faithful pictorial representation.[346]

In Pontormo's Flood, on the other hand, judging from his preparatory drawings, he pays particular attention to the destiny of the body inundated by water. Once again, what counts is movement, but not so much in the relationship between cosmic forces as in the relationship between matter and form. Giovanni Cinelli relates that "to make the figures of the choir of San Lorenzo natural," Pontormo "put corpses in troughs of water to make them swell, and he fouled the entire neighborhood with the stench."[347]

In drowning, as in bloating, water takes the upper hand over form and compels fire to reshape matter anew. In Pontormo's studies for the Flood, the drowned or drowning bodies swell, they intertwine, they blend together. The *principium individuationis* dissipates behind the outlines, and the sketch redraws the becoming of the form, its dissolution. Pontormo's Flood deals with a catastrophe; and yet, in his studies, it does not at all seem to be the anguish of death that rules, but the sleep of individuation, the spell of the return of an element to itself.

---

[346] Leonardo da Vinci, *Scritti letterari* (Milan: Rizzoli, 1974), 177. "The movements of the waters are faster the closer they are to the center. The crest of the waves of the sea descend at the front of their base, beating and coming together above the droplets of its face, and this coming together crushes the descending water into minute particles. Changing into thick fog, this mixes in the flowing of the winds like tangled smoke or revolution of clouds, and finally it rises into the air and changes into clouds." *Ibid.*, 178.

[347] Cecchi, op. cit., 143.

Places on the Scene: Three Cases

Drawing and Designing

In Pontormo's letter to Varchi, before noting the difference between the efforts of the sculptor and those of the painter, he emphasizes the fact that painting and sculpture share the same point of departure or foundation, the one thing "which is noble": "that element is *disegno*."[348] With that, Pontormo reveals the structural affinity that ties him to Michelangelo, the inner interlocutor—and rival—against whom he measures himself in the course of the work at San Lorenzo. The drawing marks out the material's limits (those of color for example, or of the marble). It sets out the shape; it is the path to its conceptualization. But if the use of drawing in the Sistine Chapel allowed Michelangelo to give power and strength to the painted figures and thus make the forms burst from the colored background—radicalizing their gestures and their conceptual force—Pontormo's use of drawing is quite different. In the preparatory sketches for the San Lorenzo frescoes, the sign seems to recede from the periphery of the depicted figures; it comes together and dissipates within the bodies in the lightness of a very fine *chiaroscuro*. Yet it is not the silhouette against the background that stands out, but the emanation of the visual matter, the appearance—surprising at every scopic moment—of the form itself, where it could be said that it is no longer the sign that indicates the movement, but the form in progress that dictates drawing.

Perhaps Pontormo's modernity also lies here, reflected in the consternation with which his contemporaries viewed the choir's frescoes. In this whole that was "full of nude figures," Vasari complains that the bodies were "deformed," and Pontormo seemed to have followed no "rules at all, either of proportion or perspective."[349] Taken to their extreme consequences the lightness and watery swelling of the figures painted in the Capponi Chapel or at Carmignano (where it was the color that dazzled and rarefied the object), Pontormo experiments here with the making of form, the form of his own body and the form, mediated and reflected by the mind's efforts, of the bodies frescoed at San Lorenzo. Perspective or geometrical point of view having fallen away, there nonetheless remains a center of the depiction, a dynamic

---

[348] J. Pontormo, "Letter to Varchi," in Mayer, op. cit., 55.
[349] G. Vasari, *The Lives of the Artists*, op. cit., 411.

Pontormo, The Flood, Study

re-centering that shatters the classic iconography and unwinds in one or more spirals that, starting from the frescoes—from their coloring "so soft that it seems to be made of breath"—seem to expand and include the spectator himself.[350]

The arrangement of the San Lorenzo frescoes had to be read starting from the center, an arrangement that left Pontormo's contemporaries perplexed and worried: "I have never understood the doctrine of this scene," declared Vasari.[351] Christ in glory was the choir's fulcrum, its reason, to which all the depicted scenes were addressed. Placed *above* God who created Eve—between the Exile from Paradise and the Original Sin—he had to his left, in the upper part of the choir, Cain and Abel, Noah constructing the arc, and Moses receiving the tablets of the commandments. To his right were the four evangelists, the sacrifice of Isaac, and the struggles of Adam and Eve. At his feet,

---

[350] *"Talmente morbido che pare finito d'alito,"* F. Bocchi, *Eccellenza del San Giorgio di Donatello* [1584], in *Trattati d'arte del Cinquecento III*. Cfr. E. Carrara, "Il manoscritto autografo del Discorso sopra l'eccellenza del S. Giorgio di Donatello di Francesco Bocchi," *Studi di Memofonte* (2014), 175.

[351] G. Vasari, *The Lives of the Artists*, op. cit., 411.

in the lower part of the choir, were the Ascension of the souls and the martyrdom of San Lorenzo, with the Flood on one side and the Resurrection of the elect on the other.

Christ, as the New Adam, was the focal point of a redemption that reconciled man with God, a salvation that brought together all of human history from Creation to the Last Judgment, suggesting a heterodox vision of faith rather distant from traditional iconography. The fall of man and his redemption, shadow and restored light, come together in a unique center in the middle of the choir, in the grace with which Christ, judging the living and the dead, invites the faithful to ascend toward him. There are no martyrs, prophets, or patriarchs; no symbols of the trinity; no interceding Madonna; no saints or symbols corresponding to them (aside from the inevitable San Lorenzo to whom the basilica was dedicated). What Pontormo depicted was not at all a traditional Judgment but, as Tolnay observed, the depiction of grace's triumph over sin.[352]

It now seems likely that the key to the frescoes' iconology was the catechism of Valdés, which appeared posthumously in an Italian version in 1545, under the title *Qual maniera si devrebbe tenere a informare insino dalla fanciulezza i figliuoli de' cristiani delle cose della religione*. This was first pointed out by Salvatore Caponetto and convincingly supported by Massimo Firpo, who followed, step-by-step, the relationship between the text and the work.[353] This correspondence between the Valdés catechism and the San Lorenzo cycle is extraordinary and precise, but not always accurate.[354] Specifically, it departs from a crucial point concerning the large fresco of the Resurrection, located at the lower right of the choir, opposite that of the Flood. In the frescoes of San Lorenzo there is no trace of the condemnation of nonbelievers and infidels, even though it is an item of the catechism. There is no depiction of hell with its wealth of devils, damned,

---

[352] C. de Tolnay, "Les fresques de Pontormo dans le chœur da San Lorenzo, Florence," *Critica d'Arte* 32 (1950), 49.

[353] S. Caponetto, *La riforma protestante nell'Italia del Cinquecento* (Torino: Claudiana, 1992), 109–14. On the Italian edition of the catechism, see M. Firpo, "Il 'Beneficio di Cristo' e il concilio di Trento (1542-1546)," *Rivista di storia e letteratura religiosa* XXXI (1995), 45–72. On the analysis of the relationship between the text and the choir's frescoes, see M. Firpo, *Gli affreschi di Pontormo a San Lorenzo*, op. cit., 92–137.

[354] "The only well-known case of a genuine translation of a religious text into images." M. Firpo, *Gli affreschi di Pontormo a San Lorenzo*, op. cit., 102.

2. Of the Heavens on Stage

Pontormo, Glory of Christ, Final Study

and tormented souls; there is no eternal suffering. Many hypotheses have been formed regarding this and Firpo evaluates them with due depth and caution, to the point of thinking that the depiction of the Judgment could be inspired by other texts by Valdés, unpublished and of limited circulation, or by a different manuscript version of his catechism. In either case, multiple facets of Valdésian thought were transmitted to the circle of the initiated, and it was found that the condemnation reserved for the infidels on the day of Judgment was not eternal suffering, but rather eternal *death*.[355] This hypothesis seems to be corroborated by the tone of the preparatory drawings for the frescoes, by the attention Pontormo gave to studying the death of the body, and by the extraordinary gracefulness of his drawing, aimed at depicting the eternal sleep of individuation more than the horror of the end. The Flood, companion to the Resurrection, carried out an essential function: it was both the logical moment of divine condemnation and the representation of the final destiny of part of humankind. This says a lot about the efforts of the artist's mind and his ideological and stylistic choices.

A Militant Work

The treatment of the frescoes demonstrates the "extraordinary capacity, on the part of those who defined the iconography of the San Lorenzo cycle, for orienting oneself in the labyrinth of Valdésian thought, for choosing between the many hermeneutic possibilities hidden within it."[356] One can measure, then, the scope of the work

---

[355] For the works by Valdés to which it may have referred, see M. Firpo, op. cit., 126–35: "All this, naturally, does not mean reviving, surreptitiously, a crypto-Anabaptist Valdés that the available documentation does not permit us to postulate, but [it does mean] distinguishing between the Spanish exile's religious reflection and his many developments and metamorphoses in Valdesianism," 133. The conviction that the souls of the wicked die with the body and those of the faithful will be saved, which figures among the Anabaptist heresies and opinions, was a question discussed in those years in Florence, as suggested by a passage of Gelli's *Capricci del bottaio*, where "it can be read that those who possess 'the light of faith' must not fear death, 'because for us other Christians, since our Savior died for us, it is that which became a sleep ... from that sleep, awakened by grace, we will return as much better beings, free from all disturbance.'" M. Firpo, op. cit., 126. G. Battista Gelli, *Opere* (Torino: UTET, 1976), 239.

[356] M. Firpo, op. cit., 133. This transcription by Pontormo into images "was not *tout court* the catechism of the heterodox Spaniard, but also the result of a reflection on his

2. Of the Heavens on Stage

Pontormo, The Flood, Study

in which Pontormo found himself engaged during politically delicate years, pulled between Reformist spiritualism and Counter-Reformist intransigence.[357] It can also be measured in the care—and not the inexplicable eccentricity—with which he insisted on protecting it, wrap-

---

spiritual legacy, a way of interpreting and using his writings, of developing their contents and implications. It was, in essence, Valdesianism" (*ibid.*). A key figure in this operation of spreading the thought of Valdés, and in support of the iconography pre-selected for the choir of San Lorenzo, was Benedetto Varchi, who dedicated a sonnet regarding this to Pontormo, mentioned in the journal on March 26, 1555: "Tuesday I did the head of the bending *putto*, and I dined on 10 ounces of bread, and I received a sonnet from Varchi." The sonnet also recites: "While I, with dark pen and humble ink / for many and many a year a live laurel form, / you with bright brush, lofty Pontormo, / make of our age an equal to antiquity." B. Varchi, "Mentre io con penna oscura e basso inchiostro," in Mayer, op. cit., 105.

[357] "The institution in 1542 of the Roman Holy Office, the first Tridentine decrees in '47, the unstoppable ascent of the intransigent party and the failed election of Pole in the conclave of '49, would prepare and finally sanction the defeat of the 'spirituals,' against whom the season of trials and condemnations would open in the following decade, and that almost none of the principal representatives of the group would manage to avoid. But in the mid 1540s, when Pontormo was beginning his frescoes at San Lorenzo, the games had (or it was believed that they had) just begun." M. Firpo, op. cit., 101.

ping it in a veil of complete discretion that resolutely denied outsiders from visiting the work in progress. The iconographic choice was certainly approved by Cosimo I and revealed a specific design, an expression of the sophisticated cultural environment of which Pontormo was a vociferous member, a member who felt authorized to transmit and interpret his own vision. The reference to the text by Valdés was the taking of a position in the ideological and religious controversies inflaming Europe: "A book and a militant fresco, then, the first published and the second begun while the Council of Trent was getting ready to meet."[358]

Vasari's negative judgment regarding the style and content of the San Lorenzo frescoes, appearing in 1568, started a defamatory tradition that would be propagated from critic to critic over the centuries until our time. The senility, extravagance, melancholy, and psychic fragility of the later Pontormo—with the wealth of hypochondria, existential angst, and sordidness attributed to the diary—were made the reasons for the "failure" of his last undertaking, a far-seeing vision that justified the work's subsequent destruction. Subjected to a careful philological reconstruction, however, Vasari's negative judgment reveals a "refined and complex cover-up operation," a political intervention aimed at saving Pontormo's person and the overall value of his work, which was of primary importance for the stylistic revolution of the sixteenth century.[359] It is also, and especially, a work of covering up directed toward Pontormo's *illustre committente*, Cosimo I. Let us not forget that this historical moment had already seen, in 1567, the Roman bonfire of Carnesecchi, when Cosimo de' Medici, getting ready to receive the grand duke's crown from the hands of Pius V, "needed to bury in oblivion a past that was not really very clear with respect to the church."[360]

The reasons behind the drafting of Pontormo's journal—and especially the necessity of maintaining a lifestyle according to the medical prescriptions of the time—are, therefore, closely and inextricably associated with the realization of a cycle of frescoes of unequaled inno-

---

[358] M. Firpo, op. cit., 102.

[359] M. Firpo, op. cit., 152.

[360] *Ibid.* "Pontormo was dead and buried. His fresco became inconvenient. But it could not be erased. It would have been an admission of complicity, embarrassing and compromising. It was necessary to have it pass through a distressing aesthetic heresy...." S. Nigro, op. cit., 25.

vation. The achievement of a life devoted to art and culture accompanied the completion of a mature and highly experimental work, with a courageous statement of principle that corresponded to the most advanced expression of stylistic, literary, and political reflection, a representative of the intellectual sophistication of the artist and his circle. Rather than "fear," "worry," "horror," "loneliness," and "inadequacy," the journal's tone seems to reflect both the style and rigor necessary to sustain an exceptional artistic effort.[361]

The San Lorenzo cycle remains, *in absentia*, not only one of the greatest compositions of the sixteenth century, but, paradoxically, also one of the most influential. The opening of a spatial multi-dimensionality thanks to the decomposing of the perspective's focal point, as well as the maintenance of one or more centers of the depiction according to a dynamic re-balancing that includes the spectator, make Pontormo's experimentation one of the era's most advanced moments of research, opening the way to the Baroque and to a syllogistic reversal of the connection to the real. This is no accident: this marks a turn in the conception of the relation of the subject to the world, in which it is already possible to recognize the impact of the new discourse of modern science. It represents a break with the classical vision of the relationship between the work of art and the viewer, one that anticipates artistic solutions developed in much later centuries.[362] This is why Pontormo remains an essential point of reference for many contemporary artists.

---

[361] Variants have recently been added to the deviant tradition that insisted that a dispirited mood showed through the pages of the diary. For Roberto Fedi (who sees in the prescriptions the expression of a "lateral" work, fruit of a literary intention that inspired the later Pontormo), thanks "to the frozen 'mirror' of writing," Pontormo tried to dominate "his worry" with a tool that was "unusual for him: writing—for which he had requested assurances and consolation at the beginning, and in which he had tried for awhile to find answers to his 'fear.' Instead ... he was demonstrating a disillusioned probing of horror." R. Fedi, op. cit., 39. Absorbed as he was in completion of his masterpiece, the hypothesis that Pontormo might have been inspired by freely-circulating medical prescriptions to dedicate himself to late and sporadic literary exercises gives us pause.

[362] The fracturing of the classical vision of the relationship between work and consumer, which reveals the role of the spectator in the very making of the representation—emphasizing his or her participation and subverting the separation between "subject" and "object"—is a subject artistically reprised over the centuries from various points of view. One might think of the Velasquez of the *Meninas*, or of the nineteenth-century *Gesamtkunstwerk*, the themes of the artistic avant-garde of the twentieth century, or the concept of "installation" that emerged in its second half.

3.
THE NEARBY AND THE OPEN ON STAGE

"Those who wish to see how the soul inhabits the body should look at how this body uses its daily dwelling-place," remarks Leonardo da Vinci.[363] We need to observe the way of dwelling to understand the way of being. However, the way of inhabiting space is not merely active, projective experience: it is also a matter of being inhabited, of being molded by the space we produce and live in. Within this two-way framework, at once projective and introjective, we may wonder what it meant to live in Viennese space at the end of the nineteenth century.

What kind of place could have led to the advent of Freud's Copernican revolution? If, in order to understand how the soul inhabits the body, one must first observe how the body inhabits its house, in what way might inhabiting the city of Vienna have influenced the birth of psychoanalysis? In what way did the architectonic transformation of the city—its urban configuration, the streets where Freud strolled—accompany, reflect, and cadence the transformation of an era, the proliferation of new points of view? How were they able to support them, to make them exist? Choosing Freud's Vienna as an example of place is a way of returning to the starting point of these pages, to the discovery of the psychic scene and of a new idea of the subject, examining them from the vantage point of the place that produced them.

The Ringstrasse and the Declaration of Styles

Bettelheim defines Vienna's setting as a "fluke of history": he remarks that the city's high point coincided with the breakup of the em-

---

[363] "Chi vuol vedere come l'anima abita nel suo corpo, guardi come esso corpo usa la sua cotidiana abitazione." Leonardo da Vinci, *Scritti letterari* (Milano: Rizzoli Editore, 1980), 73–74.

pire that had brought it its greatness.[364] At the heart of the empire and with some ten different ethnic groups, Vienna drew the contradictions of the day to it like a magnet. Behind the utopia of the "Austrian man" a clash of different ideas was taking place. Juxtaposed with the principle of the universality of the rights of man—as championed by the bourgeoisie—was the romantic inheritance of 'the blood' and natural right, a legacy that inspired the nationalistic ethnicities, and the principle of a people joined together by divine authority (the emperor being directly legitimated by the pope and the aristocracy founding its *raison d'être* in an aestheticized Catholicism). The Opera in Vienna was a convergence point for the aristocracy, steeped in the tradition of baroque sensuality, and the enlightened bourgeoisie, inspired by liberal ideas, positive science, and the spirit of the university. The set of these peculiar, varied elements—political, economic, cultural, of an obviously irreducible complexity—made the space of Vienna a veritable body evolving and decomposing, a laboratory of ideas, movements, and images, which influenced the rest of Europe and the century to come.

Carl Schorske observes that the city's grandiose building program of the 1860s was considered to have more merit as an enhancement of the city's appearance than as renovation.[365] This program indisputably derived from the wish of the liberal city fathers to give the capital a modern, functional expansion while simultaneously underlining the symbolic, representative role of certain of its areas. The Ringstrasse, as a point of departure and continual return, was obviously the cornerstone of this plan for a half-century or more. This explains the particular logic behind the affectation of the monumental buildings adorning it and the singular architectural styles used, in keeping with the reigning historical eclecticism of the day, each style destined to represent a precise function: Gothic for the municipal autonomy of the Rathaus; Renaissance for the liberal, secular rationalism of the University; early Baroque for the union of church, court, and town in the aesthetic arts of the *Burgtheater*.

Thus there appears a sort of erudite fever of styles and a simultaneous evocation of radically different historical moments. To each style its function, as if each style had a precise *raison d'être* attached

---

[364] B. Bettelheim, *Freud's Vienna and Other Essays* (New York: Knopf, 1990), 18.
[365] C.E. Schorske, "The Ringstrasse and the Birth of Urban Modernism," *Fin-de-Siècle-Vienna: Politics and Culture* (New York: Vintage Books, 1981), 24–115.

3. *The Nearby and the Open on Stage*

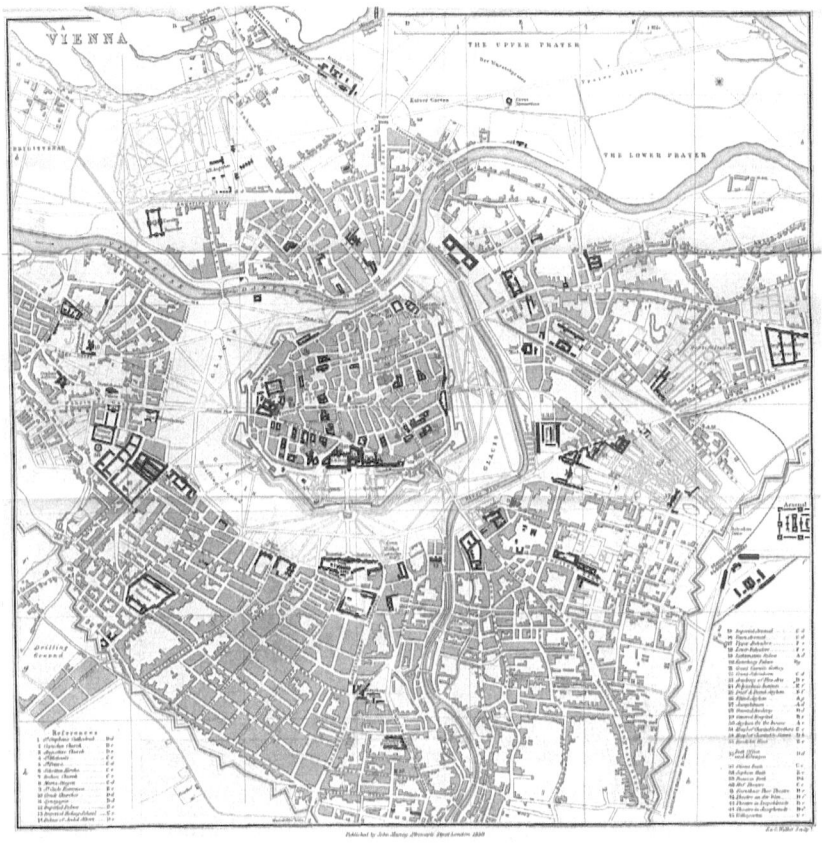

Vienna, 1858

to it, some reason thought to be the product of a certain historical moment. In this way, it was as though style arose as a declaration of principle devoted to implicit effects, the bearer of an ideology considered to be clear-cut and fixed.[366]

---

[366] That style, in this perspective, could be translated into a petrifaction of history and be used as a means of ideological persuasion, may have been a promise that captivated the eye of the young Hitler, an enthusiastic painter of the stones, buildings, and monuments of the Ringstrasse, so much so that this fascination resurfaced in the grandiose program of Nazi building, from Paul Ludwig Troost's *Haus der Deutschen Kunst* in Munich, or the re-planning of Linz and Berlin, to the styles used for the building of concentration camps.

Places on the Scene: Three Cases

We call monumental a work of great majesty or remarkable magnificence, inspired by the monument. *Monumentum* derives from the Latin *monere*: to recall, to inform, but also to alert, persuade, stimulate, punish, and announce. If the monument is meant for memory, if it is an art of memory, the monumental makes use of that art to persuade. And in every age politicians—as well as their city planners, architects, and decorators—have been fully aware of that fact. The space we inhabit has the power to influence us; throughout history, people have imagined spaces in order to elevate, sublimate, and rejoice, as well as to intimidate, subjugate, contain, and isolate.

The eclectic pageantry of the Ringstrasse was heir to the battle of styles that had marked the art theories of the eighteenth century and their impact on the beginning of the nineteenth century. One could not possibly forget the fervent quest for the "true" style that came out of the wonderment roused by the archaeological discoveries of the era, when suddenly Antiquity became pure present.[367] The polemic between the purity of classical Greek style, on the one hand, and the sublime eclecticism of imperial Rome, on the other, had given rise to various architectural interpretations and artistic stances. The Enlightenment mind and its defense of Greek rigor against the frivolities of the aristocratic Rococo had made neoclassicism, by its relation to scientific and linguistic order, the official style of the Jacobin revolution. With Napoleon, the style of republican principles was paradoxically transformed into an imperial language, with stress laid on the rhetoric of eclectic Rome. The term Historicism—first used to designate German romantic architecture and to distinguish it from nineteenth-century movements of historical revival—came to acquire a vaster significance, indicating the overall interest in history in nineteenth-century art and architecture, including the eclecticism of which the buildings of the Ringstrasse are an example. This interest arose both as a reaction to the alleged supra-historicity of the era's neoclassicism and as a manifestation of specific political credos, or out of a need to refashion

---

Alain Resnais' remarks in this regard in his 1956 film documentary *Night and Fog [Nuit et brouillard]* are highly meaningful: "A concentration camp is built like a stadium or a grand hotel, with firms competing ... the Alpine style, the garage style, the Japanese style...."

[367] The discovery of Herculaneum, for instance, dates back to 1738; that of Pompeii to 1748.

a national artistic identity in a period of political, economic, and cultural transformation.³⁶⁸

Style is, rather, a product, underlines Otto Wagner in his *Modern Architecture* (1895); it is social transformation that creates new styles. According to Wagner, the speed of social transformation in the second half of the nineteenth century prevented art from evolving at the same pace, and led to the use of "all past historical styles to fill the void."³⁶⁹ In the face of what is tellingly referred to as a "void," Vienna's architectural development in the second half of the nineteenth century appeals to historical images. Man in action, man in becoming, as Nietzsche observes, can only forget; if he refers to history, it is for some purely instrumental reason.³⁷⁰

Classical, Gothic, Baroque. The reincarnation of a past style in contemporaneity manifests the memory of history more than history itself. It expresses an *a posteriori* interpretation of the advent of a style and reveals its impact in the constructions of collective memory, whose signification is always contemporary and contingent. However atemporal and universal a style purports to be, it can never be exempt from the temporality of the context into which it is inscribed and re-inscribed; it can never cease to bespeak an interpretation, of which it becomes a new version in the present. It is thus that—through evocations summoned up by the magnificence of the Ringstrasse, where every discrete edifice offers a particular interpretation of the universe of which it is a quotation—the reincarnations of the past reveal above all the visions of the present and announce the advent of the future.

---

³⁶⁸ As pointed out in *The Dictionary of Art XIV*, ed. J. Turner (New York: Grove, 1996), 580, if historicism was interpreted as an attempt to create a historical consciousness that expresses both a continuity and a discontinuity between past and present, numerous twentieth-century critics, among them Hermann Beenken, who introduced the term *Historicism* (*Schöpferische Bauideen der Romantik*, Mainz 1952), considered eclecticism and the historical revival, which the *Ringstrasse* exemplifies, deeply contrary to the sense of history.

³⁶⁹ C.E. Schorske, *Fin-de-Siècle Vienna: Politics and Culture*, op. cit., 83. It is no accident, as Wagner observed, "that the Ringstrasse era called an architectural commission 'a style assignment' (*Stilauftrag*)."

³⁷⁰ F. Nietzsche, *Unzeitgemässe Betrachtungen, Zweites Stück: Vom Nutzen und Nachteil der Historie für das Leben* 1874.

Places on the Scene: Three Cases

The Apple That Opens

Yet in fact, beyond the representational intentions of its authors, the Ringstrasse ended up charting an utterly new and original conception of space. In this regard, let us recall that its founding decree (ordering the old city ramparts to be dismantled, signed in 1857 by the emperor Franz-Joseph) closed and reversed a centuries-old chapter of the city's history. As far back as 1529 (the date of the first Ottoman siege), the seductive emblem of temptation—the "golden apple," as the Turks sensually termed Vienna—was girded with bastions that marked off the medieval city and clearly separated it from its suburbs, which thus came to comprise the nobility's country houses. And even if the repeated assault on this coveted, impregnable object implied, on each occasion, the partial destruction of the city's interior and the sacking of its suburbs, it was always followed by a resurgence, like the boom in the years after the 1683 offensive, which made Vienna an imperial Baroque capital and one of Europe's most admired cities. Nor, for that matter, did the heart of the city ever lose its resilience. Napoleon, another conqueror, was the first to explode the city's bastions. After the post-Napoleonic recovery—with demographic, industrial, commercial expansion, and with the liberal spirit prevailing in the wake of the revolutionary movements of 1848—the Golden Apple finally had its skin peeled off by imperial decree, the old fortifications made fresh ground for creation. The Ringstrasse was inaugurated in their stead in 1865.[371]

Schorske remarks that, before the street's redesign, Baroque planners had laid out Viennese space "to carry the viewer to a central focus." On the other hand:

> The Ringstrasse designers virtually inverted Baroque procedure, using the building to magnify space. They organized all the elements in relation to a central broad avenue or corso, without architectonic containment and without visible destination. The street, polyhedral in shape, is literally the only element in the vast complex that leads an independent life, unsubordinated to any other spatial entity. Where a Baroque planner would have sought to join suburb and city—to organize vast vistas oriented toward the central, monumental features—the plan adopted in 1859, with

---

[371] According to the plan of Ludwig Forster, winner of the international competition opened up for this purpose.

few exceptions, suppressed the vistas in favor of stress on the circular flow.[372]

It is precisely this open horizontality, with no harmonizing of the spatial setting, that arouses the scorn of certain critics: the architect Camillo Sitte, for instance, a great partisan, incidentally, of the reprise of styles and of the reincarnation of history. The peculiar grandiloquence of each edifice, its forthright monumentality, blurred and faded away amid the street's open circularity. In one stroke, the monumental was made and unmade. According to Sitte, the reprise of styles had to be matched to a design and an ornamentation of open space that made the external space a meeting point, a "room outdoors."[373] For him, the construction of the exterior played the role of an "integrating myth"—on the order of the myths that came out of the *Gesamtkunstwerk* of Richard Wagner, of whom Sitte was a fervent admirer—shoring up civic, communal experience against the fragmentation of modern life.[374]

Conversely, for Otto Wagner, the Ringstrasse's open horizontality, its subversive, unexpected, and original spatial planning, became the fulcrum for Vienna's new urbanistic development. Attentive above all to the way in which circulation and traffic could feed into and redistribute the urban fabric, Wagner proposed, in 1893, "a series of four circumferential roads and rail belts, of which the Ringstrasse would constitute the first."[375] Between 1894 and 1901, with the creation of the urban rail system, Wagner underlined the relation between distribution, connection, and openness that undergirds a dynamic principle of the city. For Vienna's future, he foresaw an expansion projected to infinity; juxtaposed with the fixed, the precise, and the localized were the open, the infinite, and the idea of an evolution in progress.

---

[372] C.E. Schorske, *Fin-de-Siècle Vienna: Politics and Culture*, op. cit., 32.
[373] *Ibid.*, 64.
[374] *Ibid.*, 69.
[375] *Ibid.*, 73.

Places on the Scene: Three Cases

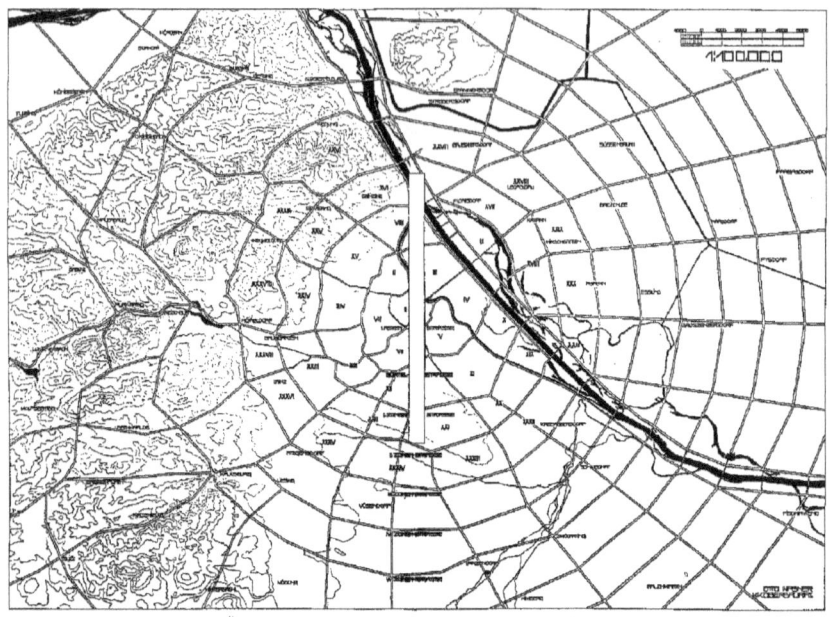

O. Wagner, Modular Plan for the Expansible City, 1911

The Particular and the Horizon

Viennese space in its transformation thus comes to contain and revolve around two different focal points: one oriented toward a specific point and the other toward the expanded horizon. This dual relation with the vision that city planning and architecture translate into the subjective experience of urban space is a nodal point in the culture of this era, observable in the realms of philosophical, literary, and artistic reflection as well as scientific discovery. The open stands side by side with the intimate, the contemplative, the precise, an echo of the sophistication of the interior celebrated in the Biedermeier style. *Weit* is "the name of the open," the "sign of breadth."[376]

This dual point of view accompanies the simultaneously inward and outward movement that characterizes the city. In the latter half of

---

[376] C. Rabant, "La pulsion du large: le phallus, horizon du sexuel," New York, Après Coup Psychoanalytic Association, February 8, 2003.

the nineteenth century, all roads in Central and Eastern Europe led to Vienna. At the same time, demographic, commercial, and industrial expansion forced the city to project itself ever outward; the city that draws in and receives also spreads out. And within this city, at the heart of a multiethnic empire, some complain that they can no longer hold a conversation in German: "Your wife is Galician, your cook is Bohemian, your valet Serbian, your driver Polish: Vienna is no longer a German city."[377] The vision of the big city becomes fragmentary, heterogeneous, explosive: the bond with tradition is accompanied by a constant relation with difference. Centralization becomes decentering.

The possibility of having both a set focal point and, at the same time, an enlargement of the visual field allowed Freud a reconceptualization of subjectivity that became the basis for the discovery of psychoanalysis. Admittedly, as Bettelheim observes, an interest in sexuality—scientific and nonscientific—was in the air at the time and other innovators paved the way for Freud. But if it is true that Krafft-Ebing's precise enumeration of sexual perversions in his *Psychopathia Sexualis* (published in 1886) prepared the cultural climate that allowed for Freud's work, it is also true that Freud approached the sexual in an unprecedented way. Instead of the focused viewpoint, such as that of the adult heterosexual sexuality considered "normal," the norm against which the perversions can be enumerated, an expanded vision is substituted that allows for all manifestations of the sexual to be placed in a single field, without exception and *equally*. The "polymorphy" Freud attributes to the forms of the sexual indicates the absence of any pre-established form as well as the production of form as a result of contingent processes set in motion by the drive. One may wonder how indebted the very possibility of this conceptualization was—so innovative that it is still subversive today—to the social context into whose core the very notion of "the open" could, literally, make its way. One cannot help but notice how greatly the very conception of immanent form—of a fashioning out of the contingency of differentiated elements—echoes the vision of the leading visual artists in the Vienna of this era. Let us recall the motto of the Secession "*Der Zeit ihre Kunst, Der Kunst ihre Freiheit*" (To the Age its Art, and to Art its Freedom), or Otto Wagner's credo "The only possible point of departure for our

---

[377] *Vienna 1900* (Video), The Museum of Modern Art, New York.

artistic creation is modern life."[378] Nor can one fail to notice that the newly emerging totalitarian political regimes vehemently attacked this same notion of immanent form, and with it both avant-garde artistic expression and psychoanalysis.[379]

To discover implies uncovering, stirring up, opening, exposing, implicitly involving an element of vulnerability, a moment of loss of reference, which is precisely what Camillo Sitte finds intolerable in modernity and what prompts him to call for a "filling up" by ornamentation, decoration, and collective myth. In contrast, Otto Wagner—who, in his idea of evolving urban space, applies the functional and the un-predetermined—responds to the vulnerability of the open, "to the painful uncertainty" of life in transformation,[380] by offering direction as an Ariadne's thread.[381]

It is no accident that the term "theory" derives etymologically from vision. Freud is interested in the visions of the world produced by the constructions of thought, to the point of enumerating them according to a hierarchy of the finite: from the most complete visions of the world, such as animism and religion, where every element is fixed and specified and finds its own coherent *raison d'être*, its certainty, to the most open vision of the world, a vision that admits the incomplete and the abandonment of the drive-satisfaction inherent in the omnipotence of thought. Such is the case, as we saw, with what Freud considers science to be, where tolerance for the open-ended implies acceptance of the temporary, the refutable, the incomplete: a practice of the not-all associated with a developing vision.

Nonetheless, the standpoint of the open does not cancel out that of the finite. Freud is very precise here: it is impossible to take a step forward without theorizing, fantasizing. Theory and a finite focal

---

[378] C.E. Schorske, *Fin-de-Siècle Vienna: Politics and Culture*, op. cit., 74.

[379] The exception here is the integration of the Futurist movement into fascist ideology. One must note that this acceptance was possible due to the convergence, more apparent than real, between aspects of Marinetti's Futurist program and those of Mussolini's political program. The Futurist spirit, though, was quickly stifled by its exploitation by the Fascist regime; realism and monumentalism became the two official forms of Italian fascist art.

[380] C.E. Schorske, *Fin-de-Siècle Vienna: Politics and Culture*, op. cit., 85.

[381] Isn't "Trouville"—"Holeville"—the very emblem of the city in which one can breathe, in which the horizon can open up, as Marguerite Duras suggests? "*Trou*," "hole," sounds like the English "true." See Marguerite Duras, "Les miradors de Poissy," in *La Vie matérielle* (Paris: Gallimard, 1987), 137–140.

point cannot be eliminated, since theory is the product of the very nature of the psychic apparatus, of secondary elaboration, of its vocation for finding answers. The fantasm is the only access to the real. The eternal challenge, then, is the constant putting-into-perspective of theory, its being called into question on the horizon of the "open," of the non-finite.

The Nearby Distant: Myth and Modernism

Such a massive presence of history, of its representativity, combined with the demands of a new economic and social reality, make the Vienna of the end of the nineteenth century an unparalleled meeting point between the past and present. To the two focal points—determinate and open, around which space is organized—are added the temporal references of past and future. The wide-open gaze turns both backward and forward.

Otto Wagner's activity is exemplary in this regard, as is his relation to the question of style. Respect for and attention to pre-established models and languages of architecture is followed by the articulation of an original language, resulting intrinsically from the very practice of fashioning. That Otto Wagner was able to keep building from the beginning to the end of his career, that he was able to accomplish most of his projects and often be his own entrepreneur, made each of his steps the result of actual experience, a characteristic that links him closely to Freud.[382] It is easy to trace the evolution of Wagner's interest in Renaissance style: from its direct celebration, as in his first projects from the 1860s and 1870s (for instance the plan for Hamburg's City Hall), or in the first buildings (the Orpheum theater and the Wasagasse complex), to its simplification (for example in the Österreichische Länderbank of 1882–1884), to its dispersal (as in the apartment buildings of Linke Wienzeile and Köstlergasse, from 1898–1899) and its final resurfacing in the never-built project of the Museum of Modern Art (1913). Nothing is more telling than the dizzying contrast between the two villas that Wagner built for himself at a distance

---

[382] "Freud's thought," observes Lacan, "is his experience." *Le Séminaire livre VII: L'éthique de la psychanalyse* (Paris: Éditions du Seuil, 1986), 262.

Places on the Scene: Three Cases

O. Wagner, Ideal Design for Twenty-Second Metropolitan District, 1910–1911

of forty years and that he wanted to place just a few meters from each other: they present us with not only the genealogy of a vision, but also a reinterpretation of building paradigms that does not fear creating opposite versions.

The archaeological discoveries of the eighteenth century and the start of the nineteenth century led not only to an immersion in history but also, equally, to a sudden awareness of what Walter Benjamin calls "the object's aura." Aura is that "which one could define as the unique apparition of a distance, however near it may be."[383] This near/distant foregrounded the notion of the object's authenticity and, at the same time, the mystery of its use, its purpose, something which greatly intrigued the collector Freud. The notion of authenticity simultaneously underscored the artist's hand, its style, and its vision. That the discovery of archaeological works and their circulation should have occurred at a historical moment of industrialization and

---

[383] W. Benjamin, "The Work of Art in the Age of Its Technological Reproducibility" (Third Version), in *Walter Benjamin: Selected Writings IV, 1938-1940*, ed. H. Eiland and M.W. Jennings (Cambridge, MA: Belknap, 2003), 255.

the sped-up production of new technologies is an essential element for understanding the era's artistic context, especially given a local artisanal tradition as refined as Vienna's was. The fact that in Vienna authenticity and reproducibility met and competed certainly had a huge impact on *Jugendstil*, on debates between originality and function, as well as the implicit aspiration to make an original of the reproducible. The idea of 'the signature' in design began to take hold.

The relation between the distant past, the unsuspected past, and the present-distant foregrounded both history and myth. The coexistence of myth and modernism is characteristic of the Vienna of this era. One may wonder to what extent the recourse to myth is not only the expression of a need for identity, a means of collective definition, but also the response to the experience of the open, the immanent. It is as if the breadth provoked by the rhythm of transformation, of the extension of the horizon, prompted the need for a fixed point, the declaration of a point of origin *prior to* history, external to that history, which could justify its course, its shaping. Myth could thus be used in radically opposed ways, as its political manipulation was in fact to prove: as a way to saturate, define, encompass, and exclude, as in the case of the identity-conferring myths of Bayreuth; and as another, contrary way to serve as a counterweight on the scales of the new, an anchorage in the practice of the open-ended (as is the case with Klimt, Freud, Hofmannsthal, Schönberg). And this too may be a characteristic trait of the Vienna of the era: opposite uses of the reference to myth.

If the presentification of history implies a reading of history, the question that modernism brings to the fore and the question it comes to interpret is that of a *practice of reading*, which comes to inform each step in its unfolding elaborations. This practice is an evolving process, as necessary to interpretation as to creation, to the very possibility of invention. In producing new versions it mingles backward and forward, the fixed and the open, and guarantees the questioning of any closed universe. It celebrates a shaping that encompasses tradition (thus, also *craftsmanship*) and transformation. Where the practice of reading stops production of idols begins, the descent back into a system of thought that excludes the not-all.[384] In this sense, a

---

[384] See B. Bernardo Fuks, *Freud and the Invention of Jewishness* (New York: Agincourt, 2008).

dividing line distinguishes the relation with history of the interpreters of modernism and of the idolaters.

Freud's unprecedented relation to reading and listening undoubtedly makes him the founder of a new conception of both subjectivity and memory, the scope and horizon of which remain partly misunderstood to these days. With Freud, memory is a process that works above all in *forward* motion, to the rhythm of a shaping that in its very elaboration gives birth to an earlier trace. We might say that this forward process was painted into the very set-design of the city of Vienna.

Psychic space is articulated by a succession of inscriptions that produce the erogenous body as well as the subject that inhabits it. At first the subject is lacking, being the result of the articulation woven around a void: the void is central, a condition so that, in view of the repression that affects the real, a *tabula rasa* can unfold and a trace can be inscribed, a condition for the beginning of memory.[385] If the inscription process of memory implies the forward movement that is life, this is all the truer given the insistence of what lies behind it, given the fixation of the original sources of pleasure. Therein lies the paradox of the apparatus animated by the drive: lazy by nature, conservative, ready to follow the shortest paths to satisfy the drive, it winds up forced into complication, extension. Evolution, then, does not imply progression; the historical process proves to be a movement that simultaneously does and undoes, never a linear development. The drive tendencies reflect its conflictual nature: one group of drives charges headlong in order to reach the ultimate end of life as soon as possible, the other group goes backward to prolong the length of the journey. A particular understanding of the historical process follows: as much in the biological as in the human domain, the historical process is articulated according to a movement at once *forward and backward*, bringing about new formations. The living world is a complex and unstable system of which the course cannot be determined in advance.

The weaving of the psychic apparatus, its immanence, reveals the existence of a fixed point, a structural element, the trace of a reality that transcends the individual in order to occupy a mythic point in the

---

[385] "There is identity," observes Lacan, "between the shaping of the signifier and the introduction into the real of a gaping, a hole." Jacques Lacan, *Le Séminaire livre VII: L'éthique de la psychanalyse*, op. cit., 146.

experience of the species. This weaving appears always as a second act: whether it is a matter of organic repression, primal repression, the "historical" appearance of the drive, *Befriedigungserlebnis*, primal *Bejahung*, or the murder of the primordial father as the antecedence of the law over subjectivity, the first moment—the inaugural act—is placed in a logical elsewhere, a mythical point that current formations account for *a posteriori*, from which temporality can be posited and the relation between signifiers emerges in cutting through atemporal constancy.[386] The immanent and projective space of the Freudian hypothesis is connected to the introjective experience of space that molds and transforms.

The Void and the Knot

The void is central to the apparatus; it is the support of psychic weaving, its extension. The Freudian model of the psyche's architecture evokes an aspect of the architectural theory that most strongly influenced the artists of Vienna in the latter half of the nineteenth century. It is hard to understand how the period's architectural language evolved (Sitte, Wagner, Fabiani, Olbrich, Loos, etc.) without taking into account the influence exerted by Gottfried Semper's *Der Stil* (1860–1863).

An intellectual of revolutionary and radical bent during his student years in Paris (1826–1830), Semper nurtured the idea that every modern discipline should imitate natural science. Impressed with Georges Cuvier's methodology of anatomical rules, which established a hierarchy of organic functions, Semper himself devised a similar method, comparative and systematic, to classify architectonic types. London's Grand Exposition of 1851 impressed him to the point of inspiring him to create the two volumes of *Der Stil*, which thus replaced the ambitious project of a *vergleichende Baule[h]re*, a comparative theory of architecture, which Eduard Vieweg had commissioned from him some years earlier.

---

[386] On the concept of organic repression, see the work of M. Antonio Coutinho Jorge, *Fundamentos da psicanálise: de Freud a Lacan* (Rio de Janeiro: Jorge Zahar, 2000).

Let us simply recall here certain key concepts of *Der Stil* that pertain to our discussion. According to Semper, identical laws govern the work of the fine and applied arts, *Kunst* and the *Kunstgewerbe*. The work originates in action. There exists a logical anteriority to the art of weaving in relation to architecture: the division of space along surfaces composed of intertwining elements is the conceptual basis of architecture. From the analogy between the practices of covering the body and covering space, *Bekleidungstheorie* (clothing theory) makes covering—at its origin interlaced fashioning, ornament—the essential artistic element synthesizing form and structure. Semper thus resolves the structure/ornament opposition of classical art and reaffirms in a new light his defense of the polychromy of classical buildings (Egyptian, Greek, Roman).[387] The essential work of art is the knot: through a simple, clever etymology, Semper links *Knoten* (knots) to *Naht* (sewing, joining-work) and to *Noth* (need, necessity), finding a common point in the Greek word *ananke*.[388] Fashioning is an immanent process whose motor is need, a process conditioned as much by the materials that compose it as by its very unfolding.[389]

Semper devises a functional theory of style and of art that rests on structural, and therefore universal, processes of fabrication; this point of view overturns Winckelmann's conception of the intrinsic priority of certain artistic manifestations. Thanks to the juncture between form and structure, art and crafts, Semper's vision allows for an integration of the era's artisanal tradition as much as for its transformation to serve contemporary needs, and thus grants free rein to the exper-

---

[387] Which he had expounded in his "Preliminary Remarks" [*Vorläufige Bemerkungen*], 1834.

[388] J. Rykwert, "Semper et la conception du style," *Macula* 5/6 (1979), 180. According to Semper, "the work of art ... is man's response to a world full of wonders and mysterious powers whose laws he seeks to understand but whose enigma he never solves; whence the perpetual state of unsatisfied tension in which he dwells." *Ibid*.

[389] This evokes an observation of Lacan's: to what extent is it possible to think of architecture as a presentification of pain? (*Le Séminaire livre VII: L'éthique de la psychanalyse*, op. cit., 74). If, as Freud says, there exists a homology between pain and motor reaction, if the area of pain emerges where the subject can no longer escape or avoid it, where s/he can no longer move, architecture may embody, among other things, the "arrested thing," its suffering. The notion of the presentification of pain perhaps offers an additional interpretation of a certain efficacy of the monumental, delegated by an experience of the intolerable that the subject unknowingly reifies or commemorates.

imentation of *Jugendstil* and modernism. Art's starting point is the knot. Fashioning is articulated around the void.

Architecture in general, like the architecture of the psychic apparatus, establishes the notion of a threshold, the relation between inside and outside, a strip that separates and unites. The structural function that Semper attributes to interlacing—to full/empty as separation, delimitation, and décor—resolves in a peculiar way not only the idea of façade, but also the concept of a wall, of partition. The theme of the wall had a central function for artists of the Baroque. We can cite the supreme example of the Church of Saints Luke and Martin in Rome where, by introducing cuts between contiguous surfaces, Pietro di Cortona eliminates the idea of wall as a limit between the interior and the exterior in order to suggest a continuity of space, a pulsation between inside and outside, a "breathing architecture."[390] Later, the Rococo fantasies of the European aristocracy offered extraordinary examples of the transformation of the inner wall into an outer skin, where the floral, vegetal, and "oriental" visions transformed walls into landscapes; we need think only of Margravine Wilhelmine's decorations for her spiritual retreat, the Neues Schloss at Bayreuth (1739–53). The subliminal calm of the wall, its ideal color and perfect pattern, made wallpaper an essential element of domestic refinement in the Biedermeier era; and if Schiller ended up dying poisoned by the arsenic that saturated the green tint of his wallpaper, it is true all the same, as Goethe had told him, that green gave the wall its ideal spiritual tone.[391]

Semper's knot between form and structure accentuates the idea of the surface's function, breaking with the fascination of the continuum between inside and outside as much as with their absolute separation. The surface has a set, contextualized function. In the knot, the discontinuous intermeshes with the continuous. Even more than Otto Wagner's Majolikahaus, the superb façade of the Wohn-und-Geschäftshaus of Max Fabiani (1899–1901) is exemplary in this regard: here every functional detail takes on a decorative value in a weaving of colors and forms. Another magnificent example is the American Bar of Adolf Loos, even if he was radically critical of Semper's idea of or-

---

[390] See P. Portoghesi, "La nascita del barocco," in *I trionfi del Barocco* (Milan: Bompiani, 1999), 44.

[391] On this topic, see S. Sangl, *Biedermeier to Bauhaus* (New York: Abrams, 2000).

nament. In this minimal space (4.45 by 6.15 meters), the wall-surface simultaneously gathers and opens out. Mirrors placed over upper panels allow a visual expansion that harkens to the open, to the limitless, but without sacrificing the intimacy of the near, the pleasure of the private, the discontinuity of points of view in its succession of select materials: onyx, marble, brass, mahogany.[392]

The One and the Other

The threshold is a point of encounter and of separation, that which, in offering itself, signals a right-here and a beyond, the one *and* the other. This *and* strikes me as an essential proposition for understanding the singular experience Vienna afforded between the last two centuries: the greatest flowering and the greatest dispersal, the determined focal point and the open, the finite and the not-all, the continuous and the discontinuous, grace and the word, immanence and a mythic elsewhere. The use of the threshold, of this "and" of continuity and discontinuity, of a passage from a here to a there, where distinct visual angles relativize the absolute and support the vulnerability of the open, is what the geniuses of Modernism may have culled from the historical contingency of Vienna, each working out some particularity according to his own style.

The knot as an essential work of art—woven and extended along the set design of the city's streets, the length of its interior spaces—illustrates to what extent full and empty are logically linked and to what extent the threshold is an edge, a border that perforates and relinks differentiated registers. The knot's "and" makes paradox a given, a permanent producer of metaphors. Thus it appears once more that the subject of Freud's Copernican revolution is the same as that of modern science, as Lacan pointed out. The lesson of baroque syllo-

---

[392] I cannot refrain from referring to the ultimate expression, at once rigorous and ironic, of 'breathing architecture': the Blur Building of Elisabeth Diller and Riccardo Scofidio, for the Swiss Expo 2002. In this structure—made of a light metal framework 100 meters long, 60 meters deep, and 25 meter tall—the main material is water. The walls are made of steam, a skin of inside-outside perpetually awaiting form. A "spaceless, massless, surfaceless, and contextless" place in which all we can see is our own dependence on sight. *Scanning: The Aberrant Architectures of Diller + Scofidio*, Whitney Museum of American Art (New York: Abrams, 2003), 93.

O. Wagner, Majolikahaus, Façade, 1899

gism is exemplary in this regard. Deriving from the calling into question of appearance, of certainty, of a shift in perspective that decenters the closed world of ancient astronomy and opens up the infinite universe of modern thought, it makes paradox—that which is contrary to common opinion—the framework for a new dimension of thought.[393] *"Prodigio tal non rimirò natura / Bagnar coi soli e rasciugar coi fiumi,"* to apply to turn-of-the-century Vienna the baroque rhyme of Giuseppe Artale.[394]

The presence of the Baroque tradition was an essential element in the cultural context of Vienna. Significant examples of this tradition are clearly present in Austrian history, especially dating from the reconstruction of Vienna in 1690. As ever, the difficulty remains in univocally understanding the notion of the baroque, particularly

---

[393] See A. Koyré, *From the Closed World to the Infinite Universe*, op. cit.
[394] "Such a wonder nature never did see / Wetting with suns and drying with rivers." Giuseppe Artale, "A Maria Maddalena Loffredo, Princess of Cardito," in *La letteratura italiana: storia e testi*, ed. R. Ricciardi (Milano-Napoli: Marino e i Marinisti, 1952), 1031.

given its varied manifestations at different historical moments. As Portoghesi observes, a theory of the baroque is in itself a contradiction in terms, since the baroque is, above all, "the pluralistic freeing from imposed bonds and the free development of a received heritage," which authorizes the "correcting of ancient rules and the inventing of new ones," a culture "of the variation as a deep need."[395] Beyond its precise manifestations, the baroque can therefore be considered, as Benjamin suggests, an opening *onto/of* modernity, independent of the historical reality in which it is expressed, an opening which, as such, occurs throughout history. The frequent binary opposition of baroque to classicism—an eminent example of which is that proposed by Eugenio d'Ors in *Du Baroque*, which sees classicism as the expression of civilization's organized balance and order and baroque as the expression of the wild, sensual, feminine side of life—risks reducing the notion of the baroque to something univocal.[396] Isn't the baroque, in fact, a culture of the multiple, of this *and* that? In embracing contraries, doesn't it produce an unpredictable dimension?[397] In this sense the figure of the *barroco* syllogism is particularly instructive: it allows for the simultaneous presence of classically or logically contradictory categories. It dares to tie reality to the unheard-of, to the impossible of the real, showing, in this way, that what surprises us is not the absurd, but rather the truth that the absurd unleashes.

Geography, said Napoleon, is destiny. We can perhaps apply that quotation to the city of Vienna. It may be no coincidence that the statement was paraphrased by Freud and became an aphorism even more famous than the original. Anatomy is destiny, he says, speaking of what is obscure, of the not-all. But if anatomy is the threshold, it is so because it implicitly underscores the inevitable radicalness of difference in the real. The "and" in "one and the other."

---

[395] P. Portoghesi, op. cit., 55.

[396] E. d'Ors, *Du Baroque* (Paris: Éditions Gallimard, 1968).

[397] Indeed, baroque artistic expressions present classical, mannerist, gothic, etc. elements. Didier-Weill has shown the importance of the passage from the logical figure of "or" (there is *or* there isn't) to the figure "and" (there is *and* there isn't) in *Lila et la lumière de Vermeer* (Paris: Denoël, 2003). As concerns the relationship between the baroque and psychoanalysis, see D. Maurano, *La face cachée de l'amour* (Paris: Presses Universitaires du Septentrion, 1999).

PUNCTUATION AT THE THRESHOLD

A surprising example of the connection between 'the one *and* the other' is provided by Philippe Petit. Among his many feats of funambulism, which involves stretching a steel wire between two high and distant points in space and creating a walking itinerary between them, his exploit of the Twin Towers in Manhattan remains unparalleled. August 7, 1974, the young Philippe Petit, 24, stretched a wire between the two buildings of the World Trade Center in New York: for 45 minutes, he walked, kneeled, waved, lay down, and turned around on it, at 412 meters from the ground.[398]

Petit talks about the detailed and indefatigable preparations for this exploit as if it were a plot, a veritable "coup." And indeed, it involved something illicit: the fact of entering a building closed to the public, with the help of accomplices, of sleeping in a place that is off-limits, of hiding from security personnel. But was the act itself illegal? Looking at it closely today, it wasn't illegal, at least not at the time; nowhere was it written that it was against the law, for no one had imagined that it was even a possibility.

Responding to the emergency of Petit's sublime stroll, the police waited for him at one of the wire's two ends. As soon as he set foot over the tower's railing, he was arrested for "disorderly conduct and criminal trespassing." *Trespassing*, exactly, in all its different meanings and connotations: among others, and not the least, the one, stretched on a steel wire, of the threshold we cross at the moment we die. As for "disorderly conduct," the disorderliness in question is food for thought. Whatever the case may be, the disproportion between the accusation and the extraordinary nature of the exploit can only make us smile. It strips bare, among other things, the incommensurability

---

[398] An extraordinary way of celebrating two not very successful buildings that disappeared under tragic circumstances, as is well known, in 2001, in a crash that constituted a threshold under our history.

Punctuation at the Threshold

Philippe Petit, World Trade Center, 1974

that exists between code and action, between the predictable and the unpredictable. In fact, it seems that Petit has been arrested more than five hundred times over the course of his high-wire exploits.

It is certain that this "and"—this conjunction drawn between the two towers, one step after the other with the sky as backdrop—is a transgression of the limits of the imagination. It transports the spectator, who is suspended in wonder, into an incredulous and ecstatic dimension. For Petit, transgression is a structural element of his relation to art. One might ask to what extent art, by achieving the unimaginable, necessarily implies the transgression of a boundary, a crossing that moves the limits of the representable. An unimaginable perishes while something new comes into existence.

Petit creates conjunctions, produces thresholds; he produces them in order to practice them, to patiently and passionately give himself over, in a subliminal balance, to the relationship with the void and, through it, to the proximity of the real. He says he believes in the void.[399] And yet we often hear that the void is frightening. For many, it is vertigo, *horror vacui*, the presentification of *absence as space*, of the real.

The real is the element that recurs in these pages, the subterranean common thread of the different figures of space drawn here. We might ask if it could be otherwise, seeing as the subjective relation to the place on the world scene, mediated as it is by the signifying articulation, ties together the imaginary, the symbolic, and the real in a transforming knot. The real is there, always present and yet always latent; and, as Lacan says, it never ceases returning to its place.

It is in the shape of the unassimilable that the real is presented in the Freudian conception of trauma; it is the foundation of the very constitution of the psychic scene and of the articulation of the registers that belong to it; it is the *jouissante* substance that *lalangue* is made of; it occupies a central role in the operations of alienation and separation thanks to which the subject emerges from the field of the Other; it belongs intimately to the process of identification and marks the gap between the body and its image; it supports the screen of the fantasm and the tracing of the coordinates of the place on the world scene. And so on and so forth.

Except that, when it makes itself felt, the encounter with the real is inopportune most of the time. This is the case with trauma, or with the manifestations of the body we inhabit, for instance when we experience the distress caused by its lack of motor coordination, or the revelation of disease, or the realization of the acephalous persistence of a drive (be it in an unexpected sexual attraction or in the lust for violence). But it is also the case with the encounter with the irreducible aspect of difference, whether it is a question of sexual difference or the difference confronted in hatred. It is the case with the encounter with the limits of the symbolizable, or with the fleeting emergence of subjective evanescence in the gap between enunciation and statement. It is the case with angst or with the sudden helplessness revealed in the *Unheimliche*, and in general with all figures that signal the temporal loss of the coordinates of place. The landscape shows a crack and, within it, the truth that belongs to it, only to close up again, almost instantly.

---

[399] P. Petit, *Credere nel vuoto* (Turin: Bollati Boringhieri, 2008).

Punctuation at the Threshold

Philippe Petit, World Trade Center, 1974

Philippe Petit Arrested by the Police, WTC, 1974

The fact that this encounter is inopportune most of the time is consubstantial with the nature of the subject of language, condemned to think where s/he isn't and to be where s/he isn't thinking, and who does not bear well his or her alterity. Most of the time, but not always. In this sense, Philippe Petit's "threshold practice" makes us think: it summons a type of relation to the subjective place which, soliciting and exploring the *di(t)mensions* that belong to it, is a practice of the proximity to the real. This exercise characterizes the way the artist or the creator inhabits the world scene, whether it is a question of poetry, music, or any of the different visual arts, from dance to performance, from painting to architecture. To provoke language in order to evoke what is beyond the sayable, or sound to summon the unheard, the material to provoke the immaterial, these are threshold practices; such practices pull the strings of the affects that testify to the primary and inaccessible matter that makes up the unconscious, echoing the *moteriality* that permeates the human being and weaves the screen of fantasm.

Philippe Petit's extraordinary exploit brings to mind enthusiasm. The Greek term ἐνθουσιασμός, *enthousiasmós*, derives from the verb *enthousiázein*, *to be inspired*, and contains the lemma ἔνθεος, composed of ἐν, "in," and θεός, "God": an inspiration that lets the god's presence be visible, the fact of having "the god in oneself." The state of exaltation that results is divine madness, a necessary condition, in ancient Greek culture, for creation and divination. The soul of poetic creation, according to Plato, allows surpassing the limits of technique and understanding and thus attains authentic lyricism, since skill alone leaves the poet "incomplete."[400]

According to the treatise *On the Sublime* by Longinus (or Pseudo-Longinus), the god's "enthusiastic breath" has an aesthetic function; it allows the creation of beautiful works.[401] Naturally, enthusiasm changes signs and connotations over the course of the history of Western thought, according to eras, cultures, and the place God occupies in them: from its ecstatic nature in the Middle Ages, it is affirmed as a heroic furor with Giordano Bruno; from the will-o'-the-wisp that

---

[400] Platon, *Ione* 533e, in *Tutti gli scritti*, ed. G. Reale (Milan: Bompiani, 2000), 53 et succ.

[401] G. Guidorizzi, *Il mondo letterario Greco* Vol. 3/2 (Turin: Einaudi, 2000), 529. Also, R. Bodei, *Le forme del bello* (Bologne: Il Mulino, 1995).

blinds us to true knowledge with Locke, it turns into an irrationality deprived of aesthetics or morality with Diderot; a consequence of the excited mind in Kant, it fuses with madness as the deep essence of the human being in Schelling's romantic vision. That said, whether it is in such and such a version, with such and such a meaning, enthusiasm signals proximity to the alterity that is our own and gives voice to the inspiration that comes from it. This alterity testifies to the presence of the Other that accompanies the subject of language. As Lacan says, overturning the premises of enlightened reason, "The real slogan of atheism is not that God is dead. It is that God is unconscious."[402]

Is enthusiasm for threshold practice an affirmation of the desire to live? Is this the "heroic" aspect of enthusiasm isolated by Giordano Bruno, the proximity and loyalty to what one has that is most *extimate* and that allows Bruno to maintain—in the wake of Nicholas de Cusas and Copernicus—the infinity of the universe and a new vision of the world, which makes of his thinking and his ethics an essential link in the configuration of modern science?[403] If that were the case, this type of enthusiasm would be situated at the opposite pole of hate, at least of one of its forms, the one Freud distinguishes as a reaction to the encounter with the living. Hate is expressed as an attachment to the frontier, a frontier opposed to threshold practice. In this sense, nothing is more distant from this type of enthusiasm than fanaticism, despite the etymological similarity of the two words: the *fanaticus* is the one who is possessed by divine inspiration, from *fanum*, "temple" (related to *fas*, sacred right), a term used most of the time in its negative connotation in the Roman world, which shows the multiplicity of signifying effects that related etymologies can produce in different cultures. Whether we consider it, with Jaspers, a pathological state resulting in self-willed blindness[404] or, with Haddad, a form of fetishizing the symbolic text of a people (be it the Bible, the Koran, the Constitution, or any founding text),[405] fanaticism is in every case a figure of closure and of the production of idols; it is the opposite, specifically, of

---

[402] J. Lacan, *Le Séminaire livre XI: Les quatre concepts fondamentaux de la psychanalyse*, op. cit., 58.
[403] G. Nolano Bruno, *De gli eroici furori: Parigi, appresso Antonio Baio l'anno 1585*, in *Dialoghi filosofici italiani*, ed. M. Ciliberto (Milan: Mondadori, 2000).
[404] K. Jaspers, *Psicologia delle visioni del mondo* (Rome: Astrolabio, 1950).
[405] G. Haddad, *Les folies millénaristes* (Paris: Grasset, Biblio essais, 1990).

the openness to the unknown, of a practice of reading that produces plural and contextualized meanings.

In this framework, one cannot help remembering one of Lacan's observations regarding the position and the formation of the analyst: "If s/he isn't borne by enthusiasm, there may well have been an analysis, but not a chance of an analyst."[406] It is a powerful observation, because it makes enthusiasm the condition for there to be an analyst, an analytic act, and transmission. It is therefore worth the trouble of returning to the opening onto the world scene created by analytical practice—by the ethical and epistemological implications of Freud's discovery—and to linger a moment on the figure of transferential space, at the heart of which the coordinates of place prepare for the advent of the analytic act.

Lacan gives a definition of the course of an analysis that is among the most evocative: "Analysis is not a simple reconstitution of the past, analysis is not a reduction to pre-established norms, analysis is not an *epos,* analysis is not *ethos.* If I had to compare it to something, it would be to a narrative that would itself be the place of the encounter that the narrative is about."[407]

It is the creation of a place, of a space-time dictated by speech, that guides the analysand's task as well as the analyst's act, the result of an attention suspended between letter and meaning. While the symptom always questions a certain knowledge, the space of transference is drawn from pre-existing knowledge, which traces the present. Unfolding according to the rhythm of the signifying articulation, the knowledge that emerges between analysand and analyst is the acting construction of the subject's history. In this sense, specifically, the past is articulated forward.

The talking cure is based on the immediacy of the relationship between saying and hearing. In the act of speech, the expressible emerges in the circuit of the invocatory drive that unfolds around the voice object; behind the equivocal nature of the signifier, the voice lets emerge the letter, the mark of the *moteriality* of the unconscious. While it summons in this way a knowledge that is otherwise inaccessible, the question becomes one of knowing how to listen to it, of

---

[406] J. Lacan, "Lettre aux italiens," 1974.
[407] J. Lacan, *Le Séminaire livre VI: Le désir et son interprétation,* op. cit., 572.

being able to read the letter in question, which is the product and the function of transferential space. The analyst's desire is founded on the stakes of the unconscious and is a desire for difference. Yet, the effects of these stakes never cease to amaze. Consenting to surprise is the element that bears the analyst's particular position—similar to that of a ballerina on a single toe, to use Freud's metaphor—a position that is at once rigorous and constantly evolving.

If, with Lacan, we consider "act" to be the entire course of a treatment, the change in subjective position that brings about the very possibility of its end, we must also note that this act, in its uniqueness and totality, is in fact cadenced by discrete punctuations dependent on the logical time particular to each session and the logical times particular to the course of a cure. These punctuations, to the extent that they bring about a change in the position of the analysand or in the listening of the analyst, are logical steps that conclude a period of repetition, opening up a new space; in this sense, they can be conceived as discrete elements of the analytical act, as its discrete representatives. They are steps in the act, crossing a threshold toward a new space.

What can be expected from an analysis at the beginning of its course does not correspond to what we find; the ultimate end does not correspond to the voyage we may have thought we were undertaking. Among other things, such a journey will involve the experience of disillusion, since it will entail a spoliation of beliefs, a questioning and a destitution of the identifications upon which the ego founds its demands. But in shaking and emptying pre-established meanings, it will also open up new meanings, new horizons; it will thus reveal a *space unhoped-for*, not yet written in the subject's history. This will reconfigure the subjective place, creating space where there wasn't any.

There will therefore have been places no longer habitable, unrecoverable places, following the extinction of this suffering of reminiscence through which Freud, as is well known, defined neurosis, places for which there will not even be nostalgia, as they will be no more. But it needs to be remarked that nostalgia is not just deadly insistence of and orientation toward the same. Barbara Cassin stresses that it is, by its very nature, polytrope, since it can express both the desire to return, as in *Heimweh*, and the predisposition to openness, as in *Sehnsucht*, and that most of the time the two extremes merge and amalgamate.[408] She rightly defines Ulysses as the one "who never stops returning," even when he doesn't cease leaving, a figure who restores the intrinsic tension between the open horizon and the point of departure, where the attraction exercised by the past necessarily involves new journeys, the extension of the subjective landscape. It is the exile endemic to the *parlêtre*, an exile that is inherently structural but most often latent. It is immediately obvious, though, to those who have actually left their country of origin. Whether it happens by force, to survive, by opportunity, or by whim, this separation necessitates breaking away from the same, from the consolation of the same; it necessitates crossing a threshold. It involves the opening to the different, the vulnerability of uncertainty, the possibility of considering one's own origin from the point of view of elsewhere; it is to become aware that the *there* we have left and came from will never be again—if it ever was—and that the *here* is never the *here* we imagined. Wherever it is, we always need to build this *here*, thus turning fate into a choice and the unexpected, the unimagined, into an opportunity.

---

[408] B. Cassin, *La nostalgie* (Paris: Éditions Autrement, 2013), 56–61.

BIBLIOGRAPHY

Agrippa, Heinrich. C., Whitehead, Wayne. F. (Éd.). *Three Books of Occult Philosophy or Magic 1.24*. Chicago: Hahn and Whitehead, 1898.

Alberti, Leon B. *De la peinture*. Paris: Macula Dedale, 1992.

Altschuler, Glenn C. "Whose Foot and Whose Throat? A Re-Examination of Melville's *Benito Cereno*." In *Melville's Short Novels*, edited by Dan McCall. New York: Norton & Company, 2002.

Anati, Emmanuel. *Il museo immaginario della preistoria: L'arte rupestre nel mondo*. Milan: Jaca Book, 1995.

--- *The Riddle of Mount Sinai: Archeological Discoveries at HarKarkom. Studi Camuni XXI*. Capo di Ponte: Edizioni del Centro, 2001.

--- *La struttura elementare dell'arte. Studi Camuni XXII*. Capo di Ponte: Edizioni del Centro, 2002.

Artale, Giuseppe. "A Maria Maddalena Loffredo, princesse de Cardito." In *La letteratura italiana: storia e testi*, edited by Riccardo Ricciardi. Milan-Naples: Marino e i Marinisti, 1952.

Audi, Paul. *Le théorème du Surmâle: Lacan selon Jarry*. Lagrasse: Verdier, 2011.

Aulagnier Spairani, Piera. "La féminité." In *Le désir et la perversion*. Points. Paris: Éditions du Seuil, 1967.

Ballerini, Luigi. "Ombre di un presente che adombra l'avvento di ombre più cupe." In Melville, Herman. *Benito Cereno*. Translated by Luigi Ballerini. Venice: Marsilio Editori, 2012.

Basaglia, Franco. "Un problema di psichiatria istituzionale: L'esclusione come categoria sociopsichiatrica." *Rivista Sperimentale di Freniatria e Medicina Legale delle Alienazioni Mentali* 90, no. 6: 1484–1503.

Benjamin, Walter. "The Task of the Translator." In *Walter Benjamin: Selected Writings I, 1913–1926*, edited by M. Bullock and M.W. Jennings. Cambridge, MA: Belknap, 2004.

--- "The Work of Art in the Age of Its Technological Reproducibility" (Third Version). In *Walter Benjamin: Selected Writings IV, 1938–1940*, edited by H. Eiland and M.W. Jennings. Cambridge, MA: Belknap, 2003.

Benveniste, Émile. "Catégorie de pensée et catégorie de langue." In *Problèmes de linguistique générale I*. Paris: Gallimard, 1966.

--- "De la subjectivité dans la langue." In *Problèmes de linguistique générale I*. Paris: Gallimard, 1966.

Bibliography

Betsky, Aaron, et al. *Scanning: The Aberrant Architectures of Diller + Scofidio*. New York: Whitney Museum of American Art, Abrams, 2003.
Bettelheim, Bruno. *Freud's Vienna and Other Essays*. New York: Knopf, 1990.
Bodei, Remo. *Le forme del bello*. Bologne: Il Mulino, 1995.
Bossière, Alain. "Vers une psychologie du mouvement: l'espace acoustique d'Erwin Strauss, entre musique et danse." *Insistance*, no. 5 (2011).
Bovillus, Carolus. *Il libro del sapiente*. Nuova universale Einaudi, 192. Turin: Einaudi, 1987.
Bréhier, Emile. *La théorie des incorporels dans l'ancien stoïcisme*. Paris: Librairie Philosophique J. Vrin, 1997.
Brini, Jean. "Du tableau au plan projectif." *Le regard: Cahiers de L'association freudienne Internationale*. Journées d'étude 7/8/9 (mai 1999).
Bruno, Giordano. N. *De gli eroici furori: Parigi, appresso Antonio Baio l'anno 1585*. In *Dialoghi filosofici italiani*, edited by Michele Ciliberto. Milan: Mondadori, 2000.
Bucciantini, Massimo. *Esperimento Auschwitz*. Turin: Giulio Einaudi, 2011.
Buckham, Phillip W. *Theatre of the Greeks*. Cambridge: J. Smith, 1827.
Campanella, Tommaso. *Metafisica*. Under the direction of Giovanni di Napoli. Filosofi Moderni 10–12. Bologne: Zanichelli, 1967.
Callen Bell, Janis. "Perspective." In *The Dictionary of Art XXIV*, edited by Janet Turner. London: Macmillian, 1996.
Cassin, Barbara. *La nostalgie*. Paris: Éditions Autrement, 2013.
Ciletti, Elena. "On the Destruction of Pontormo's Frescoes at S. Lorenzo and the Possibility that Parts Remain." In *The Burlington Magazine CXXI*, no. 921 (1979): 765-70.
Cantagalli, Roberto. *Cosimo I de' Medici: granduca di Toscana*. Milan: Mursia, 1985.
Caponetto, Salvatore. *La riforma protestante nell'Italia del Cinquecento*. Turin: Claudiana, 1992.
Capretti, Elena. *Brunelleschi*. Florence: Giunti, 2003.
Cecchi, Emilio. *Jacopo da Pontormo: Diario*. Florence: Le Monnier, 1956.
Cléro, Jean-Pierre. *Les raisons de la fiction: Les philosophes et les mathématiques*. Paris: Armand Colin, 2004.
Couthino Jorge, Marco A. *Fundamentos da psicanálise: de Freud a Lacan*. Rio de Janeiro: Jorge Zahar Editor, 2010.
Cox-Rearick, Janet. *The Drawing of Pontormo*. Cambridge, MA: Harvard UP, 1964.
da Pontormo, Jacopo. *Diario: Codice maglabechiano VIII 1490 della Biblioteca Nazionale Centrale di Firenze*, edited by Roberto Fedi. Rome: Salerno, 1996.
da Vinci, Leonardo. *Scritti letterari* (Pensieri No. 128), edited by Augusto Marinoni. Milan: Rizzoli, 1974.
--- *Trattato della pittura (dal Codice Urbinate Vaticano)*. Neuchâtel: Le Bibliophile, 1970.

de Certeau, Michel. *L'invention du quotidien: l'arts de faire.* Paris: Gallimard, 1990.

Delano, Amasa. *Narrative of Voyages and Travels, in the Northen and Southern Hemispheres. Together with a Voyage of Survey and Discovery, in the Pacific Ocean and Oriental Islands.* Boston: E. G. House, 1818.

Desargues, Girard. "Exemple de l'une des manières universelles du S.G.D.L. (Sieur Girard Desargues le Lyonnais) touchant la pratique de la perspective sans employer aucun tiers point de distance ni d'autre nature qui soit hors du champ de l'ouvrage" (1636). In *Desargues en son temps*, edited by Jacques Sakarovitch and Jean Dhombres. Paris: Libraire scientifique A. Blanchard, 1994.

de Tolnay, Charles. "Les fresques de Pontormo dans le choeur de San Lorenzo à Florence." *Critica d'arte*, no. 9: 38–52.

Didier-Weill, Alain. *Un mystère plus loin que l'inconscient.* Paris: Aubier, 2010.

--- *Les trois temps de la loi.* Paris: Éditions du Seuil, 1995.

--- *Lila et la lumière de Vermeer.* Paris: Denoël, 2003.

--- *Invocations: Dionysos, Moïse, saint Paul et Freud.* Paris: Calmann-Lévy, 1998.

Dolto, Francoise. *L'image inconsciente du corps.* Paris: Éditions du Seuil, 1984.

D'Ors, Eugenio. *Du Baroque.* Paris: Gallimard, 1968.

Dupont, Florence. *Aristote ou le vampire du théâtre occidental.* Paris: Flammarion, 2007.

Duras, Marguerite. *La Vie matérielle.* Paris: Gallimard, 1987.

Durrell, Lawrence. *Justine.* New York: Penguin Books, 1991.

Euclide. *Ottica: Immagini di una teoria della visione*, edited by Francesca Incardona. Rome: Di Renzo, 2011.

Flom, Eric L. *Chaplin in the Sound Era: An Analysis of the Seven Talkies.* Jefferson, NC: McFarland, 1997.

Fedi, Roberto. *Jacopo da Pontormo, Diario: Codice maglabechiano VIII 1490 della Biblioteca Nazionale Centrale di Firenze*, with a note by Stefano Zamponi and a comment on the sketches by Elena Testaferrata. Roma: Salerno, 1996.

--- "La cultura del Pontormo." In *Pontormo e Rosso: Atti del convegno de Empoli e Volterra*, edited by Roberto P. Ciardi and Antonio Natali. Venice: Marsilio, 1996.

Ferenczi, Sandor. "Le parole oscene: saggio sulla psicologia della fase di latenza" (1911). In *Fondamenti di psicoanalisi, Parte Prima: Teoria, Vol. I.* Rimini: Guaraldi, 1972.

Ficino, Marsilio. *Consiglio contro la pestilenza* (1481). Bologna: Cappelli, 1983.

Firpo, Massimo. *Gli affreschi di Pontormo a San Lorenzo.* Turin: Giulio Einaudi, 1997.

--- "Il 'Beneficio di Christo' e il concilio di Trento (1542-1546)." In *Rivista di storia e letteratura religiosa* 31 (1995): 45–72.

Freud, Anna. *Ego and the Mechanisms of Defense (1936).* London: International Universities Press, 1946.

Bibliography

Freud, Sigmund. *Gesammelte Werke*. Frankfurt am Main: S. Fischer Verlag.
--- *Studien über Hysterie* (1892-95). *GW I*, 1992.
--- *Die Traumdeutung* (1999). *GW II–III*, 1998.
--- *Die Traumdeutung VII:* "Zur Psychologie der Traumvorgänge" (1900). *GW II–III*, 1998.
--- *Der Witz und seine Beziehung zum Unbewußten* (1905). *GW VI*, 2000.
--- *Der Wahn und die Träume in W. Jensens „Gradiva"* (1906), *GW VII*, 1990.
--- "Der Dichter und das Phantasieren" (1908), *GW VII*, 2001.
--- *Analyse der Phobie eines Fünfjahrig Knaben* (1909), *GW VII*, 2001.
--- "Über den Gegensinn der Urworte" (1910). *GW VIII*, 1996.
--- "Formulierungen über zwei Prinzipien des psychischen Geschehens" (1911). *GW VIII*, 1996.
--- "Ratschläge für den Artzt bei der Psychoanalytischen Behandlung" (1912). *GW VIII*, 1990.
--- *Totem und Tabu* (1913). *GW IX*, 1996.
--- "Triebe und Triebschicksale" (1915). *GW X*, 1991.
--- "Das Unbewußte" (1915). *GW X*, 1991.
--- "Zeitgemäßes über Krieg und Tod" (1915). *GW X*, 1991.
--- *Metapsychologische Ergänzung zur Traumlehre* (1915). *GW X*, 1991.
--- *Vorlesung 23:* "Die Wege der Symptombildung." *Vorlesungen zur Einführung in die Psychoanalyse* (1917). *GW XI*, 1998.
--- *Aus der Geschichte einer infantilen Neurose* (1918). *GW XII*, 2006.
--- "Das Unheimliche" (1919). *GW XII*, 2006.
--- *Jenseits des Lustprinzips* (1920). *GW XIII*, 1998.
--- *Massenpsychologie und Ich-Analyse* (1921). *GW XIII*, 1998.
---- *Das Ich und das Es* (1923). *GW XIII*, 1998.
---- "Die infantile Genitalorganisation" (1923). *GW XIII*, 1997.
---- "Die Verneinung" (1925). *GW XIV*, 1991.
---- *Vorlesung 32:* "Angst und Triebleben." *Neue Folge der Vorlesungen zur Einführung in die Psychoanalyse* (1932). *GW XV*, 1991.
---- "Warum Krieg?" (1933). *GW XVI*, 2006.
---- "Konstruktionen in der Analyse" (1937). *GW XVI*, 1981.
---- "Die endliche und die unendliche Analyse" (1937). *GW XVI*, 1996.
---- *Der Mann Moses und die monotheistische Religion* (1934-37). *GW XVI*, 2006.
---- *Abriss der Psychoanalyse* (1938). *GW XVII*, 1993.
---- "Ergebnisse, Ideen, Probleme" (London, June 1938). *GW XVII*, 1993.
---- "Das Erinnern und das Urteilen." *Entwurf einer Psychologie*, *GW Nachtragsband. Texte aus den Jahren 1885–1938*, 1987.
Freud, Sigmund. *La naissance de la psychanalyse. Lettres à Fliess. Notes et plans* (1887–1902). Paris: PUF, 1956.
Freud, Sigmund. "Personaggi psicopatici sulla scena" (1905). *Opere V*. Turin: Paolo Boringhieri, 1985.

Fuks, Betty Bernardo, *Freud and the Invention of Jewishness*. New York: Agincourt Press, 2008.
Galilei, Galileo. *Il saggiatore*. Firenze: G. Barbera, 1864.
Ginzburg, Carlo. *Rapporti di forza*. Milan: Feltrinelli, 2000.
Graziosi, Paolo. *Le pitture preistoriche della grotta di Porto Badisco*. Milan: Giunti Martello, 1980.
Gropius, Walter. *Manifest des Staatlichen Bauhauses in Weimar*. Weimar: Staatliches Bauhaus, 1919.
Guidorizzi, Giulio. *Il mondo letterario greco*. Turin: Einaudi, 2000.
Haddad, Gerard, and Antonietta Haddad. *Freud en Italie: Psychanalyse du voyage*. Paris: Éditions Albin Michel, 1995.
Haddad, Gerard. *Manger le livre: Rites alimentaires et fonction paternelle*. Paris: Hachette, 1984.
--- *Les folies millénaristes*. Paris: Grasset, Biblio-Essais, 1990.
--- Tripalium. *Pourquoi le travail est devenu une souffrance*. Paris: François Bourin, 2013.
Hawking, Stephen. *Black Holes and Baby Universes and Other Essays*. New York: Bantam Dell, 1994.
Heisenberg, Werner. *Physics and Philosophy: The Revolution in Modern Science*. London: Allen and Unwin, 1959.
Heller-Roazen, Daniel. *Echolalias: On the Forgetting of Language*. New York: Zone Books, 2005.
Hippocrates. *Hippocrates IV*. Translated by W.H.S. Jones. Cambridge, MA: Harvard UP, 1931.
Jakobson, Roman. *Child Language, Aphasia, and Phonological Universals*. La Haye: Mouton, 1968.
Jaspers, Karl. *Psicologia delle visioni del mondo*. Roma: Astrolabio, 1950.
Kant, Immanuel. "Concerning the Ultimate Ground of the Differentiation of Directions in Space" (1768). In *Immanuel Kant, Theoretical Philosophy 1755-1770*. Cambridge: Cambridge UP, 1992.
Katuszewski, Pierre. *Ceci n'est pas un fantôme: Essai sur les personnages de fantômes dans le théâtre antique et contemporain*. Paris: Éditions Kimé, 2011.
Koyré, Alexandre. *From the Closed World to the Infinite Universe*. Baltimore: Johns Hopkins UP, 1957.
Lacan, Jacques. *Ecrits:* Paris: Éditions du Seuil, 1966.
--- *Ecrits: The First Complete Edition in English*. Translated by Bruce Fink (in collaboration with Héloïse Fink and Russell Grigg). New York: Norton & Company, 2007.
--- *Autres écrits*. Paris: Éditions du Seuil, 2001.
--- "L'Étourdit." *Scilicet* 4 (1973): 5–52.
--- "La troisième." VII congrès l'Ecole Freudienne de Paris (1974). *Lettres de l'Ecole freudienne, Bulletin intérieur de l'E.F.P.*, no. 16 (novembre 1975).

Bibliography

--- "Lettre aux Italiens" (1974). *Ornicar?* 25 (1982): 7–10.
--- "Conférence de Genève sur le symptôme." *Les bloc-notes de la psychanalyse* 5, Genève: Georg, 1985.
Lacan, Jacques. *Séminaires*.
--- *L'homme aux loups: Séminaire inédit* de 1952-1953.
--- *Le Séminaire livre I: Les écrits techniques de Freud*. Paris: Éditions du Seuil, 1975.
--- *Le Séminaire livre III: Les psychoses*. Paris: Éditions du Seuil, 1981.
--- *Le Séminaire livre V: Les formations de l'inconscient*. Paris: Éditions du Seuil, 1998.
--- *Le Séminaire livre VI: Le désir et son interprétation*. Paris: Éditions de la Marinière/Le Champ Freudien, 2013.
--- *Le Séminaire livre VII: L'éthique de la psychanalyse*. Paris: Éditions du Seuil, 1986.
--- *Le Séminaire livre VIII: Le transfert*. Paris: Éditions du Seuil, 2001.
--- *Le Séminaire livre IX: L'Identification*.
--- *Le Séminaire livre X: L'angoisse*. Paris: Éditions du Seuil, 2004.
--- *Le Séminaire livre XI: Les quatre concepts fondamentaux de la psychanalyse*. Paris: Éditions du Seuil, 1973.
--- *Le Séminaire livre XII: Problèmes cruciaux de la psychanalyse*.
--- *Le Séminaire livre XIII: L'objet de la psychanalyse*.
--- *Le Séminaire livre XIV: La logique du fantasme*.
--- *Le Séminaire livre XVI: D'un Autre à l'autre*. Paris: Éditions du Seuil, 2006.
--- *Le Séminaire livre XVII: L'envers de la psychanalyse*. Paris: Éditions du Seuil, 1991.
--- *Le Séminaire livre XVIII: D'un discours qui ne serait pas du semblant*. Paris: Éditions du Seuil, 2006.
--- *Le Séminaire livre XX: Encore*. Paris: Éditions du Seuil, 1975.
--- *Le Séminaire livre XXI: Les non-dupes errent*.
--- *Le Séminaire livre XXII: R.S.I.*
--- *Le Séminaire livre XXIII: Sinthome*. Paris: Éditions du Seuil, 2003.
--- *Le Séminaire livre XXIV: L'insu que sait de l'une bévue s'aile à mourre*.
Lachièze-Rey, Marc. *Au-delà de l'Espace et du temps: La nouvelle physique*. Paris: Éditions le Pommier, 2008.
Lebensztejn, Jean-Claude. *Dossier Pontormo*. *Macula* 5/6 (1980).
Levi, Primo. *Se questo è un uomo*. Turin: Giulio Einaudi, 1973.
--- "Covare il cobra." Entretien in *La Stampa*, 21 septembre 1986.
--- *I sommersi e i salvati*. In *Opere I*. Turin: Giulio Einaudi, 1987.
--- *Storie naturali*. In *Opere III*. Turin: Giulio Einaudi, 1990.
--- *The Complete Works of Primo Levi*, edited by Ann Goldstein. New York: Liveright, 2015.
Leroi-Gourant, Andre. *Le geste et la parole*. Paris: Éditions Albin Michel, 1964.
--- *Il gesto e la parola. Tecnica e linguaggio I*. Turin: Giulio Einaudi, 1977.

--- *L'homme et la matière*. Paris: Albin Michel, 2010.
Lévi-Strauss, Claude. *La pensée sauvage*. Paris: Plon, 1962.
Maestri, Delmo (Ed.). *Opere di Giovan Battista Gelli*. Turin: Utet, 1976.
Maurano, Denise. *La face cachée de l'amour*. Paris: Presses Universitaires du Septentrion, 1999.
Melville, Herman. *Benito Cereno*. In *The Piazza Tales and Other Prose Pieces, 1839*-1860, edited by Harrison Hayford, Alma A.MacDougall, Thomas. G. Tanselle, et al. Chicago: Northwestern UP and The Newberry Library, 1987.
Mieli, Paola, *A Silver Martian: Normality and Segregation in Primo Levi's Sleeping Beauty in the Fridge*. New York: CPL Editions, 2014.
--- "Jacopo da Pontormo. Un disegno del Diario," *Il Piccolo Hans* 31 (1981).
--- "See-Saw, the Most Inseparable of Companions: The Constitution of the Ego." *Littoral*, no. 31/32 (1991).
--- "Les temps du Traumatisme," In *Actualité de L'Hysterie*, edited by A. Michels. Paris: Éditions Erès, 2001.
--- "Vienne: Architecture et espace de la mémoire." In *Freud et Vienne*, edited by A. Didier-Weill. Paris: Éditions Erès, 2004.
--- "Du son qui guide l'image: notes sur pulsion, corps, espace." In *Insistance: Art, Psychanalyse, Politique*. Paris: Éditions Erès, 2005.
--- "Ein Stückchen Wahrheit: nota sul poeta portavoce." In *Balleriniana*. Ravenna: Danilo Montanari Editore, 2010.
--- "Totem et tabou: note sur la fonction de la pensee dans l'appareil psychique freudien." In *Totem et Tabou: Cent ans après*, edited by C. Basualdo, N. Braunstein, B.B. Fuks. Paris: Éditions Le bord de l'eau, 2013.
--- "El espacio de la transmisión: un acto entra linguas." In *LaPsus Calami: Revista de Psicoanalisis* 4 (Otoño 2014).
Millot, Catherine. *O solitude*. Paris: Gallimard, 2011.
Milner, Jean-Claude. *Le périple structural: Figures et paradigms*. Paris: Éditions du Seuil, 2002.
Mondzain, Marie-Jose. *Homo spectator*. Paris: Bayard, 2007.
Nasio, Juan-David. *Introduction à la topologie de Lacan*. Paris: Petite Bibliothèque Payot, 2010.
Niccolai, Giulia. "I Ballerini." In *Balleriniana*. Ravenna: Danilo Montanari, 2010.
Nietzsche, Friedrich. *La Nascita della tragedia: Considerazioni Inattuali I-III*. In *Opere di Friedrich Niezsche III*, edited by Giorgio Colli and Mazzino Montinari. Milan: Adelphi, 1972.
Nigro, Salvatore S. *L'orologio di Pontormo*. Milan: Rizzoli, 1998.
Panofsky, Erwin. *Perspective as Symbolic Form*. New York: Zone Books, 1991.
Paracelsus and Ferruccio Masini. *Paragrano*. Roma: Laterza, 1973.
--- *Paragranum: Astronomia*. In *Paracelsus (Theophrastus Bombastus von Hohenheim, 1493-1541): Essential Theoretical Writings*, edited by Andrew Weeks. Leiden: Brill, 2008.

Bibliography

Petit, Philippe. *Credere nel vuoto*. Turin: Bollati Boringhieri, 2008.
Pico della Mirandola, Giovanni. *Disputationes adversus astrologiam divinatricem 3.24*, edited by Garin Eugenio. Florence: Valecchi, 1946.
Pingree, David (Éd.). *Picatrix: the Latin Version of the Ghayat Al-Hakim; text, introduction, appendices, indices*. London: University of London, 1986.
--- *Picatrix* 1.7. Translated by John Michael Greer and Christopher Warnock. Iowa City: Renaissance Astrology Press, 2010.
Poe, Edgar Allan. "William Wilson." In *Poetry and Tales*, notes and selection by Patrick F. Quinn. New York: The Library of America, 1984.
Pollone, Marco V. *De Architectura*. Rome: Edizioni Studio Tesi, 1990.
Porge, Erik. *Se compter trois: Le temps logique de Lacan*. Paris: Erès, 1989.
--- *Transmettre la clinique psychanalytique: Freud, Lacan, aujourd'hui*. Paris: Erès, 2005.
--- "L'identification: une physique sans métaphysique." *Essaim* 24 (2010).
--- *Des fondements de la clinique psychanalytique*. Paris: Erès, 2008.
--- "Les voix, la voix." *Essaim* 26 (2011).
--- *Voix de l'écho*. Paris: Erès, 2012.
--- *Truth and Knowledge in the Clinic: Working with Freud and Lacan*. New York: Agincourt, 2016.
Portoghesi, Paolo. "La nascita del barocco." In *I trionfi del barocco: Architettura in Europa 1600-1750*, edited by Henry A. Millon. Milan: Bompiani, 1999.
Quignard, Pascal. *L'Origine de la danse*. Paris: Galilée, 2013.
Rabant, Claude. "La pulsion du large: le phallus, horizon du sexuel." Presentation at Après Coup Psychoanalytic Association, New York, February 8, 2003.
Rank, Otto. *The Double: A Psychoanalytic Study*. Chapel Hill, NC: University of North Carolina Press, 1971.
Reale, Giovanni (Ed.). *Platone: tutti gli scritti*. Milan: Bompiani, 2000.
Roux, Georges. "Greece." In *The Dictionary of Art III*, edited by Janet Turner. London: Macmillian, 1996.
Rykwert, Joseph. "Semper et la conception du style." *Macula* 5/6 (1979).
Safouan, Moustapha. *Lacaniana: Les séminaires de Jacques Lacan, 1964-1979*. Paris: Fayard, 2005.
Sangl, Sigrid. *Biedermeier to Bauhaus*. New York: Harry N. Abrams, 2000.
Schorske, Carl. *Fin-De-Siècle Vienna: Politics and Culture*. New York: Vintage Books, 1981.
--- *De Vienne et d'ailleurs: figures culturelles de la modernité*. Paris: Fayard, 2000.
Silverman, Kenneth. *Edgar A. Poe: Mournful and Never-ending Remembrance*. New York: Harper Collins, 1992.
Soler, Colette. *Lacan: l'inconscient réinventé*. Paris: Presses Universitaires de France, 2009.
--- *Les affects lacaniens*. Paris: Presses Universitaires de France, 2011.

Testaferrata, Elena. "Gli schizzi del diario e gli affreschi del coro di S. Lorenzo." In Jacopo da Pontormo, *Diario: Codice maglabechiano VIII 1490 della Biblioteca Nazionale Centrale di Firenze*, edited by Roberto Fedi. Rome: Salerno, 1996.

Teteriantnikov, Natalia. "Liturgical Arrangement." In *The Dictionary of Art VII*, edited by Janet Turner. London: Macmillian, 1996.

Trento, Dario. *Pontormo: Il diario alla prova della filologia*. Bologne: L'inchiostroblu, 1984.

Uphill, Eric P. "Temple, Egypt." In *The Dictionary of Art III*, edited by Janet Turner. London: Macmillian, 1996.

Vanier, Alain. "Faut du temps." Conclusions des Journées d'études d'Espace analytique (AFPRF) *La psychanalyse et le temps*. Paris: Maison de la Mutualité, Mars 2006. (Unpublished).

--- "Winnicott et Lacan, Lacan et Winnicott." In *Winnicott avec Lacan*, edited by Alain Vanier et Catherine Vanier. Paris: Herman Éditeurs, 2010.

--- "La musique, c'est le bruit qui pense." *Insistance: Art, Psychanalyse Politique* 6. Paris: Erès, 2011.

Vanier, Catherine. *Naître prématuré: Le bébé, son médecin et son psychanalyste*. Paris: Bayard Éditions, 2013.

Vappereau, Jean-Michel. "Le vel de la séparation." (Juillet 2006). Available on: http://jeanmichel.vappereau.free.fr/textes/Le%20vel%20de%20l%20alienation.pdf.

--- "Afin de préciser le narcissisme." (Septembre 2007). Available on: http://jeanmichel.vappereau.free.fr/textes/Afin%20de%20preciser%20le%20narcissisme.pdf.

--- "The Two Moments Prior to Narcissism: Trauma and Incorporation." Presentation at Après-Coup Psychoanalytic Association, New York, March 24–25, 2012.

Vasari, Giorgio. *Le opere* di *Giorgio Vasari VI*. Florence: Sansoni, 1973.

--- *The Lives of the Artists*. Translated by J.C. Bondanella and P. Bondanella. Oxford: Oxford UP, 1991.

Vegetti, Mario (Ed.). *Opere di Ippocrate*. Turin: Utet, 1976.

Vives, Jean-Michel. "Pour introduire la question de la pulsion invocante." In *Les enjeux de la voix en psychanalyse dans et hors la cure*, edited by Jean-Michel Vives. Grenoble: Presses Universitaires de Grenoble, 2002.

--- "La catharsis, d'Aristote à Lacan en passant par Freud: une approche théâtrale des enjeux éthiques en psychoanalyse." *Recherches en psychanalyse* 9 (2010).

Weil, Simone. *La personne et le sacré: Ecrits de Londres*. In *OEuvres de Simone Weil*. Paris: Éditions Gallimard, 1957.

Winnicott, Donald W. *Playing and Reality*. London: Tavistock, 1971.

--- *The Family and Individual Development*. London: Tavistock, 1964.

Yiannias, John J. (Ed.). *The Byzantine Tradition after the Fall of Constantinople*.

Bibliography

Charlottesville, VA: University of Virginia Press, 1991.

Zambelli, Paola. "Astrologia, magia e alchimia nel Rinascimento fiorentino ed europeo." In *Firenze e la Toscana dei Medici nell'Europa del '500*. Milan: Electa Editrice, 1980.

Zweig, Stefan. *Chess Story*. Translated by Joel Rotenberg. New York: New York Review Books, 2006.

Titles Published by the Sea Horse Imprint:

Betty Bernardo Fuks – *Freud and the Invention of Jewishness* (2008)

Gérard Haddad – *Eating the Book: Dietary Rites and Paternal Function* (2013)

Erik Porge – *Truth and Knowledge in the Clinic: Working with Freud and Lacan* (2016)

Paola Mieli – *Figures of Space. Subject, Body, Place* (2017)